Lecture Notes in Computer Science 3798

Commenced Publication in 1973
Founding and Former Series Editors:
Gerhard Goos, Juris Hartmanis, and Jan van Leeuwen

Alan Dearle Susan Eisenbach (Eds.)

Component Deployment

Third International Working Conference, CD 2005
Grenoble, France, November 28-29, 2005
Proceedings

 Springer

Volume Editors

Alan Dearle
University of St Andrews, School of Computer Science
North Haugh, St Andrews, Fife KY16 9SX, UK
E-mail: al@dcs.st-andrews.ac.uk

Susan Eisenbach
Imperial College London, Department of Computing
180 Queens Gate, London, SW7 2BZ, UK
E-mail: s.eisenbach@imperial.ac.uk

Library of Congress Control Number: 2005936342

CR Subject Classification (1998): D.2, F.3, D.1, D.3, D.4

ISSN   0302-9743
ISBN-10   3-540-30517-3 Springer Berlin Heidelberg New York
ISBN-13   978-3-540-30517-0 Springer Berlin Heidelberg New York

Springer is a part of Springer Science+Business Media

springeronline.com

© Springer-Verlag Berlin Heidelberg 2005
Printed in Germany

Typesetting: Camera-ready by author, data conversion by Scientific Publishing Services, Chennai, India
Printed on acid-free paper   SPIN: 11590712   06/3142   5 4 3 2 1 0

Preface

This volume of *Lecture Notes in Computer Science* contains the proceedings of the 3rd Working Conference on Component Deployment (CD 2005), which took place from 28 to 29, November 2005 in Grenoble, France, and co-located with Middleware 2005. CD 2005 is the third international conference in the series, the first two being held in Berlin and Edinburgh in 2002 and 2004, respectively. The proceedings of both these conferences were also published by Springer in the *Lecture Notes in Computer Science* series and may be found in volumes 2370 and 3083.

Component deployment addresses the tasks that need to be performed after components have been developed and addresses questions such as:

- What do we do with components after they have been built?
- How do we deploy them into their execution environment?
- How can we evolve them once they have been deployed?

CD 2005 brought together researchers and practitioners with the goal of developing a better understanding of how deployment takes place in the wider context. The Program Committee selected 15 papers (12 long papers, three short papers) out of 29 submissions. All submissions were reviewed by at least three members of the Program Committee. Papers were selected based on originality, quality, soundness and relevance to the workshop.

We would like to thank the members of the Program Committee (Mikio Aoyama, Noureddine Belkhatir, Judy Bishop, Paul Brebner, Wolfgang Emmerich, Thomas Gschwind, Richard Hall, Andre van der Hoek, Nenad Medvidovic, Andrea Polini and Peter Sewell) for providing timely and significant reviews, and for their substantial effort in making CD 2005 a successful workshop.

We would also like to thank the following additional reviewers: Doug Palmer, Sam Malek, Chris Mattmann, Andrew J. McCarthy, Marija Mikic-Rakic, Chiyoung Seo and Rob Chatley for their assistance in reviewing papers.

The CD 2005 submission and review process was supported by the Cyber Chair Conference Management System. We are indebted to the services of Borbola Online Conference Services and in particular Richard van de Stadt for their excellent support in managing this system. Andrew J. McCarthy must also be thanked for his diligent efforts in collating the papers in these proceedings.

The workshop was held in conjunction with Middleware 2005. We would like to acknowledge the help from the Middleware 2005 Organizing Committee for their assistance, during the organization of CD 2005, in creating this co-located event.

We would also like to acknowledge the prompt and professional support from Springer, who published these proceedings in printed and electronic volumes as part of the *Lecture Notes in Computer Science series*.

September 2005

Alan Dearle
Susan Eisenbach

Organization

Program Committee

Program Chairs

- Alan Dearle
  University of St Andrews, UK
  al@dcs.st-and.ac.uk
- Susan Eisenbach
  Imperial College, London, UK
  sue@doc.ic.ac.uk

Program Committee Members

- Mikio Aoyama
  Network Information and Software Engineering Laboratory, Japan
  mikio.aoyama@nifty. com
- Noureddine Belkhatir
  IMAG LSR, Grenoble, France
  Noureddine.Belkhatir@imag. fr
- Judy Bishop
  University of Pretoria, South Africa
  jbishop@cs.up.ac.za
- Paul Brebner
  CSIRO ICT Centre, Canberra, Australia
  Paul.Brebner@csiro.au
- Wolfgang Emmerich
  University College London, UK
  w.emmerich@cs.ucl.ac.uk
- Thomas Gschwind
  Technische Universität Wien, Austria
  thomasg@ieee.org
- Richard Hall
  IMAG LSR, Grenoble, France
  heavy@ungoverned.org
- Andre van der Hoek
  University of California, Irvine, USA
  andre@ics.uci.edu
- Nenad Medvidovic
  University of Southern California, Los Angeles, USA
  neno@usc.edu

- Andrea Polini
  CNR, Pisa, Italy
  andrea.polini@isti.cnr.it
- Peter Sewell
  University of Cambridge, UK
  Peter.Sewell@cl.cam.ac.uk
- Kurt Wallnau
  Carnegie Mellon University, Pittsburgh, USA
  kcw@sei.cmu.edu
- Alexander Wolf
  University of Lugano, Switzerland
  alexander.wolf@unisi.ch

Table of Contents

Dependability

Assembly and Packaging

Case Studies

Cooperative Component-Based Software Deployment in Wireless Ad Hoc Networks

Hervé Roussain and Frédéric Guidec

University of South Brittany, France
{Herve.Roussain, Frederic.Guidec}@univ-ubs.fr

Abstract. This paper presents a middleware platform we designed in order to allow the deployment of component-based software applications on mobile devices (such as laptops or personal digital assistants) capable of ad hoc communication. This platform makes it possible to disseminate components based on peer-to-peer interactions between neighboring devices, without relying on any kind of infrastructure network. It implements a cooperative deployment scheme. Each device runs a deployment manager, which maintains a local component repository, and which strives to fill this repository with software components it is missing in order to satisfy the deployment requests expressed by the user. To achieve this goal the deployment manager continuously interacts in the background with peer managers located on neighboring devices, providing its neighbors with copies of software components it owns locally, while obtaining itself from these neighbors copies of the components it is looking for.

1 Introduction

The number and variety of lightweight mobile devices capable of wireless communication is growing significantly. Such devices include laptops, tablet PCs, personal digital assistants (PDAs), many of which are now shipped with built-in IEEE 802.11 (a.k.a. Wi-Fi [1]) network interfaces. With such interfaces, the devices can occasionally be connected to an infrastructure network, using so-called access points that play the role of gateways. But the 802.11 standard also makes it possible for mobile devices to communicate directly in ad hoc mode, that is, without relying on any kind of infrastructure network. An ad hoc network is thus a network that can appear and evolve spontaneously as mobile devices themselves appear, move and disappear dynamically in and from the network [9].

For the users of laptops or PDAs, the prospect of deploying software applications on these devices as and when needed obviously appears as an attractive one, no matter if these devices communicate in infrastructure or in ad hoc mode. Yet, solutions for component-based software deployment have been proposed mostly for infrastructure-based environments so far, while very little effort has been devoted to software deployment in purely ad hoc networks.

In this paper we describe a model we devised in order to allow the deployment of component-based software applications on mobile devices participating in an ad hoc network. In Section 2 we motivate our approach by showing how infrastructure-based networks and ad hoc networks constitute radically different environments as far

A. Dearle and S. Eisenbach (Eds.): CD 2005, LNCS 3798, pp. 1–16, 2005.

as software deployment is concerned, and we show that solutions that prove efficient in infrastructure environments are hardly applicable in ad hoc environments. In Section 3 we present CODEWAN (COmponent DEployment in Wireless Ad hoc Networks), a middleware platform that implements our model. The main characteristics of this platform are discussed in Section 4, which also lists some directions we plan to work along in the future. In Section 5 we compare CODEWAN with other works that also address the problem of software deployment, either in infrastructure environments, or in ad hoc environments. Section 6 concludes the paper.

2   Motivations

In this section we show that deploying software components in an ad hoc network raises issues that usually do not appear in infrastructure networks. As a reminder, we first describe how software component provision and delivery are commonly performed in an infrastructure-based environment. We then show that an ad hoc network presents additional constraints that need to be addressed specifically.

2.1   Software Deployment in an Infrastructure Network

Figure 1 illustrates a typical infrastructure network, including stable and mobile hosts—typically, workstations and laptops—interconnected through gateways (such as routers and switches). In such an environment some of the stable hosts can be in charge of storing components in so-called *component repositories*, and of implementing server programs capable of delivering these components on demand. Other hosts in the network can then behave as simple clients with respect to these servers. Whenever the owner—or the administrator—of one of the client hosts initiates the deployment of a new component-based software application on this device, the problem mostly comes down to locating the server—or servers—capable of providing the components required by this application, and downloading these components so they can be installed locally.

Consider the example shown in Figure 1, and assume that the owner of device A decides to initiate the installation on this device of an application that requires components $c1$, $c2$ and $c3$. The deployment middleware running on device A must first identify

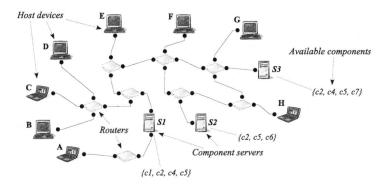

Fig. 1. Illustration of software component deployment in an infrastructure network

one or several servers capable of delivering these components. A component may actually be provided by several servers, for example in order to balance the workload in the network, or to allow fault tolerance. In any case, once a client has identified a server that can provide a component, obtaining this component simply requires its download between the server and the client. Note that in such a context the deployment of a component on a given host can usually be considered as a "real time" operation: once a user has ordered the deployment middleware to locate and download a component, this operation can usually be performed immediately. In the remaining of this section, we show that deploying components in an ad hoc environment can in contrast require a more lengthy process, which requires some middleware capable of enforcing a deployment strategy in the background on behalf of the user.

2.2 Software Deployment in a Dynamic Ad Hoc Network

Figure 2 shows a typical dynamic ad hoc network, which consists of a collection of portable communicating devices. The devices in such a network are usually highly mobile and volatile. Device mobility results from the fact that each device is carried by a user, and users themselves move quite a lot. Device volatility is the consequence of the fact that, since the devices usually have a limited power-budget, they are frequently switched on and off by their owners.

A major characteristic of wireless ad hoc networks is that communication interfaces have a limited transmission range. Consequently any device can only communicate directly with neighboring devices. Multi-hop transmissions can sometimes be obtained by implementing a dynamic routing algorithm on each device [10,13], but it is worth observing that even with dynamic routing, a realistic ad hoc network often presents itself as a fragmented network. Such a network appears as a—possibly changing—collection of so-called "islands" (also referred to as "clouds" or "cells" in the literature). Mobile devices that belong to the same island can communicate together, using either multi-hop or single-hop transmissions depending on whether dynamic routing is used or not in the network. However, devices that belong to distinct islands cannot communicate together, because no transmission is possible between islands.

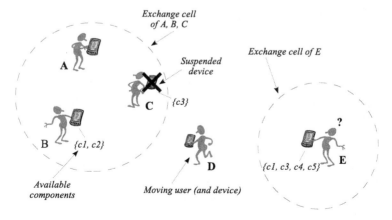

Fig. 2. Illustration of software component deployment in a dynamic ad hoc network

In such a context, a traditional client-server deployment scheme such as that illustrated in Section 2.1 is hardly applicable, as no device is stable and accessible enough to play the role of a server of components, maintaining a component repository and allowing client devices to access this repository whenever needed.

In the remainder of this paper, we present a model we propose in order to allow for these constraints. Basically, instead of being able to access a server whenever needed, each device must maintain a local component repository. A peer-to-peer interaction model then makes it possible for a device to cooperate with its neighborhood, by allowing its neighbors to obtain copies of the software components available on its local repository, while itself benefiting from a similar service offered by its neighbors.

Consider the example shown in Figure 2, and assume again that the owner of device A wishes to install on this device an application that requires components $c1$, $c2$ and $c3$. In our example, A can obtain components $c1$ and $c2$ from device B. But as devices C and E—that both own a copy of component $c3$—are (possibly temporarily) unreachable, A cannot obtain a copy of component $c3$ from any of these devices. Yet A could obtain component $c3$ from device C if this device was switched on by its user. It could also obtain this component from device E if A's user happened to walk towards E, or if E's user happened to walk toward A. A roaming device such as D may even serve as a benevolent carrier between E and A, transporting component c3—and possibly other components as well—between separate islands, and thus contributing to the dissemination of software components and applications all over the network.

This example shows that when the owner of a mobile device participating in an ad hoc network requests the deployment of a component-based application on this device, there is no guarantee that this request can be satisfied immediately, as there is no guarantee that the components required for this deployment are readily accessible in the neighborhood. Yet, since the topology of an ad hoc network can change continuously and unpredictably as devices move and are switched on or off, the fact that a given component cannot be obtained at a given time does not involve that this component will remain inaccessible in the future. There is thus a need for some deployment middleware capable of ensuring the collection of missing components in the background in order to satisfy the user's needs.

3   Towards Software Component Deployment on Mobile Devices

In this section, we present an overview of CODEWAN (*COmponent DEployment in Wireless Ad hoc Networks*), a platform we designed in order to support the deployment of component-based software applications on mobile devices communicating in ad hoc mode. CODEWAN implements a cooperative model, where neighboring devices interact in order to discover and exchange software components. Each device implements a local component repository, and a deployment manager is responsible for maintaining this repository on behalf of the user. Any component stored in the repository can be used to assemble and start an application locally. Copies of this component can also be sent on demand to neighboring devices.

3.1 Overview of the CODEWAN Platform

The platform is built as a three-layer model, as shown in Figure 3. The upper and lower layers in this model have been described in details in [7] and [3] respectively. They are thus only described briefly below, and the paper then continues with a detailed description of the model's central layer, which implements the component repository and the deployment manager that maintains this repository.

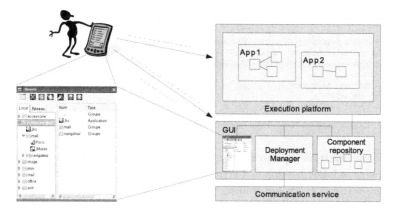

Fig. 3. Overview of the CODEWAN platform and screenshot of its GUI on a PDA

The upper layer in the platform is meant to provide a framework for assembling and running applications. Instead of defining its own component-model, CODEWAN was designed so as to rely on existing execution frameworks for component-oriented or service-oriented applications. In its current implementation it interfaces with JAMUS, a runtime framework that is primarily dedicated to hosting potentially malicious mobile applications [7], as well as with JULIA, an execution framework for applications designed using the Fractal component model [12].

The lower layer in our model was designed in order to support the asynchronous dissemination of so-called *transfer documents* in an ad hoc network. A transfer document is an XML document whose external element's attributes specify the conditions required for disseminating the document in the network. These attributes thus play approximately the same role as header fields in IP packets or in UDP datagrams. They indicate typically the document's source and destination, the expected propagation scope for this document, etc.

The "payload" of a transfer document consists of the internal XML elements that are embedded in the document. Any kind of structured information can be transported in a transfer document. In CODEWAN, though, transfer documents are used to transport software package descriptors in the network.

Figure 4 shows a typical transfer document. Attributes in this document indicate that it was sent by device *shiva*, and that it was addressed to any device in the neighborhood (notice that the communication layer CODEWAN relies on supports the use of wildcard addresses). The payload in this transfer document consists of a package descriptor, whose role and structure are detailed in Section 3.3.

```
<transfer−document
   document−id="fb54356fe468d9"
   source="device:shiva"   destination="device:*"
   hops−to−live="3"   lifetime="01:00:00"
   service−type="package−advertisement">
   <package−descriptor>
      <general−information
         type="application/java"   category="communication/messaging"
         name="JMessager"   version="1.3"
         provider="Laboratoire Valoria"
         summary="JMessager is a P2P messager"/>
      <java−application name="masc.jmessager.JMessagerImpl" />
      <dependencies>
         <required−package   name="JMessengerUI" version="1.2"/>
         <required−package   name="P2PAsyncDissemination"/>
         <optional−package   name="AddressBook" version="2.0"/>
      </dependencies>
   </package−descriptor>
</transfer−document>
```

Fig. 4. Example of an XML transfer document carrying a software package descriptor

The communication layer in CODEWAN provides services for encapsulating trans-fer documents in UDP datagrams. Large XML documents can be fragmented and then transported in distinct, smaller transfer documents that each can fit in a single UDP datagram. The communication layer of course supports the re-assembly of such frag-ments after they have been received from the network. Documents can be transferred either in unicast, broadcast, or multicast mode, and using either single-hop or multi-hop transmissions. In the latter case, all mobile devices in the network are expected to behave as routers, using algorithms for dynamic routing and flooding such as those described in [13,11,14].

Further details about CODEWAN's communication layer can be found in [3]. In the remainder of this paper we focus on the description of the central layer of the platform. The deployment manager is implemented in this layer, together with the component repository this manager is in charge of maintaining. The repository is a place where software components can be stored locally on a mobile device. Components stored in this repository are thus readily available for the execution framework that constitutes the upper layer of the platform. The deployment manager takes orders from the user, and interacts with peer managers that reside on neighboring devices in order to fill the local repository with components required by the user, while providing its peers with components they need in order to satisfy their own users.

3.2   Installation Steps in CODEWAN

The deployment manager can provide the user with information about all the applica-tions it knows about. At any time a given application is either:

– *installed locally* (meaning that this application is either already running in the local execution framework, or ready to be loaded and started in this framework);
– *installable* (meaning that all the components required for running this application are available in the local repository, so the application could be installed immedi-ately if the user requested it);

– *not installable yet* (meaning that some of the components required by this application are not present in the local repository).

Besides observing the status of each application, the user can modify this status, requesting for example that an application be started (which implies that this application be already installed locally), or that an application be uninstalled (and all its components removed from the repository). Additionally the user can initiate the deployment of an application, thus instructing the deployment manager to try to obtain any missing component for this application from neighboring devices.

CODEWAN implements a basic user interface that can run in console mode. Additionally, graphical interfaces have been designed in order to facilitate the interaction between the user and the deployment manager running on a mobile device. For example Figure 3 shows an interface that was designed specifically for personal digital assistants.

3.3 Software Components, Applications, and Packages

The deployment of component-based applications implies that components be transmitted in the network, and stored in local repositories. Before they can be loaded and executed in a runtime framework, software components are encapsulated in so-called *software packages*, that can be considered as storage and transfer envelopes for these components. Besides encapsulating the actual code of the components, software packages can additionally encapsulate some data required by a software component or application. They can also encapsulate documents describing the overall architecture of a component-based application (such as CCM component assemblies [8], or architecture descriptors in the Fractal model [12]).

Package Descriptors. Each software package in CODEWAN is associated with a package descriptor. This descriptor provides information about the package's identity, its content, its category, etc. It can be embedded in the package itself, but it can also be processed separately. For example, the transfer document shown in Figure 4 encapsulates a package descriptor as its payload. In a typical scenario such a document could be broadcast by a device in order to inform its neighbors about a software package that is available in its local repository.

The package descriptor shown in Figure 4 actually describes the main component of a Java messaging application (as specified by attribute *type* in the descriptor). It provides general information about the application, such as its name, version number, provider, etc. It also indicates that in order to be assembled the application requires components that can themselves be found in three other software packages. Two of these packages are absolutely needed for assembling the application, while the third one can be used optionally in order to improve the functionality of the application. This example shows that when the components encapsulated in a particular package depend on components that are encapsulated in other packages, this information is mentioned explicitly in package descriptors. Dependencies between packages can also appear when a package contains only the description of the architecture of an application, while other packages encapsulate components that are required for assembling this application, or data that are needed for running this application.

Software Packages. As mentioned above, software packages can encapsulate software components, as well as plain data or application architecture descriptions. A software package usually encapsulates its own descriptor, but this descriptor can also be extracted from the package and processed separately whenever needed.

In the current implementation of the CODEWAN platform, application data and the code of software components are encoded using the Base64 standard. The result of this encoding is then encapsulated as CDATA information in an XML document.

3.4   Main Functionalities of the Deployment Manager

The deployment manager running on a mobile device is notably responsible for maintaining a local component repository on this device, while interacting with peer managers located on neighboring devices. Among other things the deployment manager can:

1. *decide what packages and package descriptors should be stored in the local repository and, if necessary, what packages and descriptors should be removed from this repository;*

   Notice that since mobile devices are usually resource-constrained, the deployment manager might sometimes have to reclaim the space occupied by unused, yet potentially interesting packages.

2. *announce to its neighbors what packages are available locally, thus indicating that these packages can be delivered on demand;*

   Announcing the availability of a package is performed by broadcasting a transfer document that encapsulates the descriptor of this package, as shown in Figure 4. Such an announcement can be broadcast periodically, or when a new device appears in the neighborhood. It can also be broadcast after a request has been received from a neighbor, as described in the next three items.

3. *search the neighborhood for specific packages, or for packages that satisfy precise criteria;*

   Package searching is performed by broadcasting a transfer document that encapsulates a "request for descriptors". Such a request compares with a standard package descriptor, except that each attribute in the request defines a regular expression. Any deployment manager receiving a request can thus match this request against the descriptors of the packages stored on its local repository. If one or several of these descriptors match the request, then the deployment manager answers this request by announcing the availability of the matching packages, as described in item 2.

4. *discover what packages are available in the neighborhood;*

   This is performed by broadcasting a "request for descriptors" as explained in the former item, except that this request is not selective at all: it actually calls for the announcement of all the packages available in the neighborhood.

5. *ask a neighbor for the transmission of one—or several—particular package(s);*

   This is performed by sending the targeted neighbor a "request for packages", which is similar to a "request for descriptors" except that the neighbor is expected to return the desired packages, rather than simply announce that it owns these packages. The actual transmission of software packages can be performed either in unicast, multicast, or broadcast mode, depending on the configuration of the sending deployment manager.

6. *receive packages from a neighbor, and decide for each package if it should be stored on the local repository.*

   The deployment manager can be expected to accept and store packages it has itself requested before. But since packages can sometimes be broadcast—as explained above—the deployment manager may also receive packages it has never requested. In such a case the deployment manager can be configured so as to implement a hoarding policy, storing packages that may prove interesting in the future.

The basic operations mentioned in the above list make it possible to devise and implement a number of different strategies for cooperative component deployment. Actually, while designing the CODEWAN platform we intentionally defined a comprehensive set of functionalities so as to allow a large number of interaction patterns between neighboring deployment managers. Several alternative deployment strategies can thus be implemented based on these functionalities. Part of our current work is now devoted to devising such strategies, and observing how they perform in realistic conditions.

Although a large number of deployment scenarios can be considered, the next section describes the major steps these scenarios can be based on.

3.5   Major Steps in a Deployment Scenario

Learning About New Applications. At any time the deployment manager running on a mobile device maintains in the local repository a collection of application descriptors. As explained in Section 3.2 some of these descriptors correspond to applications that are not installable yet, meaning that some of the packages required for assembling these applications are not available locally. The deployment manager can thus "know" about the existence of an application (because it owns a descriptor of this application), even though this application is not yet installed locally.

A basic approach for a deployment manager to learn about new applications is simply to listen to the network in order to collect transfer documents that contain application descriptors, while broadcasting itself the descriptors of the applications stored in its repository. Neighboring deployment managers thus spontaneously inform each other about existing applications.

Initiation of a New Application Deployment. In order to initiate the deployment of a new application on a mobile device, the user can rely on the interface of the deployment manager, and select with this interface an application that is not installed yet. This scenario however implies that the local deployment manager must already know about the existence of this application.

Alternatively a user may know about an application the deployment manager itself has never heard about. In such a case the user can inform the deployment manager about the name of this application, and the deployment manager will then start looking for the corresponding descriptor in the neighborhood.

Identification of Missing Packages. Once the descriptor of the desired application is available, the deployment manager can examine the dependencies described in this descriptor in order to determine what other packages are needed for assembling this application.

Remember that several applications may be assembled out of the same set of components. The packages needed to assemble a new application may thus be already available locally, as they may have been collected before in order to assemble and start another application. Note also that the deployment manager may implement a hoarding policy, storing unused packages "just in case" in the local repository. Consequently, in the best circumstances, when determining what packages are needed for assembling an application the deployment manager may actually discover that all these packages are already present in the local repository. In such a case the deployment of the application can be considered as complete.

In most cases, though, when the user asks for the deployment of a new application the deployment manager is likely to discover that a number of required packages are missing in the local repository. For each application whose deployment is in progress the deployment manager maintains a list of desired packages (some kind of a "shopping list", actually). Once the packages required for a given application have been identified, their identity is appended to the corresponding "shopping list".

The deployment manager runs a background process that aims at collecting any package whose identity appears in at least one of the "shopping lists" it maintains.

Search for Missing Packages. Searching for packages is a proactive operation that consists in broadcasting "requests for descriptors". This operation can be performed either periodically, or it can be triggered by an event, such as the detection of a new device in the neighborhood.

A request is a transfer document that contains a list of desired packages. Neighboring devices that own some of these packages are expected to reply by announcing the availability of these packages.

Note that since announcements are broadcast in the network, a deployment manager can sometimes discover passively that a number of packages it is looking for are available in the neighborhood. Packages can thus be located simply by listening to broadcast announcements. CODEWAN makes it possible to combine both forms of package discovery (proactive and reactive) in a single deployment strategy.

Download of Missing Packages. Whenever the deployment manager discovers that some of the packages it is looking for are available on a neighbor device, it can react by sending a "request for packages", thus asking that the desired packages be transmitted in the network.

After receiving one of the packages it has requested, the deployment manager stores this package in the local repository, and removes its name from its "shopping lists". The descriptor of the package must also be analyzed in order to check if this package depends on other packages that are not available locally. If so, then these packages must also be considered as requested packages, and their names be appended to the deployment manager's "shopping lists".

Completion or Termination of an Application's Deployment. The deployment of an application is complete when the corresponding "shopping list" is empty, which means that all the packages required for assembling this application have been collected and are now available in the local repository. The application can then be considered as installable, and be presented as such to the user through the user interface.

The user can also decide to cancel the deployment of a particular application at any time. In that case the "shopping list" maintained by the deployment manager for this application is discarded, and the packages that have already been collected and stored in the local repository are marked as unused (unless they are indeed used by another locally installed application, and unless their names appear in another local "shopping list"). Unused packages can be maintained by the deployment manager in the local repository as long as there remains enough space to receive and store other desired packages. Otherwise the deployment manager is entitled to remove unused packages whenever there is a need to free storage space in the repository.

4 Discussion and Future Work

4.1 Efficiency Considerations

The model we propose for cooperative software deployment on mobile devices is inherently a probabilistic one. Indeed, when a user requests that a given application be deployed on a mobile device, there is no absolute guarantee that the deployment manager on this device will ever manage to collect the required packages. It is worth mentioning that this lack of guarantee is a consequence of the characteristics inherent to dynamic ad hoc networking, rather than a limitation of the model itself. However the model can be adapted in order to account for these constraints.

For example, in order to increase the chance that the requests of the user can be satisfied, the deployment manager in the CODEWAN platform was designed so as to exhibit a persistent behavior. Whenever it cannot obtain a number of packages from its current set of neighbors, the deployment manager simply persists and tries to obtain these packages later, after its neighborhood has changed. Device mobility and volatility thus become advantages in this process, as the neighborhood of a device is not limited to a fixed set of neighbors. Whenever a package cannot be found at a given time in the neighborhood, there is always a chance that it can be found in the future.

The actual efficiency of our model in realistic conditions depends on a large number of factors, such as the geographical distribution of mobile devices, their speed, the frequency at which devices are switched on and off by their users, data transmission rates, the amount of storage space available in each device's local repository, the size of software packages, the number of packages required to assemble an application, etc. Work is now in progress in order to evaluate the average efficiency of our model in different conditions, based on simulations, and based on actual experimentation with CODEWAN-enabled mobile devices.

4.2 Towards Adaptive Software Deployment

In the current implementation of the CODEWAN platform, the deployment manager running on a mobile device must be configured manually by the user of this device. For example it can be configured so as to announce periodically the packages it owns locally, and to broadcast periodically a request indicating the packages it is looking for. In both cases, though, the user is responsible for choosing the appropriate periodicity for these transmissions.

The user must likewise determine how much storage space must be assigned to the local repository (which can be implemented either in memory or in the filesystem), and whether the deployment manager should implement a hoarding policy (storing in its local repository any package it receives from the network, even if this package is not mentioned in a local "shopping list").

Future work will notably focus on the development of a strategy manager capable of adjusting the behavior of a deployment manager transparently and continuously on behalf of the user. For example the periodicity for announcing local packages and requesting desired packages could be adjusted dynamically based on the mobility of a device, on observations of its neighborhood, or on internal events (such as the local device being suspended or resumed). The hoarding policy implemented by a deployment manager may likewise be guided by statistics about the requests received from the neighborhood: a deployment manager that frequently receives requests for a package it does not own locally may decide to try to collect this package so as to help multiply its copies—and thus its overall availability—in the ad hoc network.

4.3   Security Considerations

The approach we propose for deploying software applications on mobile devices relies on the assumption that the owners of these devices may find it convenient to share software components with each other using ad hoc communication. This approach obviously raises a number of legitimate concerns regarding security, as the owner of a mobile device may for example be reluctant to run on this device pieces of software obtained from unidentified sources. We believe that this problem may be solved satisfactorily by using digital signatures so as to ascertain the origin of a software component, as well as ciphering in order to limit the use of a given component to a particular community of users. These are directions we plan to investigate in the near future.

4.4   Compatibility with Standard Component Models and Frameworks

CODEWAN is not strongly dependent on a specific execution framework, or on a particular component model. Actually the focus in this platform is put on the dissemination of software components rather than on the assembly and execution of component-based applications per se. In our opinion CODEWAN should quite easily accommodate almost any component model and any execution framework. The only condition is that components in the model considered can be transmitted and stored in packages, and that the execution framework can be adapted so as to take components from the local repository maintained by the platform's deployment manager, rather than from a legacy repository.

CODEWAN currently interfaces with two execution frameworks called JAMUS and JULIA. JAMUS is a security-oriented execution framework we designed, which provides a resource-constrained environment for untrusted Java applications [7]. JULIA is a framework that implements the Fractal component model [12]. Ongoing work aims at interfacing CODEWAN with OSCAR, a service-oriented framework for OSGi *bundles* [4].

5   Related Work

Java Web Start [17] and Apache Maven [18] both support the deployment and the update of Java-based application programs. They are primarily meant to be used on stable, fully connected, infrastructure networks, though. They rely on a client-server model: a server (or a collection of servers in Maven) maintains a repository where applications can be stored, and clients can download new applications—or new versions of applications they have already downloaded—from this server.

A number of papers have proposed to apply the client-server model for software deployment in ad hoc networks. For example, JDRUMS [2] implements a content delivery system for software components. It relies on dedicated devices that host server programs called "JSTOREs". These server programs must register with a JINI lookup service in order to be located by the devices on which some software is to be deployed. Although mobile, pervasive devices are targeted in this work, the JSTOREs and the lookup service are assumed to be stable at any time, and available whenever needed.

As explained in Section 2 we believe that the traditional client-server model is hardly applicable for deploying and updating software in an autonomous ad hoc network, although it usually performs most satisfactorily in an infrastructure network. As an alternative to the client-server model we propose to rely on cooperative, peer-to-peer interactions between neighboring mobile devices. To our knowledge, this approach has not really been investigated so far, although cooperative software deployment has been considered in infrastructure-based environments, and proposals have been made to support code mobility or information dissemination in ad hoc networks.

SoftwareDock is a framework for distributed software deployment that uses mobile agents to support the transfer of software applications between so-called producers and consumers [5]. This approach thus compares with the client-server model. Moreover SoftwareDock is primarily meant to be used in infrastructure networks, as the prime motivation in this work is to allow load balancing and fault tolerance between software producers. Tacoma [16] is another system that relies on mobile agents to deploy components. Like SoftwareDock, though, it does not specifically address the problem of component deployment in ad hoc networks.

CORBA-$\mathcal{LC}$ defines the notion of CORBA Lightweight Component, and a number of design and implementation requirements for deploying such components are identified in [15]. This paper notably suggests that components should be deployed using a "peer network" model, where the whole network acts as a repository for managing and assigning resources (including components). However, although [15] observes that spurious node failures and node disconnections should be supported, our understanding of this paper is that it too considers the deployment of components in a quasi-stable, infrastructure-based environment.

Component deployment in ad hoc networks is specifically addressed in [6], which describes a framework for service-oriented computing. The components considered in this framework are actually proxy components, which must be deployed locally in order to allow local clients to access remote services. Service directories and implementation repositories are constructed and maintained using a distributed approach that implies the opportunistic collaboration of neighboring hosts in the ad hoc network.

SATIN provides support for component-based, self organized systems on mobile devices [19]. It supports the storage and the execution of components on a device, as well as component advertisement, discovery and transfer between devices. SATIN is meant to serve as a generic platform that offers self organization through logical mobility and componentization. As such it does not readily compare with CODEWAN, which addresses specifically the problem of software deployment on mobile devices. Yet we believe that SATIN could serve as a framework for developing a deployment system similar to CODEWAN. This system would be dedicated to SATIN components, though (as SATIN defines its own component model), just like CORBA-$\mathcal{LC}$ only considers the deployment of CORBA components. In contrast CODEWAN is somehow more versatile. It processes software packages (that can encapsulate any kind of components) rather than the components themselves, and it delegates the problems of locally assembling and running components to an associate execution framework.

6   Conclusion

In this paper we presented the CODEWAN platform, which is dedicated to the deployment of component-based software applications on mobile devices participating in an ad hoc network. CODEWAN implements a peer-to-peer, cooperative model for software deployment. With this model, each mobile device maintains a local repository that can host a number of software components. The components stored in this repository are available for the execution framework that constitutes the upper layer of the platform. Neighboring devices can also exchange copies of the software components they own based on a peer-to-peer interaction scheme. A deployment manager is responsible for maintaining the local repository on a device, for interacting with peer deployment managers that run on neighbor devices, and for collecting software components in order to satisfy the requests of the owner of the local device.

The CODEWAN platform was implemented in Java and is now fully operational. It currently interfaces with the execution frameworks JAMUS and JULIA, and it thus supports the deployment and the execution of untrusted Java applications [7], as well as that of applications designed using the Fractal component model [12]. CODEWAN should also be able to support the deployment of OSGi bundles in the near future, using the service-oriented framework OSCAR [4].

Ongoing work implies using this platform in realistic conditions in order to assess its efficiency, and in order to compare the results obtained with alternative deployment scenarios. Future work should aim at augmenting the platform's functionality, for example by integrating support for digitally signed and encrypted software components.

Acknowledgements

This work is supported by the "Conseil Régional de Bretagne" under contract B/1042 /2002/012/MASC.

References

1. Information Technology, Telecommunications and Information Exchange between Systems, Local and Metropolitan Area Networks, Specific Requirements Part 11: Wireless LAN Medium Access Control (MAC) and Physical Layer (PHY) Specifications. ANSI/IEEE Std 802.11, 1999.
2. Jesper Andersson. A Deployment System for Pervasive Computing. In *Proceedings of the International Conference on Software Maintenance (ICSM'2000)*, pages 262–270, San Jose, October 2000.
3. Frédéric Guidec and Hervé Roussain. Asynchronous Document Dissemination in Dynamic Ad Hoc Networks. In *Second International Symposium on Parallel and Distributed Processing and Applications (ISPA'04)*, pages 44–48, Hong-Kong, China, December 2004.
4. Richard S. Hall and Humberto Cervantes. An OSGi Implementation and Experience Report. In *IEEE Consumer Communications and Networking Conference*, Las-Vegas, USA, January 2004.
5. Richard S. Hall, Dennis Heimbigner, and Alexander L. Wolf. A Cooperative Approach to Support Software Deployment Using the Software Dock. In *International Conference on Software Engineering*, pages 174–183, 1999.
6. Radu Handorean, Rohan Sen, Gregory Hackmann, and Gruia-Catalin Roman. A Component Deployment Mechanism Supporting Service Oriented Computing in Ad Hoc Networks. Technical Report WUCSE-04-02, Washington University, Department of Computer Science, St. Louis, Missouri, 2004.
7. Nicolas Le Sommer and Frédéric Guidec. JAMUS: Java Accommodation of Mobile Untrusted Software. In *4th Nord EurOpen/Usenix Conference (NordU 2002)*, Helsinki, Finland, February 2002. Best Paper.
8. OMG. Corba components, version 3.0, June 2002.
9. Charles Perkins. *Ad Hoc Networking*, pages 2–3. Addison-Wesley, 2001.
10. Pavel Poupyrev, Masakatsu Kosuga, and Peter Davis. Analysis of Wireless Message Broadcast in Large Ad Hoc Networks of PDAs. In *Proceedings of the Fourth IEEE conference on Mobile and Wireless Communications Networks*, pages 299–303, 2002.
11. Pavel Poupyrev, Masakatsu Kosuga, and Peter Davis. Analysis of Wireless Message Broadcast in Large Ad Hoc Networks of PDAs. In *Proceedings of the Fourth IEEE conference on Mobile and Wireless Communications Networks*, pages 299–303, 2002.
12. Éric Bruneton, Thierry Coupaye, Matthieu Leclercq, Vivien Quéma, and Jean-Bernard Stefani. An Open Component Model and Its Support in Java. In *7th International Symposium on Component-Based Software Engineering*, pages 7–22. Springer-Verlag Heidelberg, 2004.
13. Elizabeth M. Royer and Chai-Keong Toh. A Review of Current Routing Protocols for Ad-Hoc Mobile Wireless Networks. *IEEE Personal Communications Magazine*, pages 46–55, April 1999.
14. Yoav Sasson, David Cavin, and André Schiper. Probabilistic Broadcast for Flooding in Mobile Ad Hoc Networks. Technical Report IC/2002/54, Swiss Federal Institute of Technology (EPFL), 2002.
15. Diego Sevilla, José M. García, and Antonio Gómez. Design and Implementation Requirements for CORBA Lightweight Components. In *Proceedings of International Conference on Parallel Processing. Workshop on Metacomputing Systems and Applications.*, pages 213–218, sep 2001.

16. Nils P. Sudmann and Dag Johansen. Software Deployment Using Mobile Agents. In Judith Bishop, editor, *Proceedings of the IFIP/ACM Working Conference on Component Deployment (CD 2002)*, volume 2370 of *LNCS*, pages 97–107, Berlin, Germany, June 2002. Springer.
17. Sun Microsystems. Java Web Start 1.5.0 Documentation, 2004.
18. The Apache Software Foundation. Apache Maven. http://maven.apache.org/.
19. Stefanos Zachariadis, Cecilia Mascolo, and Wolfgang Emmerich. SATIN: A Component Model for Mobile Self Organisation. In *CoopIS/DOA/ODBASE (2)*, pages 1303–1321, 2004.

Infrastructure for Automatic Dynamic Deployment of J2EE Applications in Distributed Environments

Anatoly Akkerman, Alexander Totok, and Vijay Karamcheti

Department of Computer Science,
Courant Institute of Mathematical Sciences,
New York University, New York, NY, USA
{akkerman, totok, vijayk}@cs.nyu.edu

Abstract. Recent studies have shown the potential of using component frameworks for building flexible adaptable applications for deployment in distributed environments. However this approach is hindered by the complexity of deploying component-based applications, which usually involve a great deal of configuration of both the application components and system services they depend on. In this paper we propose an infrastructure for automatic dynamic deployment of J2EE applications, that specifically addresses the problems of (1) inter-component connectivity specification and its effects on component configuration and deployment; and (2) application component dependencies on application server services, their configuration and deployment. The proposed infrastructure provides simple yet expressive abstractions for potential application adaptation through dynamic deployment and undeployment of components. We report on our experience with implementing the infrastructure as a part of the JBoss J2EE application server and testing it on several sample J2EE applications.

1 Introduction

In recent years, we have seen a significant growth in component-based enterprise application development. These applications are typically deployed on company Intranets or on the Internet and are characterized by high transaction volume, large numbers of users, and wide area access. Traditionally they are deployed in a central location, using server clustering with load balancing (horizontal partitioning) to sustain user load. However, horizontal partitioning has been shown to be effective only in reducing application-related overheads of user-perceived response times, without having much effect on network-induced latencies. Vertical partitioning (e.g., running web tier and business tier in separate VMs) has been used for fault isolation and load balancing and can in principle reduce network latencies but has traditionally been considered impractical due to significant run-time overheads (even if one keeps the tiers on a fast local-area network) related to heavy use of remote invocations. The work in [1] has shown that a handful of design patterns and application skeletons can enable efficient vertical partitioning of component-based applications in wide-area networks without incurring the aforementioned overheads. Using techniques proposed in that study in conjunction with intelligent monitoring [2] and AI planning techniques [3,4], we see a potential

A. Dearle and S. Eisenbach (Eds.): CD 2005, LNCS 3798, pp. 17–32, 2005.

for dynamic adaptation in industry-standard component-based applications (e.g., J2EE-based), through demand-driven deployment of additional application components as appropriate for changing application usage patterns.

However, in order to achieve such dynamic adaptation, we need an infrastructure for automating component-based application deployment in distributed environments. Taking the J2EE framework as an example, this need is quite evident to anyone who has ever tried deploying a J2EE application even on a single application server, which is a task that involves a great deal of configuration of both the application components and system services they depend on. For example one has to set up JDBC data sources, messaging destinations and other resource adapters before application components can be configured and deployed. In a deployment that spans multiple server nodes, this process proves even more complex, since more system services that facilitate inter-node communications need to be configured and started and a variety of configuration data, like IP addresses, port numbers, JNDI names and others have to be consistently maintained in various configuration files on multiple nodes.

In general, a distributed deployment infrastructure must be able to:

- support inter-component connectivity specification and define its effects on component configuration and deployment,
- address application component dependencies on application server services, their configuration and deployment,
- provide simple but expressive abstractions to control adaptation through dynamic deployment and undeployment of components,
- enable reuse of services and components to maintain efficient use of resources on application server nodes,
- provide these facilities without incurring significant additional design effort on behalf of application programmers.

In this paper, we describe an infrastructure for automatic deployment of J2EE applications, that addresses all of the aforementioned issues. The infrastructure defines two architecture description languages (ADL) for component and link description and component assembly respectively. The *Component Description Language* is used to describe application components and links. It provides clear separation of application components from system components. A flexible type system is used to define compatibility of component ports and links. A declaration and expression language for *configurable component properties* allows for specification of inter-component dependencies and propagation of properties between components. The *Component (Replica) Assembly Language* allows for assembly of replicas of previously defined components into application paths by connecting appropriate ports via link replicas and specifying the mapping of these component replicas onto target application server nodes. In addition, the infrastructure incorporates a *Component Configuration Process*, which evaluates an application path's correctness, identifies the dependencies of application components on system components, and configures component replicas for deployment. An attempt is made to match and reuse any previously deployed replicas in the new path based on their configurations.

We have implemented the infrastructure as a part of the JBoss open source Java application server [5] and tested it on several sample J2EE applications – Java Pet-

Store [6], RUBiS [7] and TPC-W-NYU [8]. The infrastructure implementation utilizes JBoss's extensible *micro-kernel* architecture, based on the Java Management Extensions (JMX) specification, to allow incremental service deployments depending on the needs of deployed applications. We believe that dynamic reconfiguration of application servers through dynamic deployment and undeployment of system services is essential to building a resource-efficient framework for dynamic distributed deployment of J2EE applications.

The rest of the paper is organized as follows. Section 2 provides necessary background for understanding the specifics of the J2EE component technology which are relevant to this study. Section 3 gives a general description of the infrastructure architecture, while Section 4 goes deeper in describing particularily important and interesting internal mechanisms of the infrastructure. Section 5 describes the implementation of the framework. In Section 6 we report on our experience with using the infrastructure and we conclude with a discussion of related work is Section 7.

2 J2EE Components

The infrastructure differentiates between application components and system components (system services).[1]

Application components are typically custom developed for a given application, like web-tier components (e.g., servlets and JSPs) and business-tier components (e.g., EJBs). The infrastructure also treats certain resources that are technically provided to the application by system services as application components, since they tend to represent resources that are in exclusive use by the application. Such application components are exemplified by JMS messaging destinations (e.g., topics and queues), and data sources (e.g., JDBC connection pools managed by the application server).

System components are typically services or resources that are part of the underlying application server and are shared by several applications running in the same application server. System components are exemplified by the JMS Messaging Service and the Transaction Manager service.

2.1 Links Between Components

Remote Interactions. J2EE defines only three basic inter-component connection types that can cross application server boundaries:

- *Remote EJB invocation:* synchronous EJB invocations through EJB Home and EJB Object interfaces.
- *Java Connector outbound connection:* synchronous message receipt, synchronous and asynchronous message sending, database query using ConnectionFactory and Connection interfaces.
- *Java Connector inbound connection:* asynchronous message delivery into Message-Driven Beans (MDBs) only, utilizing ActivationSpec objects.

---

[1] For space reasons, the paper does not provide a high-level description of the J2EE framework. The reader is referred to [9] for additional details.

In all scenarios, communication between components is accomplished through special Java objects. In the first two cases, an application component developer writes the code that performs lookup of these objects in the component's run-time JNDI context as well as code that issues method invocations or sends and receives messages. The component's run-time JNDI context is created for each deployment of the component. Bindings in the context are initialized at component deployment time by the deployer (usually by means of a component's deployment descriptors). These bindings are assumed to be static, since the J2EE specification does not provide any contract between the container and the component to inform of any binding changes.

In the case of Java Connector inbound communication, ActivationSpec object lookup and all subsequent interactions with it are done implicitly by the MDB container. The protocol for lookup has not been standardized, though it is reasonable to assume a JMX- or JNDI-based lookup.

Assuming the underlying application server provided facilities to control each step of the deployment process, establishment of a link between J2EE components would involve: (1) deployment of target component classes (optional for some components, like destinations), (2) creation of a special Java object to be used as a target component's proxy, (3) binding of this object with the component's host naming service (JNDI or JMX), (4) start of the target component, (5) deployment of referencing component classes, (6) creation and population of the referencing component's run-time context in its host naming service, and finally (7) start of the referencing component.

However, none of the modern application servers allow detailed control of the deployment process for all component types beyond what is possible by limited options in their deployment descriptors.[2] Therefore, our infrastructure uses a simplified approach that relies on the following features currently available on most application servers:

- ability to deploy messaging destinations and data sources dynamically,
- ability to specify initial binding of EJB Home objects upon EJB component deployment,
- ability to specify a JNDI *reference* in the referencing component's run-time context to point to the EJB Home binding of the referenced EJB component.

In our infrastructure, which is currently limited to operating on homogeneous application servers, these options are sufficient to control inter-component links through simple deployment descriptor manipulation. Note however that for heterogeneous application servers, simple JNDI references and thus simple descriptor manipulation are insufficient due to cross-application-server classloading issues.

Local Interactions. Some interactions between components can occur only between components co-located in the same application server JVM and sometimes only in the

---

[2] For example, creation of EJB Home objects is usually automatically handled by the container, as well as its binding into JNDI. Some servers, notably JBoss, allow custom creation of multiple EJB Home objects (utilizing different remote invocation transport protocols) for a single EJB deployment, however their deployment is still coupled with deployment of the component itself. Ideally, one should be able to deploy the EJB component and then dynamically deploy any number of transport-specific EJB Home objects.

same container. In the Web tier, examples of such interactions are servlet-to-servlet request forwarding. In the EJB tier, such interactions include CMP Entity relations and invocations via EJB local interfaces. Such local deployment concerns need not be exposed at the level of a distributed deployment infrastructure other than to ensure colocation. Therefore, our infrastructure treats all components requiring colocation as a single component.

2.2 Deployment of System Components (Services)

While some of the issues of application component deployment were addressed with the introduction of the *J2EE Application Component Deployment Specification* in J2EE version 1.4, the J2EE standard falls short with respect to deployment of system services (components). Not only is a standardized deployment facility for system services not specified, the specification, in fact, places no requirements even on life cycle properties of these services, nor does it address the issue of explicit specification of application component dependencies on the underlying system services.

For example, an EJB with container managed transactions that declares at least one method that supports/requires/starts a new transaction would require the presence of a *Transaction Manager* service in the application server. Similarly, a message-driven bean implicitly requires an instance of a messaging service running somewhere in the network that hosts the messaging destination for the MDB and a Java Connector based hook-up from within its hosting application server to this messaging service.

Given that applications would typically use only a subset of services provided by the application server, componentized application servers that allow incremental service deployments allow for most efficient utilization of server resources. There are some J2EE application servers that are already fully or partially componentized, including open-source application servers JBoss [5] and JOnAS [10]. We feel that dynamic reconfiguration of application servers through deployment and undeployment of system services is essential to building a resource-efficient framework for distributed deployment of J2EE applications. Therefore we advocate and will use as a model a micro-kernel application server design used by JBoss [11]. In this model a minimal server consists of a service invocation bus, a robust classloading subsystem, and a dynamic deployment subsystem. All other services are hot-deployable and communicate through the common invocation bus. Such an application server design facilitates explicit handling of application component dependencies on system services and proper configuration and deployment of only required system services.

3   Infrastructure Architecture

Table 1 introduces the definition of key infrastructure elements and terms used throughout this paper. The infrastructure consists of a network containing multiple application server nodes. Each application server node runs an infrastructure-controlled *Agent Service*. These agents communicate with an instance of a *Replication Management Service* (consisting of *Component Registry*, *Replica Configuration* and *Replica Deployment* Services) running on one application server node (which can be dedicated). In addition,

Table 1. Definition of key infrastructure elements and terms

application server (target) node	computer system or a cluster of computers that run an instance of the infrastructure-controlled application server
application path	abstraction that represents a deployment (potential or actual) of component replicas on infrastructure nodes such that these replicas are configured to properly communicate with each other preserving original application semantics
deployment specification	description of application paths as used by the infrastructure; it is written in the infrastructure-defined language and can be written manually, constructed by a planning algorithm, or generated from a visual representation of an application path using special visual editors
component replica	deployment of a component; there could be multiple deployments of the same component on different nodes and with different configurations
link	abstraction of connectivity between two components
link replica	instance of a link used to connect specific ports of specific component replicas in a deployment specification

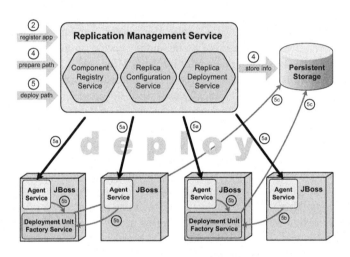

Fig. 1. Infrastructure architecture

a *Deployment Unit Factory Service* (one or more) runs on some subset of the nodes (see Fig. 1).

The infrastructure defines two architecture description languages (ADL) for component and link description and component assembly respectively. The main features of the *Component Description Language* are (1) a clear separation of system components from application components, (2) a flexible type system for component ports and links, (3) the ability to specify dependencies of both application and system components on other system components, and (4) a declaration and expression language for configurable component properties. The *Component (Replica) Assembly Language* allows for assembly of replicas of previously defined components into application paths by connecting appropriate ports via link replicas and specifying the mapping of these component replicas onto target application server nodes.

3.1 Infrastructure Usage

The usage of the infrastructure consists of the following set of steps (see also Fig. 1):

1. **Initialization.** The infrastructure is initialized with a description of available application server nodes. This description is supplied by a network administrator, alternatively, the nodes may be configured to register themselves with the infrastructure and provide sufficient information about themselves.
2. **System components and application registration.** The infrastructure has to be initialized with descriptions of system and application components as well as links prior to any requests for deployment of replicas of these components. These descriptions (written in the Component Description Language) are registered with the *Component Registry Service*. It is expected that an application server provider prepares and registers a description of system services (system components) and links that are available for dynamic deployment on compatible target nodes, while the application vendor prepares a description of application components.
3. **Writing the deployment path specification.** The application deployer writes a deployment path specification in the *Component Assembly Language*. In it s/he specifies the placement of components on the target nodes and links that connect them. The deployer may choose to write the specification by hand, or to use a GUI-based path editing tool, which also serves as a user-friendly portal to the Replication Management Service.
4. **Preparing deployment path.** After the initial registration, the infrastructure is ready to accept deployment requests. First, a deployment specification for an application path is submitted for *preparation* to the *Replication Management Service*. This service performs initial validation and passes the deployment specification to the *Replica Configuration Service*. The Replica Configuration Service, in turn attempts resolution of application component dependencies on system components and recursively, dependencies of newly discovered system components on other system components. If all component dependencies successfully resolve, the Configuration Service then configures each component replica. During configuration, the Configuration Service attempts to match any previously deployed replicas to replicas in the new path based on their configurations. All new replica deployment configurations are then persistently stored and any matched replicas that exist in other deployments are reused. This last step is called *committing the prepared path*.
5. **Deployment of prepared path.** If the path preparation and committing steps succeed, the infrastructure client can subsequently request deployment of the prepared path. Upon a deployment request from the user, the *Replica Deployment Service* issues deployment requests to appropriate agents on nodes involved in providing services for this path (step 5a). These agents, in turn, request deployable bundles of component replicas scheduled for deployment from a *Deployment Unit Factory Service*, located on a nearby node (step 5b). For each requested component replica's deployment bundle, the Deployment Unit Factory service locates the corresponding

replica configuration in persistent storage and generates a properly configured deployment bundle (step 5c). This bundle is then shipped to the requesting agent. The agent, upon receiving all deployable bundles for components and services scheduled for deployment on its node, deploys them in an order that respects deployment dependencies.

6. **Management of deployed paths.** The infrastructure maintains a registry of prepared paths, deployed paths and current state of application and system component replica deployments. Clients may request undeployment of previously deployed paths which will result in undeployment of component replicas that are exclusively used by the undeployed path.

4   Infrastructure Internals

In this section we describe in greater detail particularly important and interesting internal mechanisms of the infrastructure.

4.1   Component Description Language

The primary goal of the *Component Description Language* is to describe components and links between them. The components and links are grouped into applications. An application defines a namespace for components and links that it contains.

Ports. The most significant difference between the application components and system components is that application components declare *ports*, while system components do not. Ports of application components fall into two categories: *required* or *provided*. Declaration of a required port in a component description means that this component requires communication with another component. A declaration of a provided port means that the component can accept communication from another component (which in turn must have a matching required port). A port must declare a *type* (the port type) and a *link type*, these are used to check for semantic consistency of an assembly.

Port Type. Port type is a one of two mechanisms for assuring semantic consistency of component assembly. One can think of port types as interfaces to the component functionality. Port types are used in typechecking deployment specifications, so that a required port and a provided port can be connected to each other only of their types match. The infrastructure may use a pluggable type system and each application may define its own custom type system. The minimal requirements on a typesystem are that it implements checks for subtypes and exposes proper typesystem interfaces defined by the infrastructure.

```
<component name="ItemEJB">
    <provides>
        <port name="InvocationPort" type="Item"
              link-type="jboss.system.EJBLink">
            <property name="EJBObjectJNDI">Item-${systemId}</property>
        </port>
    </provides>
</component>
```

Fig. 2. Example of a component specification written in the Component Description Language

Port Link Type. Link types specify what link may connect this port to another port. It is the second mechanism for assuring semantic consistency of a component assembly. The intuitive understanding of a link type is of a communication protocol through which functionality of a component may be accessed. A port link type's value must be a name of a well-defined link, known to the infrastructure. Typically there are only a few link types defined by an application server provider, corresponding to the three basic remote connectivity options available to components (see section 2.1). Fig. 2 shows the usage of the *Port*, *Port Type*, and *Port Link Type* declarations.

Property Declaration Mechanism. This feature of the Component Description Language allows definition of adjustable component replica deployment configurations and at the same time expression of component dependency on system components.

Properties can be defined for components (application and system), ports and links. All application components implicitly define the systemId property. Property values are strings, they can be a constant string or a *property value expression* which evaluates to a string. Constant property values are simplest to understand, they remain constant for all replicas of the given component.

The same way that an application acts as a namespace for its components, components themselves act as namespaces for properties and ports, and ports act as namespaces for properties only. The values of properties are computed for each component replica and stored in a *replica configuration* during path preparation. More precisely, a *configuration* is a container for resolved property-value pairs from the corresponding property scope. Configurations corresponding to component-wide scope and port scope are linked in a parent-child relationship for the purpose of property value query delegation. The delegation is from child to parent and is very similar to standard programming languages that allow nested scopes, where variables declared in the outer scopes are visible in the inner scopes. For example, in case of the ItemEJB component (Fig. 2), a lookup of the systemId property against the configuration of the InvocationPort port would succeed because it will be delegated to the component-wide scope, where the systemId property is declared and stored.

A component replica's configuration (with nested subconfigurations for its ports), filled with resolved property values, completely defines this replica's deployment configuration. This configuration is subsequently used by the infrastructure to configure this replica's deployment descriptors.

Property Value Expression Language. The expression language for property values allows for concatenation of constant strings with values of other properties (of the same

```
<CompositeExpression>  ::= <SubExpression> |
                           <CompositeExpression><SubExpression>
<SubExpression>        ::= <string> |
                           ${<CompositeExpression>}|
                           ${<CompositeExpression>@<Namespace>}
<Namespace>            ::= <string>
```

Fig. 3. Backus-Naur definition of the property value expression language

```
<component name="ItemInvalidationTopic">
    <provides>
        <port name="DestinationPort"
              type="ItemInvalidationTopic"
              link-type="jboss.system.jbossmq.DestinationLink">
            <property name="DestManagerObjName">
                ${DestManagerMBeanName@jboss.system.jbossmq.Service}
            </property>
        </port>
    </provides>
</component>
```

Fig. 4. Example of a specification of component dependency on a system component

component replica or other components and links). Backus-Naur definition of the expression language is shown in Fig. 3. The ${...} operator is a *value of* operator, which performs value lookup of a named property that is specified inside the braces. The full name of a property has the form of <name>@<namespace>, where the @ symbol separates the property name from the namespace in which the property is to be looked up. For example, EJBObjectJNDI@OnlineStore.ItemEJB.InvocationPort is the full name of a EJBObjectJNDI property declared in the InvocationPort subscope of the ItemEJB component of the OnlineStore application. Alternatively, the namespace may be omitted, then the lookup will be done in the same namespace that contains the property whose expression is being evaluated.

Component Dependency Specification Through Property Value Expressions. As we have already described, the value of a property may depend on values of properties from other namespaces. External references to properties in namespaces other than the component's own, is the mechanism by which a component expresses dependency on a system component. The descriptor snippet in Fig. 4 contains a declaration of property DestManagerObjName in the scope of the DestinationPort port. The expression value for this property is a lookup of another property value, namely DestManagerMBeanName@jboss.system.jbossmq.Service. In this case, the referred namespace, jboss.system.jbossmq.Service, is in fact a name of a system component. This reference means that the ItemInvalidationTopic requires a replica of jboss.system.jbossmq.Service component running on the same node and it must be fully configured before we can properly configure the ItemInvalidationTopic component replica.

Propagation of Property Values. Imagine a situation where a component (CatalogEJB, in our example) has a required port that points to another component (ItemEJB). A link of type jboss.system.EJBLink (corresponding to the synchronous EJB invocation) connects these components. In order to properly connect to the ItemEJB component, the CatalogEJB component needs to know the value of some properties from the ItemEJB component's namespace, for example the JNDI name of the ItemEJB's Home Object.

We solve this problem by propagating property values between components, through properties of the link connecting the components. The ItemEJB component specifies an EJBObjectJNDI property of its provided port (Fig. 2). The link type `jboss.system.EJBLink` has a property `EJBObjectJNDI`, which, in the example below, evaluates in the context of the *target port*, that is, the provided port of the `ItemEJB` component:

```
<link type="jboss.system.EJBLink">
  <property name="EJBObjectJNDI">${EJBObjectJNDI@_targetPort}</property>
</link>
```

Now when the property value has been propagated to the link namespace, the last step in the chain is achieved by the following rule: if the property whose value is being evaluated is declared in the scope of a required port, and if the external namespace matches the link type of the port, it is then a reference to the link property:

```
<component name="CatalogEJB">
  <requires>
    <port name="PortToItem" type="Item" link-type="jboss.system.EJBLink">
      <property name="EJBObjectJNDI">
        ${EJBObjectJNDI@jboss.system.EJBLink}
      </property>
    </port>
  </requires>
</component>
```

Primary Component Properties. Sometimes a component's semantic role in the application may depend not only on components it references but on references to entities not modeled as components by the infrastructure. For example, a data source application component has no required ports, however, it has properties that define database connection parameters that this data source uses to connect to the external RDBMS. In order to handle such cases, we introduce the notion of *primary component properties*. Primary properties are usually the properties that need to be explicitly specified by the application deployer, such as the database host name for a data source application component.

4.2   Component Replica Assembly Language

The *Component (Replica) Assembly Language* is used for writing a deployment (path) specification. This relatively straightforward language (see Fig. 5) allows to request that a replica of a given component be deployed on a particular node and specify how its

```
<deployment-path path-id="...">
  <component-replica replicaId="93" name="CatalogEJB" targetId="hostB">
    <port-configuration name="PortToItem" .../>
  </component-replica>
  <component-replica replicaId="57" name="ItemEJB" targetId="hostA">
    <port-configuration name="InvocationPort" .../>
  </component-replica>
  <link-replica replicaId="152" link-type="jboss.system.EJBLink"
                _sourceEndpoint_id="93"
                _sourceEndpoint_portId="PortToItem"
                _destEndpoint_id="57"
                _destEndpoint_portId="InvocationPort"/>
</deployment-path>
```

Fig. 5. Component Replica Assembly Language code snippet for a 2-component path

ports are connected to ports of replicas of other components within the deployment specification. Only application components can be assembled using the assembly language. This design choice is intentional in order to allow the application path planner to focus only on application aspects of the path without worrying about system components needed to support correctness of the application components' operation. It is the role of the infrastructure to resolve dependencies of the application components on system components, and subsequently to configure and deploy the required system components.

4.3   Component Configuration Process

A deployment specification for an application path is a directed acyclic graph of replicas of components connected via links from required to provided ports.[3]

The component configuration process (preparing a deployment path) is a *leaf-to-root, post-order* processing of the DAG. *Leaf* replicas are ones that have no required ports and thus have no outgoing links. However, they may depend on system components through the property value expression mechanism (Section 4.1). So the algorithm in turn attempts resolution of application component dependencies on system components and recursively, dependencies of newly discovered system components on other system components. It then proceeds in the direction opposite to link direction. In this way, necessary property values are propagated from a component scope to the scope of its provided port, then to the link, then to the required ports of the connected components, according to the property value propagation mechanism (Section 4.1).

A replica in the graph is processed only after all component replicas that it connects to via its required ports are already processed. When configuring a replica, the following order of property resolution within component scopes is adopted: (1) component-wide scope, (2) provided ports, (3) required ports. This means that component-wide scope will be filled with resolved property-value pairs first, and only after that all properties for all provided and required ports are resolved. The order was chosen so that ports' properties may rely on component-wide properties being configured, so as to use their property values.

Component Reuse. A component's replica on a given node can be safely reused by multiple deployment paths if the same sequence of communications with the replica will result in the same application state. Replica reuse is an obvious optimization that allows for decreased deployment overheads and consistency management. Such reuse is permitted because in the J2EE component model, a component is unaware of any components that require it. Moreover, in J2EE, any references to other components required by a given component must be set at this component's deployment time, so a component is configurable only at deployment time. The infrastructure adopts the following component reuse algorithm, which is performed as a part of the preparing of an application deployment path, after component dependencies have been resolved and all components' properties have been evaluated:

---

[3] The acyclicity of the component graph is a simplifying assumption used in the current version of the algorithm. We believe the algorithm can be extended to allow cycles.

Component replica $R1$ of component C deployed on node N can be reused in place of component replica $R2$ of C on node N only if primary property values of these replicas are the same and subgraph of $R1$'s referenced component replicas can be reused in place of $R2$'s corresponding subgraph.

5   Implementation

We have implemented the infrastructure as a part of the JBoss open source Java application server [5], utilizing its extensible *micro-kernel* architecture, based on the JMX specification.

All infrastructure nodes run an instance of the JBoss application server. These JBoss instances are configured to start a custom *Agent MBean*, which serves as the infrastructure-controlled Agent Service (Section 3, see also Fig. 1). The Agent MBean plugs into the JBoss deployment mechanism.

One master node runs a JBoss instance with the *XmlBlaster Service*, which acts as a persistence back-end, to store the information of prepared application paths, deployed paths and current state of application and system component replica deployments. Xml-Blaster [12] is a Publish/Subscribe and Point-To-Point (PTP) Message-Oriented middleware (MOM) server, which exchanges messages between publishers and subscribers. Messages are described with XML-encoded meta information. A lot of features are supported, among them is a persistence support for messages. It is also equipped with the full text search capabilities – subscribers can use *regular expressions* to filter the messages they wish to receive. Our persistence and inter-node messaging is accomplished through XmlBlaster.

Any number of infrastructure nodes may serve as hosts to codebase and deployment generation services. This functionality is encapsulated in a deployable Web application (J2EE WAR) – *Deployer* – serving as the Deployment Unit Factory Service. It contains the codebases of the applications preregistered with the infrastructure, in the JAR format. An Agent MBean requests the predefined Deployer for the deployable bundles for components and JBoss services scheduled for deployment on its node. The Deployer queries the XmlBlaster storage back-end for the replica configurations, produces deployable bundles and returns them back to the Agent, which in turn deploys them on the node in the order preserving component dependencies.

As a part of the infrastructure, we have also implemented a GUI tool serving as a Replication Management Service client. With this tool, infrastructure users may:

– compose and edit application deployment path specifications for preregistered applications, rather than writing them manually using the Component Replica Assembly Language;
– interact with the Replication Management Service for preparing, committing, deploying and removing application deployment paths.

The Replication Management Service should run as a JBoss service or as a stand-alone application. In the current implementation, it runs as an application bundled with the GUI tool, with the *Java Event Notification* as the messaging mechanism between them. However, their codebases are decoupled and all necessary support for other pluggable (remote) communication mechanisms is available. Our future plans include implementation of a JMX-based communication mechanisms between the Replication Management Service and its clients (e.g., the GUI tool). Additional details of the implementation can be found in the documentation and by inspecting the source code of the infrastructure, which is available publicly from http://www.cs.nyu.edu/pdsg (follow the Software tab).

6   Infrastructure Usage Experience

The infrastructure was tested on several sample J2EE applications at hand – Java Pet-Store [6], RUBiS [7] and TPC-W-NYU [8] – to produce several multi-host distributed deployments of these applications. The code of Java PetStore and RUBiS was augmented with the design patterns, which were proposed in [1] for enabling efficient distribution of component-based applications. This also gave us an opportunity to test the infrastructure's configuration capabilities applied to messaging components (the original code of all three tested applications did not utilize JMS messaging at all). The infrastructure worked correctly and produced valid multi-node deployments of the tested applications. The preparation work included the writing of the application component descriptions using the Component Description Language, which was easy to achieve based on the original J2EE deployment descriptors.

Note that the Replication Management Service and the XmlBlaster persistent storage are centralized services. This fact introduces single points of failure into the system, and might slow down infrastructure performance in WAN environments. In principle, these services can be replicated to allow the infrastructure to scale, however, the current version of the infrastructure has not focused on this issue.

7   Related Work and Discussion

The *deployment* and *dynamic reconfiguration* of (distributed) component-based applications has been the subject of extensive research in the software engineering and distributed systems communities. Research efforts in this direction can be broadly divided into two camps. The first [3,13] try to construct a general model for a relatively broad class of systems, by identifying the required functionality for dynamic reconfiguration, but rarely provide immediately applicable mechanisms for actual reconfiguration. The second [18,15,16] provide practical mechanisms for carrying out certain kinds of reconfigurations, but usually assume a specialized system architecture to do so. The work presented in this paper belongs to the second category.

It has been acknowledged that *component dependencies* represent an important aspect of component-based systems, from the fault-tolerance, management and reconfiguration perspectives. In [13] the authors present a generic model of reifying dependencies in component systems. They identify two distinct kinds of dependencies: (1) requirements for loading a component into the system (called *prerequisites*), and (2) *dynamic dependencies* between loaded components in a running system. *Component prerequisites* are further subdivided into the three categories: (a) the *nature* of the hardware resources the component needs, (b) *capacity* of the hardware resources it needs, and

(c) the software services (such as other components) it *requires*. With regards to this generic dependency classification, the J2EE component model we are working with has only static dependencies (prerequisites of type (c)), which come as a specification of system and application components that are required for a given component to execute. J2EE does not allow for dynamic reconfiguration of deployed components, so J2EE deployment descriptors are sufficient for describing static deploy-time dependencies. In this work we do not address component hardware and QoS requirements at all, partly because it lies beyond the scope of the J2EE specification.

Augmenting middleware with additional services that simplify the tasks performed by application developers, deployers and system administrators naturally follows the spirit of the middleware paradigm. Several previous studies have proposed mechanisms of dynamic application reconfiguration through component redeployment and implemented them as middleware services. The work in [2,17] proposed active monitoring and micro-reboots for fast automatic recovery and fault isolation. Authors of [14] advocated the approach of running multiple versions of the component at the same time, to reliably upgrade the system. The authors of [18] built a middleware service for *atomic* redeployment of EJB components across multiple servers. Our work follows this path, by proposing an infrastructure that facilitates and automates component deployment in distributed environments. However, this paper is different from the previous work in component deployment in that it specifically addresses the problem of efficiently expressing dependencies of portable J2EE application components and connectors on services provided by the middleware. We are working strictly within the constraints imposed by the J2EE programming model and do not propose extensions to the J2EE specification.

The variety of deployed components resulting from the usage of our infrastructure represents an *application-level overlay network* of J2EE components analogous to that of [3], [14], and [1], where several instances of the same component may coexist together. We believe that J2EE limitations on component lifecycle, concurrency and state may allow for efficient models of consistency between multiple versions of the same stateful J2EE component. The proposed infrastructure may form a foundation for a tool for J2EE *component replication*, analogous to the replication of CORBA components [19]. Replication of J2EE components can be used for different purposes, ranging from failover and increased availability to differentiation of the service among several client groups.

Acknowledgments

This research was sponsored by DARPA agreements N66001-00-1-8920 and N66001-01-1-8929; by NSF grants CAREER:CCR-9876128, CCR-9988176, and CCR-0312956; and Microsoft. The U.S. Government is authorized to reproduce and distribute reprints for Government purposes notwithstanding any copyright annotation thereon. The views and conclusions contained herein are those of the authors and should not be interpreted as representing the official policies or endorsements, either expressed or implied, of DARPA, Rome Labs, SPAWAR SYSCEN, or the U.S. Government.

References

1. Llambiri, D., Totok, A., Karamcheti, V.: Efficiently distributing component-based applications across wide-area environments. In: Proceedings of the International Conference on Distributed Computing Systems (ICDCS). (2003) 412421
2. Chen, M. et al.: Pinpoint: Problem determination in large, dynamic, Internet services. In: Proc. of the International Conference on Dependable Systems and Networks. (2002)
3. Arshad, N., Heimbigner, D.,Wolf, A.L.: Deployment and dynamic reconfiguration planning for distributed software systems. In: Proceedings of the 15th International Conference on Tools with Artificial Intelligence (ICTAI03). (2003)
4. Kichkaylo, T., Ivan, A., Karamcheti, V.: Constrained component deployment in wide-area networks using AI planning techniques. In: Proceedings of the International Parallel and Distributed Processing Symposium (IPDPS). (2003)
5. JBoss Group: JBoss Application Server. http://www.jboss.org
6. Sun Microsystems Inc.: Java Pet Store Sample Application. http://java.sun.com/developer/releases/petstore/
7. ObjectWeb Consortium: RUBiS: Rice University Bidding System. http://rubis.objectweb.org/
8. TPC-W-NYU: A J2EE implementation of the TPC-W benchmark. http://www.cs.nyu.edu/ totok/professional/software/tpcw/tpcw.html
9. Sun Microsystems Inc.: *Java 2 Enterprise Edition.* http://java.sun.com/j2ee/
10. ObjectWeb Consort.: JOnAS Application Server. http://jonas.objectweb.org/
11. Fleury, M., Reverbel, F.: The JBoss extensible server. In: Proceedings of the ACM/IFIP/USENIX International Middleware Conference. (2003)
12. XmlBlaster Open Source Project: http://www.xmlblaster.org/
13. Kon, F., Campbell, R.H.: Dependence management in component-based distributed systems. IEEE Concurrency 8 (2000) 26–36
14. Rutherford, M. et al.: Reconfiguration in the Enterprise JavaBean component model. In: Proceedings of the Working Conference on Component Deployment. (2002) 67–81
15. Batista, T., Rodriguez, N.: Dynamic reconfiguration of component-based applications. In: Proceedings of the International Symposium on Software Engineering for Parallel and Distributed Systems. (2000)
16. Magee, J., Tseng, A., Kramer, J.: Composing distributed objects in CORBA. In: Proceedings of the Third International Symposium on Autonomous Decentralized Systems (ISADS97). (1997) 257–263
17. Candea, G. et al.: JAGR: An autonomous self-recovering application server. In: Proceedings of the 5th International Workshop on Active Middleware Services. (2003)
18. Cook, J.E., Dage, J.A.: Highly reliable upgrading of components. In: Proceedings of the 21st International Conference on Software Engineering (ICSE99). (1999)
19. Marangozova, V., Hagimont, D.: An infrastructure for CORBA component replication. In: Proceedings of the Working Conference on Component Deployment. (2002) 257–263

Component Deployment Using a Peer-to-Peer Overlay

Stéphane Frénot and Yvan Royon

INRIA Ares - CITI Lab - INSA Lyon,
Bat. Leonard de Vinci, 69621 Villeurbanne cedex, France
{stephane.frenot, yvan.royon}@insa-lyon.fr

Abstract. The deployment of component-based software applications usually relies on a centralized repository where the components are stored. This paper describes a peer-to-peer approach for components distribution. The software components are distributed among a set of nodes participating in the execution of services. When a node wants to install a component which is not present locally, this component is both searched and installed using a peer-to-peer network. The proposed architecture is an underlayer for OSGi application (*bundles*) deployment and execution management.[1]

1 Introduction

The installation of software component-based systems requires an infrastructure for the search and distribution of these components. Typically, an HTTP or FTP server hosts these components, and provides an indexation mechanism.

We describe a peer-to-peer (p2p) infrastructure implementation for the management of "installable" software components. This decentralized and distributed infrastructure dispatches the installable components, their index mechanism and their versioning system over a set of peer network nodes. The expected benefits are the distribution of storage and bandwidth load, as well as robustness due to peer-to-peer inherent characteristics.

We propose an application of this approach to the OSGi world, which currently has no standardized component deployment mechanism.

The OSGi technology is a proposition to standardize the way local services and peripherals are remotely operated. The OSGi specifications [1] define Java-like APIs for the execution of applications in a service-oriented programming way. An OSGi component (the deployment unit) is called a bundle. It is a Java jar archive, described by a Java manifest file. The OSGi Service Platform manages the bundles' life cycles, *i.e.* their state: stopped, installed, resolved, started.

Deployment within the OSGi context is summarized in section 2, while section 3 proposes an approach for deployment management, based on self-organized peer nodes.

---

[1] This work is partially supported by the IST-6thFP-507295 MUSE Integrated Project.

A. Dearle and S. Eisenbach (Eds.): CD 2005, LNCS 3798, pp. 33–36, 2005.

2 Deployment in the Context of OSGi Technology

The OSGi specifications do not currently address the deployment issue. Bundles
are retrieved using a provided URI, but no deployment mechanisms are proposed.

We use OSGi platforms with a specific actors model in mind: users own
a single OSGi service platform within their homes. Depending on subscriptions
the users contract, several service providers may want to install bundles on these
unique service gateways.

The only deployment architecture currently available is OBR (Oscar Bundle
Repository), from the Oscar [2] open source implementation of the OSGi specifications. With OBR, an XML descriptor file lists and details all bundles hosted
on a remote repository. The client service gateway retrieves this file and parses it
to mount a memory representation of the bundle it can install. The installation
is performed using HTTP requests with the URIs provided by the descriptor file.

OBR is a centralized repository. It is therefore weak to denial of service attacks, as well as peaks in CPU or bandwidth loads. Also, if the central repository
crashes, a potentially huge number of service gateways have no way to update
their bundle index.

All these problems are addressed by peer-to-peer networks. A peer network
comprised of all these service gateways would be a good way to distribute both
bundles and their index. We cast our choice upon a Pastry [3] network, since it
offers an effective way to locate resources (bundles in our case) among a set of
peer nodes. It also has interesting resource replication features, which make the
whole deployment infrastructure less error-prone.

A second problem we address is the versioning system. With the OSGi specifications and OBR, bundle version numbers are internal, *i.e.* they only appear
inside the bundle's manifest file. This makes it impossible for a lower-layer deployment system to include version management. We propose to include the
version number in the bundle name, and to integrate this information within
the peer-to-peer search mechanism. This enables service gateways for automated
and integrated bundle updates.

3 Implementing a Peer-to-Peer Deployment Network

3.1 OSGi Components Deployment

General Network Architecture. Our p2p deployment infrastructure for
OSGi platforms uses a Pastry network. It is composed of 3 layers. The IP layer
identifies the participating OSGi service platforms. The Pastry layer allocates
each of these platforms a node identifier. The component layer locates OSGi
components on the Pastry peer network.

Diffusion of a Component. Any peer node can share a software component
on the network. To do so, the source node sends a **deposit request** for the
resource. A root node identifier is computed from the resource hash key, using
a function known to all peer nodes: `hash(<bundleName>)` ⇒ `root node ID`.

The route between the current node diffusing the resource and the root node is automatically calculated by the network: the component is routed hop by hop until the node which identifier is the closest to the root node ID is found. This last node then hosts the component.

This procedure is extended to include version management. In this case, resource publication requires 2 steps (see listing **??**). Firstly, the node with nodeID the closest to hash(<bundleName>) hosts the current version number for the bundle. This is obtained with the 1st call. Secondly, The actual bundle is named <bundleName>-<version>.jar instead of <bundleName>.jar. Its root node is the one with nodeID closest to hash(<bundleName>-<version>). The 2nd call which achieves this.

```
1. publish(hash(<bundleName>), <version>);
2. publish(hash(<bundleName>-<version>), bytecode);
```

Listing 1.1. Calls for publishing with version management

Installation of a Component. An OSGi bundle is a Java jar archive. Its name is its identifier. To install a component, the user types the **start** <bundleURI> command. For coherence reasons, the URI we use follow this pattern: p2p://<bundleName>. Hence, typing **start p2p://log.jar** retrieves the latest version of the **log.jar** bundle from the network and installs it locally.

More precisely, the client node requesting the bundle computes a hash key from the bundle's name (3rd call, listing **??**). This call returns the current version for this bundle. The second step is call number 4, which returns the actual bundle in its latest version.

```
3. retrieve(hash(<bundleName>));
4. retrieve(hash(<bundleName>-<version>));
```

Listing 1.2. Calls for retrieving a versioned bundle

Node Insertion. A node needs to know one node of the peer network in order to join the community. Once again, during a node insertion, Pastry's features are used: resources are redistributed among the nodes for balance reasons.

3.2   Implementation with FreePastry/Oscar

Our implementation uses the open source Oscar [2] implementation of OSGi specification, and FreePastry [4] for peer-to-peer distribution. We provide 3 OSGi bundles.[2]

---

[2] Available at http://ares.insa-lyon.fr/~sfrenot/devel/

The first one (pastryWrapper) is used by the OSGi service platform to declare itself to the peer network. The bundle manager also uses it to publish or retrieve bundles.

The second bunlde (p2pHandler) extends bundleRepository from the Oscar distribution. The usual bundleRepository (OBR, Oscar Bundle Repository) is the centralized index presented in section 2. We extend this system to integrate a protocol handler for `p2p://` URIs. Thus, if the bundle location follows the `p2p://<bundleName>` pattern, nodes using OBR directly search the peer-to-peer network.

Finally, the third bundle (posgiCommand) provides commands for Oscar's shell.

4   Comments and Conclusions

We have developed an infrastructure for deploying and downloading OSGi components, called bundles, over a peer-to-peer network. These bundles are downloaded from a `p2p://` URI, which we implement inside the OSGi service platform.

Future works include testing our implementation wide-scale. We still need to check Pastry's behavior within the OSGi context. We plan to run tests within the MUSE [5] project, which aims to define home connectivity and service delivery for European citizens.

We would also like to investigate the simultaneous use of several publish/discovery protocols, depending on the context. It would then be possible to use a broadcast search on the local area network. If no node replies, then the search is extended to routing mode. This is what Sun's JXTA framework does. In our case, this is interesting when deploying applications in computer rooms: remote downloading is done only once, and the remaining downloads are done locally.

References

1. Open Service Gateway initiative: Osgi specifications. http://www.osgi.org (2002)
2. Hall, R.S.: Oscar: Object service container architecture. http://oscar.objectweb.org (2004)
3. Rowstron, A., Druschel, P.: Pastry: Scalable, distributed object location and routing for large-scale peer-to-peer systems. In: Proceedings of IFIP/ACM Middleware. (2001) 33–34
4. FreePastry: http://freepastry.rice.edu. Rice University, Houston, Texas (2004)
5. MUSE Project: Ist-507295 fp6. http://www.ist-muse.org/ (2004)

A Methodology for Developing and Deploying Distributed Applications

Graham N.C. Kirby, Scott M. Walker, Stuart J. Norcross, and Alan Dearle

School of Computer Science, University of St Andrews,
North Haugh, St Andrews, Fife KY16 9SX, Scotland
{graham, scott, stuart, al}@dcs.st-and.ac.uk

Abstract. We describe a methodology for developing and deploying distributed Java applications using a reflective middleware system called RAFDA. We illustrate the methodology by describing how it has been used to develop a peer-to-peer infrastructure, and explain the benefits relative to other techniques. The strengths of the approach are that the application logic can be designed and implemented completely independently of distribution concerns, easing the development task, and that this gives great flexibility to alter distribution decisions late in the development cycle.

1 Introduction

This paper presents a methodology for developing and deploying distributed applications. This exploits many features of the RAFDA middleware system [1-4], the most significant of which is its ability to separate distribution concerns completely from the core application logic. The middleware allows any application object to be made remotely accessible. This means that any changes to distribution boundaries within the application do not require re-engineering of the application, making it easier to change the application's distribution topology. This separation of concerns simplifies the software engineering process to the programmer's advantage both when creating a new distributed application and when introducing distribution into an existing application.

In outline, the methodology involves three successive phases:

- The application is designed, implemented and tested without taking any account of how it will be distributed.
- Various mandatory details of distribution are defined, including how application objects should be partitioned across the network, which should be remotely accessible, and how they are initially connected.
- Other optional issues may be addressed—or may be ignored—including error handling of network-related failures, parameter passing semantics, and the insertion of monitoring probes.

Code written during the second and third phases is logically separated from the original application code written during the first phase; the original code executes unchanged, whether locally or distributed. Although the additional effort required to distribute the application is non-trivial, because the extra code resides in newly

A. Dearle and S. Eisenbach (Eds.): CD 2005, LNCS 3798, pp. 37–51, 2005.

written classes rather than pervading the application logic, it is relatively straightforward to write, and to change at any time, including late in the development cycle.

2 Related Work

Industry-standard middleware systems—CORBA [5], Java RMI [6], Microsoft COM [7], Microsoft .NET remoting [8] and Web Services [9]—are complex, making the creation of distributed applications difficult and error-prone. Programmers must ensure that application classes supporting remote access correctly adhere to the particular rules of the middleware system in use, for example, extending certain base classes, implementing certain interfaces or handling distribution-related error conditions.

This affects inheritance relationships between classes and often prevents application classes from being remotely accessed if their super-classes do not meet the necessary requirements. At best, this forces an unnatural or inappropriate encoding of application semantics because super-classes are often required to be accessible remotely for the benefit of their sub-classes and, at worst, application classes that extend pre-compiled classes cannot be made accessible remotely at all.

The above systems all require programmers to follow similar steps in order to create the remotely accessible classes. Programmers must specify the interfaces between distribution boundaries then decide which classes will implement these interfaces. Thus classes are hard-coded at the source level to support remote accessibility; programmers must therefore know how the application objects will be distributed at run-time when defining classes—early in the design cycle.

The difficulties inherent in creating and configuring distributed applications are addressed by several second-generation middleware systems. These allow programmers to employ code transformation techniques to generate the distribution-related code automatically. J-Orchestra [10] and Pangaea [11] transform non-distributed applications into distributed versions based on programmer input. They perform static code analysis and employ tools to help programmers choose suitable partitions. Distributed versions of applications are automatically generated from the local versions and so the re-engineering process is simplified, making a trial and error approach to creating applications more feasible.

ProActive [12] and JavaSymphony [13] allow objects to be exposed to remote access dynamically. However, both subtly alter application threading semantics and force programmers to ensure referential integrity manually through their use of active objects [14]. This requires programmers to consider both application distribution and the middleware system's threading model at class creation time in order to ensure that thread safety is retained after objects are exposed to remote access or migrated to other address-spaces.

In all current middleware systems, the parameter-passing semantics employed during remote method calls are determined statically, often at design-time. Programmers cannot take advantage of run-time knowledge or application-specific information to alter these semantics dynamically. Generally, semantics are based on the remote accessibility of the application classes [6, 8] or defined in the classes explicitly [5].

3   The RAFDA Middleware System

By contrast with existing middleware systems, the RAFDA Run-Time [1-4] (RRT) permits arbitrary application objects to be dynamically exposed for remote access. Object instances are exposed as Web Services through which remote method invocations may be made. The RRT has four notable features that differentiate it from other middleware technologies:

1. The programmer need not decide statically which classes support remote access. Any object instance from any application, including compiled classes and library classes, can be deployed as a Web Service without the need to access or alter application class source code.
2. The system integrates the notions of Web Services, Grid Services and Distributed Object Models by providing a remote reference scheme synergistic with standard Web Services infrastructure, and extending the pass-by-value semantics provided by Web Services with pass-by-reference semantics. Specific object instances rather than object classes are exposed as Web Services, further integrating the Web Service and Distributed Object Models. This contrasts with systems such as Apache Axis [15] in which classes are deployed as Web Services.
3. Parameter passing mechanisms are flexible and may be controlled dynamically. Parameters and result values can be passed by-reference or by-value and these semantics can be decided on a per-call basis.
4. When objects are passed by-reference to remote address-spaces, the system deploys them automatically. Thus an object b that is returned by method m of deployed object a is automatically deployed before method m returns.

Although the RRT is written in Java and is designed to support Java applications, it does not rely on any features unique to Java.

4   Development and Deployment Methodology

The methodology is designed to support a separation between core application logic and the details of its distribution. It focuses specifically on the implementation and testing phases of the software engineering process. The steps involved are as follows:

1. Design and implement the application code, without taking any account of how it will be distributed.
2. Deploy, test and debug the (currently non-distributed) application within a single address-space.
3. Define how the application will be (initially) distributed.
4. Define how the new failure modes introduced by distributing the application should be handled (optional).
5. Define particular object transmission, caching and exception handling policies (optional).
6. Deploy, test and debug the application in multiple address-spaces on a single physical host.
7. Deploy, test and debug the application in a fully distributed setting.
8. Design and deploy probes to monitor the execution of the distributed application (optional).

For simplicity, these steps are described as a linear progression from start to finish. In practice the developer will often return to previous steps, as is common in many software engineering approaches. Indeed, it is a distinct benefit of this methodology that it is very simple to revisit and alter earlier decisions made regarding distribution policy. This is possible because the distribution policy and logical code structure are orthogonal to each other; furthermore the different policies, for example distribution policy and parameter-passing policies are also orthogonal to each other. In most middleware systems these orthogonal issues are conflated.

4.1 Implementation of Application Logic

The initial step is to design and implement the application logic, without taking any account of how the application will be distributed. The entire application at this stage will run within a single Address Space (AS). Interaction between components of the application, which may involve remote calls over the network in the final distributed version, is implemented using standard inter-object method calls.

This allows the developer to concentrate on the core logic, ignoring distribution issues[1]. In particular, the developer need not:

- (ever) write any networking code
- consider which application objects will communicate with remote objects
- extend or implement any special base classes or interfaces to enable remote communication

Although this is described as a single step in the methodology, it would typically represent most of the development effort.

The methodology will be illustrated in the context of developing JChord, an implementation of the Chord peer-to-peer protocol [16]. This employs a global ring topology to link all participating nodes, with additional inter-peer links to support resilience and efficient routing. Each node has a unique key; the node keys are used to order the nodes in the ring. The fundamental operation provided by the peer-to-peer network is *lookup()*, which maps a key to the node currently "in charge" of that key.

Although a Chord network may contain a large number of participating nodes, the intrinsic symmetry of the peer-to-peer model means that the software running on most of the nodes is identical. In the JChord implementation, four principal node types can be identified:

- the initial network node
- any other network node
- a diagnostic console node that receives events from network nodes
- a control node that is able to start and stop network nodes

The first and second node types differ only in the way that they are initialised: the initial node needs no configuration information, whereas all nodes subsequently joining the network must be configured with a reference to a node already in the network. Fig. 1 shows an (extremely simplified) outline of a class *P2PNode* that implements a

---

[1] With the exception that all fields in any class that may be accessed remotely must be **private**. This is often regarded as good coding practice anyway.

```
public class P2PNode {
    private final Key key;
    private IP2PNode successor;
    public Key getKey(){...}
    public IP2PNode getSuccessor(){...}
    public void setSuccessor(IP2PNode successor){...}
    public IP2PNode lookup(Key key){...}
    public void route(Key key, Message msg){...}
    public void start(){...}
    public void stop(){...}
    public void setConsole(IConsole console){...}
}
```

Fig. 1. Outline of peer-to-peer node implementation

```
public class ConsoleNode {
    public void receiveEvent(Event event){...} }
```

Fig. 2. Outline of console node implementation

network node. At this stage the focus is on application logic rather than distribution, so although instances of the class are likely to be remotely accessible, the class does not implement any special interface or extend any base classes.

The methods respectively: return the key of a node; get and set the successor node in the ring; lookup the node corresponding to a key; route a message to the node for a given key; start and stop the node; and set the diagnostic console to which events should be sent. The interfaces *IP2PNode* and *IConsole* are defined in Fig. 5.

Fig. 2 shows the outline of a class *ConsoleNode* that implements a diagnostic console. The method *receiveEvent* allows a diagnostic event to be delivered to it by a network node.

A class *ControlNode* defines the control node type; details are omitted here. The completion of the implementation of these classes concludes the first development step. At this point it is possible to deploy and test the application in a single AS as described in step two. In contrast to most common middleware systems, the design and implementation thus far has not required the developer to consider distribution boundaries, extend base classes or implement particular interfaces. This eases the development task and retains flexibility with respect to how the resulting objects will be distributed.

4.2 Local Deployment and Testing

The next step is to deploy the application in a single AS and design a test suite for the core application logic, using conventional tools such as JUnit [17]. This may, of course, be integrated with the previous step for a test-driven development approach. Tests are run and any defects corrected.

The key point here is that although the entire application runs within a single AS at this stage, it is the real application code that is executing rather than a simulation. Few changes will be made to that logic during the later steps that introduce distribution, giving little scope for the introduction of further programming defects. In particular, there is no need to transform or translate the original code into a distributed form.

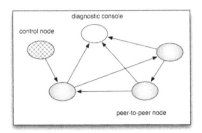

Fig. 3. JChord objects running in single AS

Fig. 3 shows a minimal JChord network in a testing configuration within a single AS. Three peer-to-peer node objects are linked in a ring; each of these refers to a diagnostic console object; a control node object refers to one of the peer-to-peer nodes in order to control it.

This configuration is created by a test program that instantiates the five objects and then establishes the connections among them. Testing checks that the ring is correctly formed, that *lookup()* and *route()* work as expected, that diagnostics are displayed by the console, etc.

The benefit of the methodology at this testing stage is that the developer can focus exclusively on verifying the application logic, ignoring issues of distribution.

4.3 Definition of Initial Application Distribution

Once a functional local version of the application has been produced in the previous steps, the developer defines its distribution. This involves:

- deciding how the application objects should be partitioned across the available ASs,
- deciding which objects should be made available for remote access (i.e. objects whose methods can be called by objects in remote ASs), and
- deciding the initial inter-AS object "wiring" (i.e. which pairs of objects located on different ASs should be connected by references)

These decisions feed into a number of coding activities. First, multiple entry points must be defined for the application, corresponding to each of the ASs on which part of the application will run. Thus whereas the initial version of the application may contain only a single class with a *main()* method, now a separate class with a *main()* is required for each entry point[2]. Execution of the application via the appropriate entry point on a particular AS results in instantiation of the appropriate application objects for that AS[3]. The partititioning for the JChord application is straightforward: each of the JChord objects described previously is placed in a separate AS, as illustrated in Fig. 4.

---

[2] Depending on the symmetry of the application, it is often possible for a particular entry point class to be used for multiple hosts.

[3] Support for remote object instantiation according to specified policies is under development.

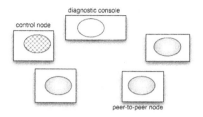

Fig. 4. JChord objects partitioned across ASs

Implementation of this partition involves writing an application entry point (a class with a *main()* method) for each of the four distinct node types. In each case the *main()* method creates an instance of the corresponding class (*P2PNode*, *ConsoleNode* or *ControlNode*). Where some configuration of the new object is required—for example, a *P2PNode* joining an existing network needs to be given references to an existing peer-to-peer node and to the console node—the configuration information is passed in the command line parameters.

Next, for each entry point, additional *deployment* code must be written to make the appropriate objects remotely accessible. Typically only a relatively small number of objects need be made remotely accessible; these will act as entry points. A deployed object may expose one or more *deployment interfaces*. Deployment interfaces are defined using Java classes or interfaces whose methods are structurally compatible with those defined in the object's actual class. The class need not have been defined as extending those classes or implementing those interfaces. This means that an interface through which a deployed object is exposed may be decided after the object already exists. The RRT provides the following API:

```
void deploy(Object objectToBeDeployed,
            Class interfaceToBeExposed, String deploymentName)
```

In the JChord application, three logically distinct interfaces can be identified: one exposing peer functionality to other peers, one supporting remote control of a peer from any other object, and one allowing peers to send events to the console. Fig. 5 shows the definitions of the corresponding interfaces *IP2PNode*, *IManage* and *IConsole*.

```
public interface IP2PNode {
    public Key getKey();
    public IP2PNode getSuccessor();
    public void setSuccessor(IP2PNode successor);
    public IP2PNode lookup(Key key);
    public void route(Key key, Message msg); }

public interface IManage {
    public void start();
    public void stop(); }

public interface IConsole {
    public void receiveEvent(Event event); }
```

Fig. 5. JChord remote interfaces

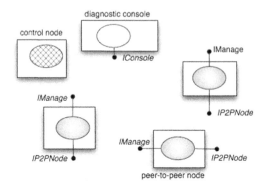

Fig. 6. JChord objects deployed for remote access

```
P2PNode p2pNode = new P2PNode();
// initialisation code omitted for brevity
RAFDARunTime.deploy(p2pNode, IManage.class, "Manage");
RAFDARunTime.deploy(p2pNode, IP2PNode.class, "P2P");
```

Fig. 7. Code to deploy remote interfaces

As shown in Fig. 6, interfaces *IP2PNode* and *IManage* are both exposed by each peer-to-peer node; *IConsole* is exposed by the console; while the control node need not expose any remote interface. It should be emphasised again that the classes *P2PNode* and *ConsoleNode* were not declared as implementing any of these interfaces. This means that the decision as to what interfaces are exported can be made later in the development cycle than the definition of the functionality[4].

The code to deploy the appropriate remote interfaces is added to the *main()* method in the corresponding application entry point class. This is illustrated in Fig. 7, which shows the deployment of *IP2PNode* and *IManage* interfaces for a new *P2PNode*.

Finally, wiring code is needed to establish connections between objects on different ASs. Each connection consists of a remote reference held by an object, denoting another object in a remote AS. Since remote references are indistinguishable from local references, this is sufficient to allow methods on the remote object to be called. Each remote reference is obtained by a method call to the local middleware infrastructure, passing it a description of the remote AS identified by IP address and port, and a name or identifier for the required object. The RRT provides the following API for this purpose:

```
Object getObjectByName(SocketAddress rrt, String name)
```

Further connections can be established dynamically, through a remote method call returning a reference to another object. Thus the initial wiring code can be fairly minimal; only one connection into every AS is necessary to give connectivity between the different parts of the application.

---

[4] It also means that instances of library classes can be made remotely accessible even if the source code of those classes cannot be modified.

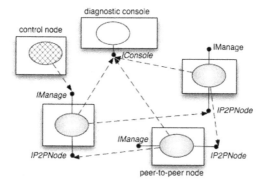

Fig. 8. Remote connections established between JChord objects

```
public static void main(String[] args {
    P2PNode p2pNode = new P2PNode();    // As in Fig. 7
    ... // deployment code omitted
    SocketAddress successorAddr = ...   // extract from args
    SocketAddress consoleAddr = ...     // extract from args
    IP2PNode succ = (IP2PNode)RAFDARunTime.getObjectByName(
                successorAddr, "P2P");
    p2pNode.setSuccessor(succ);
    IConsole cons = (IConsole)RAFDARunTime.getObjectByName(
                consoleAddr, "Console");
    p2pNode.setConsole(cons);
    p2pNode.start();
}
```

Fig. 9. Setting up inter-AS references in entry point for P2PNode joining ring

Since these distribution policy decisions are specified independently of the main application logic, they can be altered easily. The partition of objects across ASs can be changed between successive builds of the application[5]. Furthermore, the deployment of objects for remote accessibility, and the inter-AS connections, can be changed dynamically.

Fig. 8 shows an initial configuration for the JChord application equivalent to that shown for single AS testing in Fig. 3.

At this point, the necessary application components are extant in the appropriate ASs and available for remote access, but do not reference each other. The method *getObjectByName()*, described above, is used in order to establish remote references between the components. The only information that is required is the address of the RRT hosting each remote component, and the logical name. This code is added to each entry point class, taking details of the required network addresses from the command line parameters. Fig. 9 sketches the code to set up the references for a new peer-to-peer node joining the ring, from the node to its successor node and to the console node. The final *start()* call starts the node, so that it accepts remote calls and periodically executes its fault tolerance algorithms (not described here).

---

[5] Support for dynamic object migration is under development.

For ease of management it may be preferable instead for the network addresses of the various connection end-points to be specified in a configuration file, copied to all participating hosts, rather than reading them from the command line.

4.4   Definition of Distribution-Related Error Handling (Optional)

Distributing a hitherto non-distributed application introduces new failure modes: a method call to a remotely accessible object may now fail due to network or remote host failures. If the developer wishes to specify in detail how such failures should be handled, this can be achieved by specifying appropriate exception handlers for remote method calls.

However, the RRT middleware can handle such errors automatically, in which case failure of a *void* remote method call will be invisible to the calling object, while failure of a remote method call that returns a result will lead to a default value (e.g. null, 0 etc) being returned. This capability is designed to increase distribution flexibility, in that code calling a method need not differ between local and remote calls. If used, however, the developer should be aware that remote calls may now return default values without warning. Automatic handling of distribution-related exceptions is disabled by default. This facility is especially useful in prototyping where different topologies can be easily explored without regard to application resilience.

To allow dynamic choice as to whether automatic handling is used, distribution-related exceptions are *unchecked*, achieved by sub-classing *RuntimeException*. The significance of this is that Java does not enforce the specification of handlers for code in which such exceptions may occur. Thus the developer has three choices:

- to enable automatic handling via a single API call
- to write no additional code at all
- to specify exception handlers in the normal way

In the first case, no network-related exceptions will be thrown, and default values will be returned from a remote call. In the second case, exceptions will be thrown and the calling application will fail. In the final case, exception handlers are written by the developer to catch network exceptions.

The first option is not appropriate for JChord, since network errors need to be detected and handled explicitly. With the second option, any error arising from network or remote node failure would throw an unchecked exception, which, not being caught, would terminate execution of the AS in which it occurred. This is unacceptable in the JChord application, which is designed to provide fault tolerance. If a peer-to-node is unable to communicate with its successor, for example, it should initiate action to locate a new successor.

```
try {
        IP2PNode nextButOne = successor.getSuccessor();
        ... }
catch (RafdaRuntimeException e) {
        // call to successor failed; initiate recovery actions
        Exception cause = e.getCause();
        ... }
```

Fig. 10. Handling a distribution-related error

Fig. 10 shows an example of exception handling code added for a call to *getSuccessor()* on a peer-to-peer node's successor, within the definition of the *P2PNode* class. Since the *successor* field holds a remote reference, calls performed on it may fail. Similar code is added for each remote call. The considerable developer effort required is the price paid for fault tolerance. Without it, the application would still function correctly on a reliable network, but would not be able to handle node or network failure.

4.5 Configuration of Middleware Policies (Optional)

The RRT middleware permits control of the following policies:

- whether parameters and result values for remote method calls should be passed by-reference or by-value (default: *by-reference*)
- whether particular fields of objects denoted by remote references should be cached locally, and if so whether methods of such objects that access cached fields should be executed locally (default: *not*)
- whether network-related errors should raise exceptions or be handled automatically (default: *raise exceptions*)

Default settings for these policies are designed such that the developer may omit this step and still obtain a functioning distributed application.

By default, all objects passed to and from a remote method call are passed by-reference. This preserves object identity and involves minimal change in application semantics between the initial local implementation and the distributed version. However, where it is known that an object's state will change infrequently, it may be desirable for it to be passed by-value so that future operations on it may be performed without the need for a remote call. This may improve efficiency and eliminate potential network-related errors. When an object is passed by-value, a copy is created in the receiving AS. The middleware does not currently provide any automatic coherency control, hence it is the responsibility of the application to maintain coherency of object copies in the event of update.

Parameter passing policy is controlled by the sending side. Thus the policy in effect within a particular AS controls the passing of parameters **to** remote calls to other ASs, and the returning of results to remote calls made **from** other ASs. The policy can be specified at various levels of granularity as appropriate: for all instances of a given class, for all parameters of a given method, or for specific method parameters. The RRT provides the following API for class-level control (others omitted here):

```
void setClassPolicy(Class c, int policy)
```

Field caching allows a reference transmitted to a remote AS to include copies of particular fields of the referenced object. Typically this is used in cases where fields are not expected to be updated. As with passing by-value, this may improve efficiency and eliminate potential network-related errors. Method caching allows a method call on a remote object to be evaluated locally, in cases where all the fields accessed by the method are locally cached. Again, the motivations are efficiency and fault-tolerance. Setting all fields to be cached would have the same effect as passing

```
TransmissionPolicyManager.setClassPolicy(
    Key.class, BY_VALUE, LOW);
// LOW priority allows this to be overridden
// by more specific policies
TransmissionPolicyManager.setClassPolicy(
    Message.class, BY_VALUE, LOW);
```

Fig. 11. Setting transmission policy for particular classes

```
TransmissionPolicyManager.setFieldToBeCached(
    P2PNode.class.getField("key"));
TransmissionPolicyManager.setMethodToBeCached(
    P2PNode.class.getMethod("getKey"));
```

Fig. 12. Setting field and method caching

by-value, thus this mechanism may be viewed as giving finer control than the by-reference / by-value distinction. The RRT provides the following API:

```
void setFieldToBeCached(Field field)
void setMethodToBeCached(Method method)
```

In the JChord implementation, instances of classes *Key* and *Message* are candidates for being transmitted by-value, since they are immutable and likely to be relatively small. This is specified by further code added to the entry point classes, illustrated in Fig. 11.

The intention here is to set the transmission policy for these classes for the duration of the application execution. It is also possible to change the policy more dynamically. For example, the *route()* method might set the policy for *Message* instances to *BY_VALUE* for small messages, and to *BY_REF* for larger messages [3].

For this application it is also beneficial for each remote reference to a *P2PNode* to cache the value of the *key* field locally, and for calls to the *getKey()* method to be evaluated locally. This improves efficiency since keys are accessed frequently. The code to specify this is shown in Fig. 12.

A further benefit of this caching is that diagnostic code reporting failure of a peer node is able to access the peer's key even though the peer is inaccessible. Thus the exception handling block in Fig. 10 can include:

```
console.receiveEvent(new Event(
    "successor failed - key: " + successor.getKey()));
```

4.6   Local Distributed Deployment and Testing

The initial testing of the distributed version of the application can be performed on a single host, by instantiating multiple ASs locally. Communication between the RRT instances in the various ASs will take place via the loopback network interface in the same way as for genuinely distributed ASs. This allows testing of the object partitioning, the deployment of selected objects for remote access and the initial inter-AS object wiring in a reliable context, before the introduction of potential time-outs and other failures in the fully distributed setting.

Fault tolerance to distribution-related errors can be tested to some extent by killing various AS processes, producing a similar effect to the abrupt failure of a remote host or network connection in a genuinely distributed deployment. Since such errors are always possible, the developer should verify at this stage that the parts of the application on the surviving ASs handle such events in an acceptable way. The RRT also allows the developer to specify the class of *Socket* used for inter-RRT communication, allowing the use of *Socket* implementations which emulate connections that are low bandwidth, high latency, etc.

For repeated testing, it is useful to write scripts containing the Java commands to instantiate a number of ASs. Each command includes the entry point class for that AS, and parameters such as descriptions of other ASs (specified by IP address and port) to be used by the application in performing initial inter-AS object wiring. The command also specifies a Java classpath that includes the RRT *.jar* file.

Testing at this stage can be further automated using tools such as JUnit. It then becomes necessary to be able to initialise an entire collection of ASs under control of a running test program. This may be achieved using Java's *Runtime.exec()* to create ASs running within new processes. The test code can then establish inter-AS remote references to objects in other ASs, and proceed to carry out application tests. The only difference in the form of these application tests from those performed during single AS testing is that remote calls are, naturally, restricted to use only the interfaces through which the remote objects have been deployed.

Section 4.3 described how a separate entry point class can be written for each distinct variety of node, with a *main()* that instantiates and configures an instance of the appropriate class. This approach presents the problem of orchestrating the deployment and execution of the appropriate entry points on appropriate hosts. To ease this, it may be preferable to combine the entry points into a single class, which reads details from a local configuration file as to which variety of node is required. The problem is then reduced to one of distributing a single application image to all hosts, and tailoring the configuration file appropriately on each.

4.7 Full Distributed Deployment and Testing

The final testing phase involves genuine distribution of the application. This requires no changes to the code or the tests developed in the previous step, but the deployment infrastructure must be adapted. Two actions are required: copying of the application code and the RRT release *.jar* file onto each host, and execution of the appropriate application entry point on each host. On a small scale this can be performed manually. For a more scalable solution these tasks can be automated using a deployment application written in Java. This uses an SSH library [18] to establish a secure connection to each of the remote hosts and create a process that copies the required files and runs a AS with the appropriate application entry point.

An interactive tool has been developed to support simple launching of a JChord ring with any number of nodes. Each node runs in a separate AS, created either locally or remotely via SSH. AS processes can be killed to simulate failure. The tool also provides an API.

4.8 Monitoring (Optional)

It may be useful to monitor the state of a running distributed application, for the purposes of debugging or for gathering ongoing diagnostics. The RRT middleware offers two approaches:

- the RRT instance running on a particular host/AS may be queried via a web browser
- probe objects, tailored to the application, may be dynamically deployed within a particular AS

Each RRT instance runs a web server, which can be accessed using a conventional web browser to obtain information about deployed objects. Each deployed object is listed, showing the deployment interface, service class, service name and a string representation of the service object[6]. This interface can be used to verify which objects have been successfully deployed within a particular AS.

Fig. 13 shows the web interface provided by the instance of the RRT running in a particular AS. It lists the deployed interfaces, with the corresponding classes and objects. In this example each interface is accessible both via a logical deployment name and via a generated unique identifier.

Fig. 13. Web interface for RRT instance

Probe objects to monitor particular aspects of the application's execution can be installed and accessed remotely, either by another Java application via the RRT middleware, or by any Web Services client—by virtue of the fact that the RRT uses Web Services as its remote invocation mechanism.

Probes may be deployed by the application itself, or installed remotely under administrator control. In the latter case, the application must expose an interface that supports the integration of probes.

5 Conclusions

This paper has presented a methodology for developing and deploying distributed applications, exploiting many of the features of the RRT middleware. The strengths of the approach are that the application logic can be designed and implemented completely independently of distribution concerns, easing the development task, and that

---

[6] Support for automatic generation of WSDL for each deployed object is under development, as is a facility to allow object method invocation from the web browser.

this gives great flexibility to alter distribution decisions late in the development cycle. The RRT middleware is available for download [1].

Plans for further development include support for policy-driven object placement, support for transparent object migration, a distributed naming service, improved resilience to transient network failures, an improved security model, and improvements in performance.

Acknowledgements

This work was supported by EPSRC grants GR/R51872 and GR/S44501/01 and by EC Framework V IST-2001-32360.

References

1. Dearle A., Kirby G.N.C., Rebón Portillo A.J., Walker S. Reflective Architecture for Distributed Applications (RAFDA). 2003. *http://www-systems.dcs.st-and.ac.uk/rafda/*
2. Rebón Portillo Á.J., Walker S., Kirby G.N.C., Dearle A. A Reflective Approach to Providing Flexibility in Application Distribution. In: Proc. 2nd International Workshop on Reflective and Adaptive Middleware, ACM/IFIP/USENIX International Middleware Conference (Middleware 2003), Rio de Janeiro, Brazil, 2003, pp 95-99
3. Dearle A., Walker S., Norcross S., Kirby G.N.C., McCarthy A. RAFDA: Middleware Supporting the Separation of Application Logic from Distribution Policy. University of St Andrews Report CS/05/3, 2005.
4. Walker S.M. RAFDA Run-Time (RRT) Beginner's Guide v1.0. University of St Andrews Report CS/05/4, 2005.
5. OMG. Common Object Request Broker Architecture: Core Specification, 2004
6. Sun Microsystems. Java™ Remote Method Invocation Specification, 1996
7. Microsoft Corporation. The Component Object Model Specification. 1995.
8. Obermeyer P., Hawkins J. Microsoft.NET Remoting: A Technical Overview. Microsoft Corporation, 2001.
9. W3C. Web Services Architecture. 2004. *http://w3c.org/2002/ws/*
10. Tilevich E., Smaragdakis Y. J-Orchestra: Automatic Java Application Partitioning. In: Proc. European Conference on Object-Oriented Programming (ECOOP), Malaga, 2002
11. Spiegel A. Automatic Distribution of Object-Oriented Programs. PhD thesis, 2002
12. Caromel D., Klauser W., Vayssiere J. Towards Seamless Computing and Metacomputing in Java. Concurrency Practice and Experience 1998; 10,11-13:1043-1061
13. Fahringer T., Jugravu A. JavaSymphony: A New Programming Paradigm to Control and to Synchronize Locality, Parallelism, and Load Balancing for Parallel and Distributed Computing. Concurrency and Computation: Practice and Experience 2002; 17,7-8:1005-1025
14. Lavender R.G., Schmidt D. Active Object - An Object Behavioral Pattern for Concurrent Programming. In: J. Vlissides, J. Coplien and N. Kerth (ed) Pattern Languages of Program Design 2. Addison-Wesley, 1996
15. Apache Axis. 2004. *http://ws.apache.org/axis/*
16. Stoica I., Morris R., Karger D., Kaashoek F., Balakrishnan H. Chord: A Scalable Peer-To-Peer Lookup Service for Internet Applications. In: Proc. ACM SIGCOMM 2001, San Diego, CA, USA, 2001, pp 149-160
17. JUnit, Testing Resources for Extreme Programming. 2005. *http://www.junit.org*
18. AppGate Network Security. MindTerm. 2005. *http://www.appgate.com/products/80_MindTerm/*

Crosslets: Self-managing Application Deployment in a Cross-Platform Operating Environment

Stefan Paal [1], Reiner Kammüller [2], and Bernd Freisleben [3]

[1] Fraunhofer Institute for Media Communication,
Schloss Birlinghoven, D-53754 St. Augustin, Germany
stefan.paal@imk.fraunhofer.de
[2] Department of Electrical Engineering and Computer Science, University of Siegen,
Hölderlinstr. 3, D-57068 Siegen, Germany
kammueller@pd.et-inf.uni-siegen.de
[3] Department of Mathematics and Computer Science, University of Marburg,
Hans-Meerwein-Strasse, D-35032 Marburg, Germany
freisleb@informatik.uni-marburg.de

Abstract. The Sun Java Runtime Environment (JRE) is used for developing applications which can be run in a cross-platform operating environment. The underlying Java Virtual Machine (JVM) facilitates the execution of Java applications, but it still requires manual application deployment. There are various approaches, such as the Java Network Launch Protocol (JNLP), which address dynamic application deployment, but are limited in scope. In this paper, we present a new approach towards self-managing application deployment in a cross-platform operating environment. It is based on the idea of dynamically deducing an appropriate deployment process without user intervention. We present a self-descriptive deployment unit called *crosslet* and introduce *crossware archives (XAR)* to package and distribute it. The Java realization of the approach is described and its application for nomadic desktop computing is illustrated.

1 Introduction

The Sun Java Runtime Environment (JRE) is available for a variety of hardware platforms and operating systems. It is often used for developing applications which are supposed to be run in a heterogeneous environment, such as the Internet [1]. A prerequisite is the installation of a suitable variant of the Java Virtual Machine (JVM), which is typically performed by an administrator for each individual computing system. While the JVM facilitates the development and execution of applications following the *Write-Once-Run-Anywhere (WORA)* principle, it leaves a basic problem up to the user: How are Java applications deployed on a computing system if they are not known by the time the JRE is installed? This leads to further issues, e.g. code distribution, module composition and runtime configuration, which are not directly addressed by the JRE. Certainly, there are various approaches, such as Java Web Archives (WAR) and Java Enterprise Archives (EAR) which address selected problems, e.g. code distribution and application configuration. However, an administrator has to manually install and update related applications, e.g. from a CDROM or a remote software repository, as shown in fig. 1.

A. Dearle and S. Eisenbach (Eds.): CD 2005, LNCS 3798, pp. 52–66, 2005.

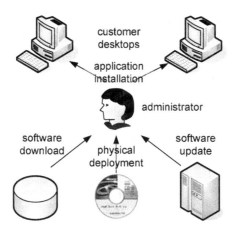

Fig. 1. Manual Application Deployment in a Cross-Platform Operating Environment

However, *manual application deployment* is not well-suited for a large-scale environment with a large variety of applications. A remedy is *dynamic application deployment* offered by approaches like Sun Java Web Start. Instead of installing the applications on each node, they are deployed into particular application repositories. From there, the required application components are dynamically retrieved and installed when an application is requested. Updated components are automatically downloaded each time the application is started, which keeps the local installation up-to-date without user intervention. Although approaches using particular deployment descriptions, e.g. based on the Java Network Launch Protocol (JNLP), release the administrator from maintaining the application deployment process, they are typically limited to a deployment-per-application level. Common components are not shared but individually downloaded for each application. There is no support for multiple code repositories, and dynamic composition requests are not addressed. In addition, the deployment process typically cannot be modified by the application, by the runtime environment or by the customer, e.g. selecting a different code repository or choosing a compatible component already downloaded by another application.

In this paper, we present an approach towards *self-managing application deployment* in a cross-platform operating environment. We introduce a novel principle called *Deploy-Once-Compose-Anywhere (DOCA)* which is based on the separation of concerns in terms of platform setup, code distribution, module composition and application configuration. We present a cross-platform application system and propose the use of so called *crosslets* to enable spontaneous application deployment. It adjusts itself according to platform capabilities and application requirements. We describe the realization in Java on top of legacy JVMs and illustrate the use of the approach. Finally, we demonstrate its application in an ongoing project.

The paper is organized as follows. In section 2, we discuss the goal of self-managing application deployment, outline the requirements and examine related work. In section 3, we introduce our approach towards self-managing application deployment, propose the new deployment unit called *crosslet* and describe the realization in Java using *crossware archives (XAR)*. In section 4, we demonstrate the application of the approach for nomadic desktop computing in a cross-platform operating environment. Finally, section 5 concludes the paper and outlines areas for future work.

2 Self-managing Application Deployment

In this section, we discuss the overall goal of self-managing application deployment. We outline the requirements with respect to the use in a cross-platform operating environment and examine related work.

2.1 Goal

In our understanding, application deployment encompasses the entire process from the development of an application up to its execution in a suitable runtime environment on a customer computing system. At the first look, an application is composed of smaller parts, e.g. libraries, modules and components which may be distributed by developers in separate packages or within a common deployment unit. In turn, each customer computing system is set up by administrators with an appropriate JVM and configured according to the specific environment, e.g. passing the address of the proxy server a JVM has to use. When an application should be run, the required application components are retrieved and a suitable runtime environment is provided to run the corresponding application components.

From this point of view, the deployment process in a cross-platform operating environment is basically influenced by two distinct factors, the platform and the application configuration, as shown in fig. 2.

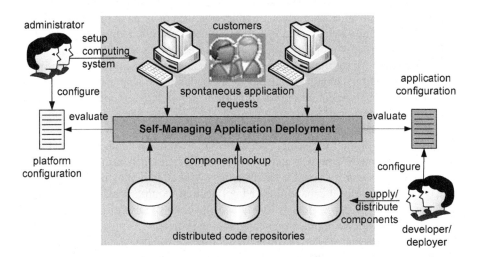

Fig. 2. Self-Managing Application Deployment in a Cross-Platform Operating Environment

The developers supply the application components and put them in distributed code repositories. The administrators set up the computing system supposed to run the application. Both developers and administrators perform their tasks without considering each others' configuration. Concerning self-managing application deployment, the overall goal is the dynamic evaluation of the platform configuration and the application configuration and the subsequent deduction of an appropriate deployment process without user intervention.

2.2 Requirements

Comparable Deployment Units. The distribution of application code is the first step in the deployment process. An essential requirement is the introduction of comparable deployment units which may be concurrently introduced and managed by different authorities. A self-managing deployment approach should be able to synchronize multiple code repositories and to identify compatible variants, e.g. while evaluating and updating already downloaded deployment units.

Custom Composition. Applications are typically composed of smaller units, such as libraries or components, which may be offered in different variants and may be updated individually. A concern is the customizable selection and resolution of required components according to the requesting application and the current hosting environment. A self-managing deployment approach queries the code repositories for suitable components and dynamically selects and retrieves the most appropriate ones.

Seamless Execution. A particular requirement is the provision and configuration of a suitable runtime environment, e.g. selecting a compatible JVM and passing specific environment settings such as the address of the proxy server. A self-managing deployment approach should also be able to alter the deployment process without affecting the application execution, e.g. switching from one code repository to another or selecting a compatible variant already installed on the host computing system.

On-Demand Operation. The heterogeneity of computing nodes found in a cross-platform operating environment makes it practically impossible to create a one-for-all solution. An application developer cannot consider every computing system on which the application will be hosted. In turn, a platform administrator is not able to set up a runtime environment which is suitable for every application. A self-managing approach should support on-demand operation without particular user intervention.

Legacy Runtime Environment. In a cross-platform operating environment, it is not feasible to provide and support proprietary JVM implementations for different types of operating systems and hardware platforms. The same is valid for custom deployment approaches which require the manual installation of particular frameworks or invent particular programming models. A self-managing deployment approach should rely on a legacy runtime environment and support legacy applications.

2.3 Related Work

There are many Java deployment approaches available which mainly differ in the way how Java classes are packaged, distributed and retrieved. In the following section, we review related work with respect to the discussed concerns and their applicability in a cross-platform operating environment.

The native Java deployment approaches are basically characterized by using the Java system class loader. A simple option is to put the Java classes in a directory structure following the package hierarchy and set the CLASSPATH accordingly. This approach is suitable for development time but fails to support remote code distribution. A refinement is the use of a Java archive (JAR) which is built by packaging the directory structure into a single file [1]. On the one hand, a JAR file can be easily distributed and used to add extra information about the contained classes, such as version statements in the manifest file. It is compatible with each legacy JVM and is therefore well-suited for a cross-platform operating environment. On the other hand, it lacks support for dynamically configuring the composition, customization and execution. Once started, the JVM cannot be easily reconfigured to consider additional JAR files that were not added to the CLASSPATH. The customization of an application is not possible without modifying the JAR files, and the runtime configuration is not addressed at all by this approach.

There are framework approaches which emerged from standardized application scenarios, such as *CORBA Components* [2] and *Java Servlets* [3]. They address specific deployment and composition scenarios which are defined by the framework implementation. For example, web modules are packaged in *web archives (WAR)* files which are JAR files containing particular configuration directories and files, such as Java classes, HTML and XML files. They are supposed to be exclusively used by a servlet engine for the deployment of Java servlets. The *Enterprise Java Beans (EJB)* approach introduces *enterprise archives (EAR)* which add an additional abstraction level to group various WAR and JAR files into a single entity [4]. This makes it easy to reuse components in new J2EE applications and distribute them to another application server. Both approaches focus on the support of specific server-side application scenarios and are not suitable for different kinds of applications, e.g. legacy Java desktop applications. While a WAR file does not basically differ from a JAR file concerning deployment configuration, an EAR file can be used to configure the composition, customization and execution of a J2EE application. Though it separates the concerns of application deployment and supports different user roles, such as application assembly, it is not able to dynamically modify the deployment and composition process during runtime. It lacks support for remote code repositories and always bundles the code along with the configuration files as a single entity.

A dynamic approach is specified by the *Java Network Launch Protocol (JNLP)* and used by various implementations for client-side deployment, such as *Sun Java Web Start*, *Netx* [5] and *Object Component Desktop* [6]. Instead of distributing code and application configuration as a single unit, a JNLP configuration file is retrieved from a remote application repository and used to dynamically configure the deployment process. The approach supports local caching of downloaded JAR files and checking for updated versions which are transparently downloaded when the application is started next time. In addition, it supports the configuration of the application composition by introducing particular server-side JNLP handlers and the parameterization of the application execution. The dynamic selection and configuration of a suitable runtime environment is possible. Although the JNLP approach supports many issues of dynamic application deployment in a cross-platform operating environment, it is basically limited to a fixed deployment scenario, e.g. using well-known JNLP repositories. The distribution and composition configuration is tightly coupled, and there is no way to dynamically include or query other code repositories. There is no support for self-managing customization of the deployment process such as the selection of the most appropriate component according to application requirements and platform capabilities.

There are several custom deployment approaches which address different application scenarios. *Deploy Directory* [7] and *Power Update* [8] are designed to manage auto-updating of Java clients and use a proprietary deployment protocol. The approaches are able to customize the deployment process but are not supposed to be used in different application scenarios. A different deployment approach is introduced by the OSGi service platform [9] which focuses on the installation and management of software components. It introduces so called *bundles* as deployment units and covers a broad range of use cases, such as service deployment on smart and embedded devices. It supports the concurrent execution of multiple applications within the same JVM and addresses the customized sharing of common components. While it is supposed to foster a standardized computing environment for networked services, it relies on a well-known deployment scenario. Bundles are provided at specific locations and cannot be dynamically selected and retrieved from concurrent repositories. The service composition and dependency resolution is based on Java packages but not on custom component units.

Another custom deployment approach is represented by *SmartFrog* [10]. It defines an application as a collection of possibly distributed components which are automatically deployed and configured. A particular specification language is introduced to define the lifecycles and dependencies of components and how they should be deployed, run and connected. The major drawback of this approach is the encapsulation of each instantiated component in a separate process or JVM. A certain middleware approach, such as RMI, must be used to connect the components. Moreover, there is no way to share commonly required software libraries which increases the resource requirements. A further custom approach is *Software Dock* [11]. It enables cooperative software deployment by introducing particular servers, release dock and field dock, which represent software producers and software consumers, respectively. Agents implement the actual software deployment functionality and use the servers to deploy and to retrieve software systems. While this approach introduces an advanced software deployment infrastructure, it heavily relies on a well-known deployment scenario and specific agents to perform certain operations, such as checking for software updates. The approach supports the installation and removal of separate software systems but does not explicitly address custom application composition. A different approach is *SATIN* [12] which provides a lightweight component model supposed to be used in mobile devices. It adapts itself to changing requirements and enables self organization based on logical mobility and the introduction of Logical Mobile Units (LMU). An inherent drawback is the compulsory use of the component model which actually turns this approach unfeasible for the deployment of legacy Java code.

2.4 Summary

In this section, we have discussed the goal of self-managing application deployment and have outlined the requirements with respect to cross-platform operating environments. There are various requirements which have to be addressed by a self-managing deployment approach. An overall issue is the ability to dynamically modify the deployment process, e.g. selecting another component instead using the one which has been actually configured by the developer. This raises the general requirement to separate the concerns, e.g. decoupling code distribution from application composition.

We have examined related work which focuses on different concerns. Native approaches are commonly used to encapsulate and distribute application classes, such as Java archives (JAR), but do not support distributed scenarios. Framework approaches such as Java servlets add particular features but are typically limited to standardized application scenarios. Dynamic approaches based on JNLP are able to customize the deployment process but depend on well-known environments. Custom approaches tend to be specific for a certain application scenario and fail for different ones. They typically require particular installations, such as the OSGi framework, and lack support for legacy Java applications, such as SATIN.

To summarize, the basic requirement of self-managing application deployment is the customizable evaluation of platform configuration and application configuration. Although there are approaches which support single features required for dynamic application deployment in a well-known scenario, none of them is currently suitable for the use in a dynamic and uncertain cross-platform operating environment.

3 Crosslets

In the following, we present our proposal towards a self-managing cross-platform application system. We illustrate the conceptual approach of so called *crosslets* and describe a realization in Java. The use of *crossware archives (XAR)* to distribute Java crosslets is demonstrated.

3.1 Conceptual Approach

The key stone of the conceptual approach is the proposal of a self-descriptive deployment unit called *crosslet*. It represents a platform-independent configuration of the deployment process. As shown in fig. 3, a self-managing cross-platform application system is introduced which evaluates the crosslet and configures the deployment process with respect to the platform configuration. The crosslet covers the cross-platform issues concerning code distribution, module composition and application configuration, whereas the platform configuration contains the local settings of the computing system, e.g. platform-specific path to native executables. In this context, the provided runtime environments are not tightly bound to the application system but may also be started in a separate process. In general, a crosslet can be used to configure a deployment process. This is possible as long as a suitable platform configuration can be found, e.g. indicating how to access remote code repositories.

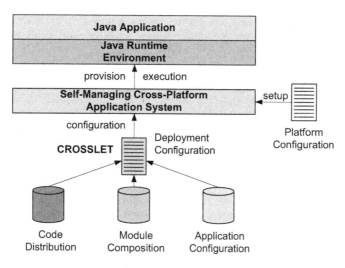

Fig. 3. Conceptual Approach

3.2 Java Realization

While the crosslet approach is basically not limited to Java applications, in the following we will focus on self-managing Java application deployment. The presented approach benefits from our previous work concerning code distribution and module composition (i.e. Distributed Application Repositories [13] and Java Loadable Modules [14]). It separates the concerns of distribution, composition and execution of a Java application, as shown in fig. 4.

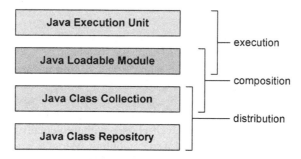

Fig. 4. Separation of Concerns

Java Class Repository. The notion of a *class repository* is used for any source which provides access to a group of Java classes, such as a JAR file or a network link. In this context, a basic problem of concurrent code distribution across distributed application repositories is the lack of determining identical class repositories. A common workaround is the comparison of file size and date, e.g. used in JNLP. However, this is only applicable if the class repository is located on the same file system but fails if the class repository is distributed on different locations. We propose to use a unique identifier to determine identical class repositories. When a new Java class repository, e.g. a JAR file, is uploaded to a remote code repository, an extra configuration is supplied, as shown in fig. 5.

```
<repository id="{B8FA2E24-CFFF-49DC-AB4C}">
  <jarfile url="http://crossware.org/editor-1.0.jar"/>
</repository>
```

Fig. 5. Deployment of a Java Class Repository

The attribute `id` tags this Java class repository; the `id` is later used to reference and identify it. The attribute `url` denotes the location which may be used by the application system to download the JAR file and to put it into the local cache. If a class repository with the passed `id` has already been uploaded to the code repository, a warning is issued and the deployment request is ignored. In turn, if an application system determines a copy of the class repository in the local cache, it is not downloaded.

Java Class Collections. The overall goal of *class collections* is the invention of virtual class groups which may be created without modifying existing Java class repositories [15]. Class collections can be marked with certain attributes and support the concurrent declaration of similar variants. An example of a related configuration file is shown in fig. 6. It illustrates how the classes from the application *editor* are grouped into a new collection and tagged with custom properties.

```
<collection id="{06FBE205-DF61-40ea-AF12}">
  <variant>
    <property name="name" value="editor"/>
    <property name="release" value="1.0"/>
    <property name="vendor" value="crossware"/>
    <repository id="{B8FA2E24-CFFF-49DC-AB4C}">
      <package name="org/crossware/editor/.*"/>
    </repository>
```

Fig. 6. Grouping Java Classes using Class Collections

The collection is decorated with the name `editor`, the release parameter `1.0` and the vendor name `crossware`. The `repository id` specifies the class repository which actually contains the code. In case only a subset of classes should be considered, regular expressions can be used to address certain classes. As a result, class collections can be used to define groups of classes without actually knowing how to access the classes on the currently employed computing system.

Java Loadable Modules. The particular composition issues are handled by introducing an abstract deployment and composition unit called *module*, as detailed in [14]. In essence, the composition of a Java application is described by specifying the required modules and their properties like version, vendor or compatibility parameters, as shown in fig. 7. The module editor is marked with a unique identifier id and defined to use the class collections editor and xerces with the given properties. The attribute handler points to a class which represents the module handler of the current module, e.g. performing the initialization of the module.

```
<module name="editor" id="{515D0F0D-C215-4f43}"
                handler="org.crossware.editor.CModule">
  <property name="vendor" value="crossware" />
  <property name="release" value="1.0.0" />
  <dependency>
    <module id="{B283663C-C97F-491b-8E03}"/>
  </dependency>
  <collection id="{06FBE205-DF61-40ea-AF12}">
    <property name="name" value="editor" />
    <property name="vendor" value="crossware" />
    <property name="release" value="1.0" />
  </collection>
  <collection id="{945A69A2-ECCA-4da6-97D9}">
    <property name="name" value="xerces" />
    <property name="vendor" value="apache " />
    <property name="release" value="2.4.0" />
  </collection>
</module>
```

Fig. 7. Module Composition using Class Collections

The module may also define properties like vendor which can be used to query this module. Finally, the dependency section indicates which modules have to be loaded before the current module can be used. In contrast to class collections which are related to code distribution and are not directly accessed by applications, modules address code composition and may be dynamically requested by applications, e.g. using the unique module id or querying an appropriate module by its properties.

Java Execution Units. Another issue is the provision and configuration of a suitable runtime environment for running a Java execution unit. An example of an execution configuration for a legacy Java application is shown in fig. 8. It requests a runtime environment denoted by native-java and indicates to start the execution unit at org.crossware.editor.Main. The parameter args is passed to the application during startup. The rest of the configuration file may contain additional information about the application such as its title to be used for display purposes.

A corresponding platform-specific runtime configuration is shown in fig. 9. It is provided by the platform administrator and configured to meet the capabilities of the platform installation. It is decorated with various parameters such as native-java which indicates that this configuration starts a separate Java process using the parameter command given as /usr/sdk/sun-jdk-1.4.2/bin/java.

```
<runtime-environment id="{DBEBA020-89EB-4ca0-B084}">
    <runtime="native-java" />
    <main-class="org.crossware.editor.Main" />
    <args="col=80,row=50" />
    <title>Editor</title>
</runtime-environment>
```

Fig. 8. Execution Configuration of a Java Execution Unit

```
<application-runtime id="{A19800A4-5AE7-4f27-B5E8}">
    <property name="runtime" value="native-java" />
    <property name="type" value="process" />
    <property name="version" value="1.4.2" />
    <property name="command"
        value="/usr/sdk/sun-jdk-1.4.2/bin/java" />
</application-runtime>
```

Fig. 9. Platform-Specific Runtime Configuration

The purpose of the Java execution unit is the encapsulation of the execution configuration of a Java application. It does not refer to any local resource or configuration but is dynamically evaluated by the self-managing deployment approach along with the platform-specific runtime configuration. As a result, the configuration of Java execution units may be dynamically passed to various computing systems in a cross-platform operating environment and the appropriate runtime environment is dynamically selected and set up.

3.3 Use

After having illustrated the Java realization, we show how the approach is used to define Java crosslets as self-descriptive deployment units. Basically, we want to reuse existing deployment approaches and tools. Similar to a WAR file, we introduce a *crossware archive (XAR)* which contains the crosslet definition, as shown in fig. 10.

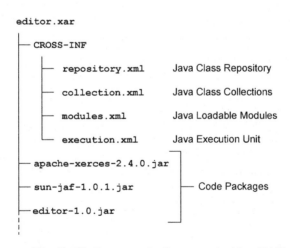

Fig. 10. File Structure of a Crossware Archive (XAR)

The XAR file can be created using the standard JAR tool or any other ZIP compliant compression tool. It contains a particular folder CROSS-INF which in turn may contain various XML configuration files. They describe the content of the crosslet and are evaluated during the deployment process. In addition, a XAR file can be used to group various code packages into a single file and to deploy them at once, e.g. including third-party libraries.

The crosslet may be used in different ways. In a simple deployment scenario, the XAR file consists of code packages and a class repository configuration file only. There is no definition of class collections or modules. This addresses the need to distribute shared legacy code packages independent of any application, such as Apache Xerces. The related code repository can be queried without actually downloading the XAR files, and an application system may retrieve a missing code package referred but not included in a different crosslet. Another crosslet may define an execution unit but without containing any code package. Instead, the application system is free to retrieve related module, collection and repository configurations from the local cache or different code repositories. This supports the reuse of already downloaded software packages, e.g. using a locally stored Java class collection which is compatible with the requested one.

The employment of crosslets requires the installation of a particular cross-platform application system which manages the platform configuration and is able to evaluate the deployment configuration found in a crosslet. For client-side scenarios, we use an existing deployment infrastructure based on Sun Java Web Start, as shown in fig. 11.

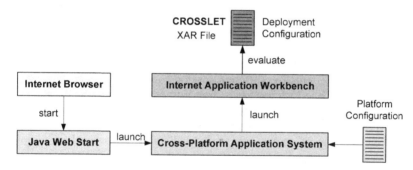

Fig. 11. Installation of a Cross-Platform Application System

At the initial setup of the system, the user visits a link with a regular Java enabled Internet browser. This launches a core application system on the client computer and retrieves further modules from remote code repositories using the presented approach. Although there are command line tools to interact with the cross-platform application system, we have spent many efforts to create a graphical user interface which eases the overall use of the system. The *Internet Application Workbench* is part of the CROSSWARE project and aims to provide a pervasive desktop interface in a cross-platform operating environment [16].

3.4 Discussion

The presented approach enables the self-managing application deployment in a cross-platform operating environment based on the dynamic evaluation of the application configuration with respect to the platform setup. Concerning the discussed requirements, it supports distributed code repositories, custom composition and seamless execution. Administrators can prepare the platform setup without actually knowing which applications will be launched on the computing system. In turn, application developers can distribute software packages; define module compositions and runtime configurations independent of the current deployment scenario and platform setup. The required cross-platform application system can be dynamically installed by using a Java-enabled browser and Java Web Start. Another option is the manual installation, e.g. as part of an application server setup. Legacy Java applications are supported and related class repositories, such as JAR files, are not modified but wrapped and reused. A suitable runtime environment is selected and configured on the fly without user intervention. As a result, the presented approach supports the on-demand operation in an unmanaged and heterogeneous cross-platform operating environment.

Clearly, there are some limitations. The current realization introduces a custom deployment unit which can only be evaluated by our proprietary cross-platform application system. Due to the use of custom class loaders, it cannot be easily bundled with other deployment approaches relying on a particular class loading strategy, such as used by servlet engines or J2EE application servers. Furthermore, the use of advanced composition features requires particular knowledge and may require the modification of the application. Finally, the introduction and dynamic evaluation of XML configuration files decreases the overall performance in a large-scale application scenario.

4   Application of the Approach

In this section, we present an application of the approach for nomadic desktop computing. A nomadic user employs different desktop computing systems while he or she is on the move from one location to another. In the project CROSSWARE [17], we work on an autonomic cross-platform operating environment for on-demand Internet applications. A particular part of this project is the provision of a graphical desktop interface which seamlessly moves with the nomadic user. The related Java implementation is called *Internet Application Workbench* and shown in fig. 12.

Fig. 12. Internet Application Workbench

The workbench is composed of a launch bar to start already installed applications, a common navigation side bar to explore local and remote repositories and individual windows for each started application. From this point of view, the workbench mimics the appearance of well-known graphical operating systems such as MS Windows. However, the workbench and the related applications are not installed and configured in advance but dynamically deployed and configured each time the user starts the workbench. The presented approach of self-managing application deployment is a key stone for launching the workbench and deploying the applications in a cross-platform operating environment. It is used to install new and to update already downloaded application components without actually knowing the current deployment scenario. The user selects a XAR file via the file explorer or the Internet browser running in the workbench and starts the deployment process by a double-click. The configuration files of the crosslet are evaluated, the crosslet is stored in the local cache and related code is downloaded, if required. As a result, the workbench may not only be used to deploy and launch an application on-demand, but also to seamlessly install application components in advance, e.g. due to offline operation. A demo version of the workbench and the presented approach can be retrieved from [16].

5 Conclusions

In this paper, we argue that self-managing application deployment is a prerequisite to enable the on-demand execution of applications in a cross-platform operating environment. We have shown that existing approaches partially address self-managing application deployment but none of them is currently suitable for the use in a heterogeneous and uncertain cross-platform operating environment. An approach towards self-managing application deployment has been presented which is based on the separation of concerns in terms of code distribution, module composition, runtime configuration and platform setup. Based on previous work, such as Java Class Collections [15] and Distributed Application Repositories [13], it introduces a self-descriptive deployment unit called crosslet which is used to configure the deployment process. Based on the common JAR file format, it is encapsulated in a crossware archive (XAR) which can be easily created and evaluated using standard tools. It is used to bundle related code libraries, component specifications and execution configurations in a single file, e.g. deploying legacy JAR files and configuring the required runtime environment. Finally, we have illustrated the application in an ongoing project for the support of on-demand application execution in a nomadic computing environment.

There are various areas for future research. First, the presented approach relies on the concurrent use of remote code repositories. A particular concern is security which has been not yet addressed at all. We currently examine how existing code signing approaches, such as *jarsign*, can be transparently applied to a XAR file. This would smartly ensure the authenticity and the integrity of a crosslet without inventing a proprietary code security framework. A different issue is the extension of the crosslet format for custom application scenarios, e.g. ad hoc execution migration. We work on a related implementation which extends the XAR file with migration data. A particular crosslet is dynamically created and transmitted from one host to another while the application migrates.

Acknowledgements

The presented approach is based on a cross-platform operating environment which has been evaluated and used in various projects, such as CAT [18], AWAKE [19] and CROSSWARE [16]. They are funded by the German Federal Ministry for Education and Research and conducted by the research group MARS of the Fraunhofer Institute for Media Communication, Sankt Augustin in cooperation with the University of Siegen and the University of Marburg, Germany.

References

1. Venners, B. Inside The Java 2 Virtual Machine. McGraw-Hill 1999.
2. Marvic, R., Merle, P., Geib, J.-M. Towards a Dynamic CORBA Component Platform. Proc. of 2nd International Symposium on Distributed Objects and Applications (DOA). Antwerpen, Belgium. pp. 305-314. IEEE 2000.
3. Hunter, J., Crawford, W., Ferguson, P., Java Servlet Programming, O'Reilly 1998.
4. Monson-Haefel, R. Enterprise Java Beans. O'Reilly 2000.
5. Netx. http://jnlp.sourceforge.net/netx/compare.html
6. Object Component Desktop. http://ocd.sourceforge.net/docs/index.html
7. Deploy Directory. http://www.quest.com/deploydirector/
8. PowerUpdate. http://www.zerog.com/products_pu.html
9. OSGi Service Platform Release 3. Open Service Gateway Initiative 2003. http://osgi.org
10. Goldsack, P., Guijarro, J. et al. SmartFrog: Configuration and Automatic Ignition of Distributed Applications. HP Labs, Bristol, UK. http://www.hpl.hp.com/research/smartfrog/
11. Hall, R. S., Heimbigner, D, Wolf, A. L. A Cooperative Approach to Support Software Deployment Using the Software Dock. Proc. of the 21st Intl. Conference on Software Engineering (ICSE 1999). Los Angeles, USA. ACM 1999. pp. 174-183.
12. Zachariadis, S. Mascolo, C., Emmerich W. SATIN: A Component Model for Mobile Self-Organisation. Proc. of the 5th Intl. Conf. on Distributed Applications (DOA 2004). LNCS 2888. Agia, Napa, Cyprus. pp. 1303-1321.
13. Paal, S., Kammüller, R., Freisleben, B. Dynamic Software Deployment with Distributed Application Repositories. 14. Fachtagung Kommunikation in Verteilten Systemen (KiVS 2005). Informatik aktuell. Kaiserslautern, Germany. Springer 2005. pp. 41-52.
14. Paal, S., Kammüller, R., Freisleben, B. Separating the Concerns of Distributed Deployment and Dynamic Composition in Internet Application Systems. Proc. of the 4th Intl. Conf. on Distributed Applications (DOA 2003). LNCS 2888. Italy. Springer 2003. pp. 1292-1311.
15. Paal, S., Kammüller, R., Freisleben, B. Java Class Deployment with Class Collections. Proc. 2003 Conf. on Objects, Components, Architectures, Services, and Applications for a Networked World. LNCS 2591. Erfurt, Germany. Springer 2003. pp. 135-151.
16. CROSSWARE - An Autonomic Cross-Platform Operating Environment for On Demand Internet Applications. Marburg, Germany. 2005. http://crossware.org
17. Paal, S., Kammüller, R., Freisleben, B. Crossware: Integration Middleware for Autonomic Cross-Platform Internet Application Environments. International Journal on Computer Aided Engineering. 2005 (to appear).
18. Fleischmann, M., Strauss, W., Novak, J., Paal, S., Müller, B., Blome, G., Peranovic, P., Seibert, C., Schneider, M. netzspannung.org - An Internet Media Lab for Knowledge Discovery in Mixed Realities. In Proc. 1st Conf. on Artistic, Cultural and Scientific Aspects of Experimental Media Spaces, St. Augustin, Germany. pp. 121-129., 2001.
19. AWAKE - Networked Awareness for Knowledge Discovery. Fraunhofer Institute for Media Communication. St. Augustin, Germany. 2003. http://awake.imk.fraunhofer.de

DAnCE: A QoS-Enabled Component Deployment and Configuration Engine*

Gan Deng, Jaiganesh Balasubramanian, William Otte,
Douglas C. Schmidt, and Aniruddha Gokhale

Department of Electrical Engineering and Computer Science,
Vanderbilt University, Nashville,
TN 37203, USA

Abstract. This paper presents two contributions to the study of component deployment for distributed real-time and embedded (DRE) systems.
First, it uses an inventory tracking systems (ITS) as a case study to elicit
challenges involved in deploying DRE systems to account for their quality
of service requirements. Second, it describes how we designed and implemented the Deployment And Configuration Engine (DAnCE), which is
QoS-enabled middleware that addresses the challenges that arose in the
context of our ITS case study. Our experience shows that DAnCE provides an effective platform for deploying DRE system components using
a standard runtime environment and metadata.

1 Introduction

Component middleware platforms are an effective way of achieving systematic
reuse and composition of software artifacts [1]. In these platforms, *components*
are units of implementation and composition that collaborate with other components via *ports*, including (1) *facets*, which define interfaces that accept point-to-
point method invocations from other components, (2) *receptacles*, which indicate
dependencies on point-to-point method interfaces provided by other components,
and (3) *event sources/sinks*, which enable the exchange of typed messages with
one or more components. Groups of related components can be connected together via their ports to form component *assemblies* that can be deployed to
particular nodes in a *target domain*. Implementations of component assemblies
are bundled into *packages* that can contain (1) multiple binary executables of the
same component written in different languages and for different OS platforms
and (2) metadata that describes the package contents.

In large-scale distributed real-time and embedded (DRE) systems, such as
shipboard computing environments [2], inventory tracking systems [3], and intelligence, surveillance and reconnaissance systems [4], component middleware
features can help make the software more flexible by separating (1) application

---

* This work is supported in part by funding from DARPA, NSF, LMCO ATC, LMCO
ATL, LMCO Eagan, Raytheon, and Siemens CT.

A. Dearle and S. Eisenbach (Eds.): CD 2005, LNCS 3798, pp. 67–82, 2005.

functionality from (2) system lifecycle activities, such as component configuration and deployment. Conventional component middleware platforms, such as J2EE and .NET, is not well-suited for these types of DRE systems since they do not provide real-time quality of service (QoS) support. *QoS-enabled component middleware*, such as CIAO [5], Qedo [6], and PRiSm [7], have been developed to address these limitations by combining the flexibility of component middleware with the predictability of Real-time CORBA.

QoS-enabled component middleware, however, also introduces new complexities that stem from the need to (1) deploy component assemblies into the appropriate DRE system target nodes, (2) activate and deactivate component assemblies automatically, (3) initialize and configure component server resources to enforce end-to-end QoS requirements of component assemblies, and (4) simplify the configuration, deployment, and management of common services used by applications and middleware. The lack of portable, reusable, and standard mechanisms to address these challenges is hindering the adoption of component middleware technologies for DRE systems.

To meet these challenges, we have developed the *Deployment and Configuration Engine* (DAnCE), which is an open-source (`www.dre.vanderbilt.edu/CIAO`) QoS-enabled middleware framework compliant with the OMG Deployment and Configuration specification [8] that enables the deployment of DRE system component assemblies by addressing various QoS-related concerns, such as collocation, memory constraints, and processor loading. The deployment and configuration of components in DAnCE, therefore, involves mapping known variations in the *application requirements space* (such as variations in QoS requirements) to known variations in the *software solution space* (such as configuring the underlying network, OS, middleware, and application parameters to satisfy the end-to-end QoS requirements).

The key capabilities provided by DAnCE to support deployment and configuration of DRE systems include:

- One-time parsing and storing of component configuration and deployment descriptions (which are represented as metadata in XML format) so that runtime parsing overhead is not incurred during component deployment.
- Automatic downloading of component packages so that the implementations can be changed seamlessly as components migrate from one node to another, even in a heterogeneous target domains.
- Automatic configuration of object request brokers (ORBs), containers, and component servers to (1) meet the desired QoS requirements and (2) reduce human operator mistakes introduced while configuring middleware and application components.
- Automatic connection[1] of component ports so that developers need not be concerned with these low-level details.

---

[1] In the context of this paper, a *connection* refers to the high-level binding between an object reference and its target component, rather than a lower-level transport (*e.g.*, TCP) connection.

- Automatic deployment and lifecycle management of common middleware services, such as directory, event, security, and load balancing services, so that developers can concentrate on component business logic, rather than tedious and error-prone programming activities concerned with managing these common services.

The remainder of this paper is organized as follows: Section 2 provides an overview of inventory tracking system (ITS) case study that elicits many challenges of deploying large-scale DRE systems; Section 3 describes how we designed and applied DAnCE to resolve key challenges in our ITS case study; Section 4 compares our work with related efforts; and Section 5 presents concluding remarks.

2 Deployment and Configuration Challenges in Component-Based DRE Systems

To illustrate the deployment and configuration challenges in DRE systems, this section presents a case study of a representative component-based DRE system called the *inventory tracking system* (ITS) [3]. An ITS is a warehouse management infrastructure that monitors and controls the flow of goods and assets within a storage facility. Users of an ITS include couriers (such as UPS, DHL, and Fedex), airport baggage handling systems, and retailers (such as Walmart and Target). This section first provides an overview of the structure/functionality of our ITS case study and then uses the case study to describe configuration and deployment challenges.

2.1 Overview of ITS

An ITS provides mechanisms for managing the storage and movement of goods in a timely and reliable manner. For example, an ITS should enable human operators to maintain the inventory throughout a highly distributed system (which may span organizational boundaries), and track warehouse assets using decentralized operator consoles. In conjunction with colleagues at Siemens [3], we have developed the ITS shown in Figure 1 and deployed it using DAnCE.

Figure 1 shows how our ITS consists of the following three subsystems:

- **Warehouse management**, whose high-level functionality and decision-making components calculate the destination locations of goods and delegate the remaining details to other ITS subsystems.
- **Material flow control**, which handles all the details (such as route calculation and transportation facility reservation) needed to transport goods to their destinations. The primary task of this subsystem is to execute the high-level decisions calculated by the warehouse management subsystem.
- **Warehouse hardware**, which deals with physical devices (such as sensors) and transportation units (such as conveyor belts, forklifts, and cranes).

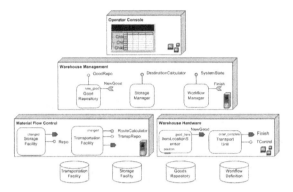

Fig. 1. Key Components in the ITS Case Study

After the ITS components comprising the ITS subsystems described above are developed, they must be configured and deployed to meet warehouse operating requirements. In our ITS case study, ~200 components must be deployed into 26 physical nodes in the warehouse. We focus on a portion of this system to motivate key challenges DAnCE faced when deploying and configuring the ITS. Figure 2 shows a subset of key component interactions in the ITS case study shown in Figure 1. As shown in this figure, the `WorkflowManager` component of the material flow control subsystem is connected to the conveyor belt and crane transportation units of the warehouse hardware subsystem. We focus on the scenario where the `WorkflowManager` contacts the `ConveyorBelt` and `Crane` components using the `move_item()` operation to move an item from a *source* (such as a loading dock) to a *destination* (such as a warehouse storage location). The `move_item()` operation takes source and destination locations as its input arguments. When the item is moved to its destination successfully, the `ConveyorBelt` and the `Crane` inform the `WorkflowManager` via the `finish_mov()` event opera-

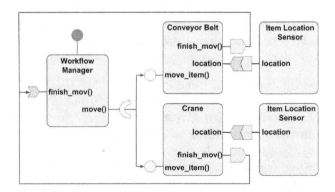

Fig. 2. Component Interactions in the ITS Case Study

tion. `ConveyorBelt` and `Crane` components are also connected to various `Item-LocationSensor` components, which periodically inform the other components of the location of moving items.

2.2   Challenges in Configuring and Deploying ITS

Using the ITS case study described in Section 2.1, we now illustrate the deployment and configuration challenges in component-based DRE systems.

Challenge 1: Efficiently storing and retrieving component implementations. Large-scale DRE systems need capabilities that enable application developers and deployment runtime tools to (1) upload component implementations to storage sites and/or (2) fetch component implementations from storage sites for installation. These capabilities should allow multiple implementations of a component written in different programming languages and run on different OS platforms. Moreover, it should be possible to pre-stage component implementations to avoid downloading selected implementations from central storage sites during the deployment process.

As shown in Figure 2, it is conceivable that how an ITS `ConveyorBelt` component could have implementations for Linux in Java and Windows in C++, which will require that these implementations be fetched and deployed appropriately on a particular node in a small and bounded amount of time.

Challenge 2: Activation, passivation, and deactivation of component assemblies. To manage shared resources in a DRE system effectively, components in an assembly need to be activated to become functional, passivated when they will not be accessed for an extended period of time, and deactivated when they are no longer needed. A key challenge is to coordinate these operations in a complete assembly, rather than in an individual component or node. For example, components in an assembly that collaborate by sending messages or events must be *preactivated* to configure the necessary environment and resources so that messages are exchanged in the intended fashion. In particular, all collaborating components in an assembly must be preactivated before any component is activated. Similarly, all collaborating components need to be passivated before any component is deactivated so that no component tries to communicate after its recipient has been deactivated.

For instance, when the `ConveyorBelt` component in Figure 2 is being removed, the `WorkflowManager` component must already be passivated since otherwise it could continue to make `move_item()` invocations on the `ConveyorBelt`.

Challenge 3: Configuring NodeApplication component server resources. In large-scale DRE systems, QoS requirements (such as low latency and bounded jitter) are often important considerations during the deployment process since component (re)deployment may occur throughout the lifecycle of a large-scale system. To enforce these QoS requirements, component servers and containers must be configured in accordance with QoS properties, such as those defined in Real-time CORBA [9]. Component deployment and configuration tools must therefore be able to (1) specify the middleware configurations needed to configure components, containers, and component servers and (2) set the QoS policy options provided by the underlying middleware into semantically consistent configurations.

For instance, in the ITS case study (Figure 2), whenever a `ConveyorBelt` component's hardware fails, it should notify the `WorkflowManager` in real-time to minimize/avoid damage. Likewise, ITS `ConveyorBelt` and `Crane` components may need to be collocated with `WorkflowManager` in some assemblies to minimize latency.

Challenge 4: Configuring and deploying common middleware services. Traditional object-oriented middleware (such as CORBA 2.x) provides DRE systems with access to common middleware services (such as Naming and Trading) through the underlying Object Request Broker (ORB) and Portable Object Adapter (POA). Component-based middleware, such as Lightweight CORBA Component Model (CCM) [10] enables (1) reusability of components by implementing only application logic and (2) easier integration into different applications and runtime contexts. Component deployers thus need to support the integration of common middleware services into component-based applications for which no standard mechanisms yet exist.

For instance, Figure 2 shows how the ITS `ItemLocationSensor` and the `ConveyorBelt` components exchange messages using *event sources/sinks*, which may require the configuration of some middleware publish/subscribe services, such as the CORBA Real-time Notification Service or the Data Distribution Service (DDS).

Section 3.2 describes how DAnCE addresses these challenges for DRE systems and how our solutions have been applied to the ITS case study.

3   The Design of DAnCE

This section describes the *Deployment And Configuration Engine* (DAnCE), which is middleware we developed based on the OMG's Deployment and Configuration (D&C) specification [8]. This specification standardizes many aspects of configuration and deployment for component-based distributed systems, including component configuration, component assembly, component packaging, package configuration, package deployment, and target domain resource management. These aspects are handled via a *data model* and a *runtime model*. The data model can be used to define/generate XML schemas for storing and interchanging metadata that describes component assemblies and their configuration and deployment characteristics. The runtime model defines a set of managers that process the metadata described in the data model during system deployment. This section shows how the design and implementation of DAnCE has been tailored to address the D&C challenges of component-based DRE systems described in Section 2.2.

3.1   The Structure and Functionality of DAnCE

The architecture of the Deployment and Configuration Engine (DAnCE) is shown in Figure 3. This section describes how DAnCE provides a reusable middleware framework for deploying and configuring components in a distributed target environment, using the ITS case study in Section 2.1 to motivate its key capabilities. DAnCE is built atop The ACE ORB (TAO) [11] and CIAO [5], which makes it portable to most hardware and OS platforms in use today.

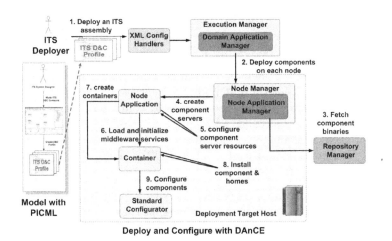

Fig. 3. Overview of DAnCE

As shown in Figure 3, an ITS deployer creates XML descriptors that convey application deployment and configuration metadata, using external model driven development (MDD) tools [12]. This metadata is compliant with the data model defined by the OMG D&C specification. To support additional deployment and configuration concerns not addressed by this specification, we enhanced the spec-defined data model by describing additional deployment concerns (such as real-time QoS requirements and middleware service configuration and deployment) discussed in Section 3.2.

All the metadata to describe these concerns is captured in an XML file called the *deployment plan*, which describes (1) the DRE system component instances to deploy, (2) what properties of these components should be initialized, (3) what QoS policies these components must contain, (4) what middleware services the components use, and (5) how the components are connected to form component assemblies. The various entities of DAnCE shown in Figure 3 are implemented as CORBA objects[2] that collaborate as follows:

---

[2] The DAnCE deployment infrastructure is implemented as CORBA objects to avoid the circular dependencies that would ensue if it was implemented as components, which would have to be deployed by DAnCE itself!

ExecutionManager runs as a daemon and is used to manage the deployment process for one or more domains. In accordance with the D&C specification, DAnCE defines a *domain* as a target environment composed of *nodes, interconnects, bridges*, and *resources*. An ExecutionManager uses the *factory* and *finder* design patterns to manager a set of `DomainApplicationManagers`.

DomainApplicationManager manages the deployment of components within a single domain (to manage multiple domains, an `ExecutionManager` can coordinate with multiple `DomainApplicationManagers`). A `DomainApplication-Manager` splits a deployment plan into multiple subplans, one for each node in a domain. In DAnCE, the `ExecutionManager` and `DomainApplicationManager` objects reside in the same daemon process to improve deployment performance by leveraging the collocation optimizations provided by TAO.

NodeManager runs in a daemon on each node and manages the deployment of all components that reside on that node, irrespective of which application they are associated with. Components are created by containers, which are hosted in component server processes called `NodeApplications`. The `NodeManager` creates the `NodeApplicationManager`, which in turn creates the `NodeApplication` processes that host containers, thereby enhancing the reuse of components shared between applications on a node.

NodeApplicationManager is collocated with a `NodeManager` to manage the deployment of all components within a `NodeApplication` which is a server process that hosts a group of related components in a particular application. To differentiate deployments in a node, DAnCE's `DomainApplicationManager` uses the node's `NodeManager` to create a `NodeApplicationManager` for each deployment and sends it the metadata it needs to deploy components.

NodeApplication plays the role of a component server process that provisions the computing resources (*e.g.*, CPU, memory and network bandwidth) for the components it hosts. Based on metadata provided by other DAnCE managers in the deployment process, the `NodeApplication` creates the initial containers that provide an environment for creating and instantiating application components. Components in a node are thus deployed in one or more `NodeApplications` in accordance with a deployment plan.

RepositoryManager runs as a daemon dedicated to a domain and is used by (1) deployer agents to store component implementations and (2) DAnCE's `NodeApplicationManager` to fetch necessary component implementations on demand. Each `NodeApplicationManager` uses its `RepositoryManager` to search component implementation binaries (stored in the form of dynamic linking libraries) and fetches them into the local node's storage cache.

3.2   Applying DAnCE to Address DRE Systems D&C Challenges

The remainder of this section describes how (1) the DAnCE managers in Figure 3 address key DRE systems D&C challenges described in Section 2.2 and (2) our solutions are applied to the ITS case study presented in Section 2.1.

**Resolving Challenge 1: Storing and Retrieving Component Implemen-
tations Via a Repository Manager.** DAnCE's `RepositoryManager` provides
efficient mechanisms where applications can (1) store component implementations at any time during the system lifecycle and (2) retrieve different versions of
implementations as components are (re)deployed on various types of nodes. As
shown in Figure 4, the `RepositoryManager` can also act as an HTTP client and
download component implementations specified as *URLs* in a deployment plan.
It caches these implementations in the local host where the `RepositoryManager`
runs so they can be retrieved by `NodeApplicationManagers`.

Over a system's lifetime, a component could be migrated and redeployed
on a node whose type is different than its earlier host(s), in which case a different component implementation must be provided. To support efficient deployment, DAnCE's `NodeApplicationManagers` periodically contact the `Repo-
sitoryManager` to download the latest implementations of designated compo-
nents. When a component is redeployed, therefore, all its implementations can
be cached locally on the target nodes, so downloading overhead need not be
incurred during the deployment process.

DAnCE's `RepositoryManager` uses ZIP compression and file archiving mechanisms (`debin.org/zzip`) to provide an efficient representation of the contents of
a ZIP archive and (de)compress all the implementations in a packaged format. It
uses CORBA operation invocations to transfer the ZIP-encoded component assembly packages to the node(s) in a domain that run `NodeApplicationManagers`.

In the ITS case study, an initial deployment might write the `ConveyorBelt`
component in Java and host the component on an Embedded Linux node. As
the system runs, ITS developers could create a C++-based Win32 implementation of `ConveyorBelt` and submit it to DAnCE's `RepositoryManager`. At some
point during the ITS lifecycle, the `ConveyorBelt` could be stopped at the current
Linux node and moved to a Windows node. To execute that deployment request,
DAnCE's `NodeApplicationManager` running on the Windows node could contact the `RepositoryManager` to retrieve the Windows implementation of the

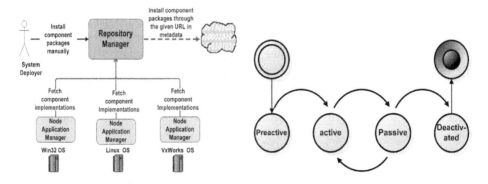

Fig. 4. Downloading implementations using the Repository Manager

Fig. 5. Different States of a Component

ConveyorBelt component and deploy it. The RepositoryManager thus helps decouple when and how ITS component implementations are developed from when they are deployed.

Resolving Challenge 2: Using the DomainApplicationManager to Coordinate the Component Assembly Lifecycle. During the lifecycle of the component assembly, DAnCE's DomainApplicationManager maintains PREACTIVE, ACTIVE, PASSIVE, and DEACTIVATED runtime state information on each component in the component assembly, as shown in Figure 5. The PREACTIVE state indicates that the component has been created and has been provided its environment settings. The ACTIVE state indicates that the component has been activated with the underlying middleware. The PASSIVE state indicates that the component is idle and all its resources can be used by other components. The DEACTIVATED state means that the component has been deactivated and removed from the system.

During the deployment process, DAnCE's DomainApplicationManager ensures that components are not connected and activated until all the components are in the *preactive* state. Similarly, during assembly deactivation, DAnCE's DomainApplicationManager ensures that components in an assembly are deactivated only when all the components are in the *passive* state.

To ensure that a component's ongoing invocations are processed completely before it is passivated, all operation invocations on a component in CIAO are dispatched by the standard Lightweight CCM Portable Object Adapter (POA), which maintains a *dispatching table* that tracks how many requests are being processed by each component in a thread. CIAO uses standard POA reference counting and deactivation mechanisms to keep track of the number of clients making invocations on a component. After a server thread finishes processing the invocation, it decrements the reference count in the dispatching table. Only when the count is zero, is the component passivated. CIAO therefore ensures that the system is always in a consistent state to ensure that no invocations are lost. To prevent new invocations from arriving at the component while it is being passivated, the container blocks new invocations for this component in the server ORB using standard CORBA portable interceptors.

In the ITS case study, DAnCE's DomainApplicationManager ensures that the ItemLocationSensor components does not make operation invocations on the ConveyorBelt components unless both are active. Similarly, during the deactivation of the ConveyorBelt component, the DomainApplicationManager ensures that WorkflowManager components are passivated, which ensures that all move_item() requests are handled properly. Finally, the ConveyorBelt component's POA ensures that all requests being processed by the component are dispatched before deactivating the component.

Resolving Challenge 3: Configuring NodeApplication Component Server Resources. To enforce QoS requirements, DAnCE extends the OMG D&C [8] specification to define NodeApplication server resource configurations, which heavily influence end-to-end QoS behavior. Figure 6 shows the different cate-

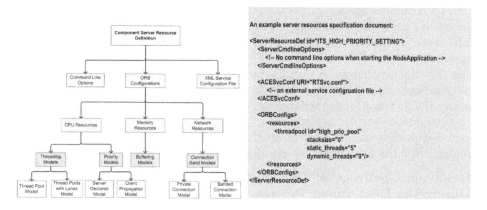

Fig. 6. Specifying RT-QoS requirements

Fig. 7. Example Server Resources Specification

gories of server configurations that can be specified using the DAnCE *server resources XML schema*, which are related to system end-to-end QoS enforcement. In particular, each server resources specification can set the following options: (1) *ORB command-line options*, which control TAO's connection management models, protocol selection, and optimized request processing, (2) *ORB service configuration option*, which specify ORB resource factories that control server concurrency and demultiplexing models. Using this XML schema, a system deployer can specify the designated ORB configurations.

As described in Section 3.1, components are hosted in containers created by the *NodeApplication* process, which provides the run-time environment and resources for components to execute and communicate with other components in a component assembly. The ORB configurations defined by the *server resources XML schema* are used to configure *NodeApplication* processes that host components, thereby providing the necessary resources for the components to operate. Since the deployment plan describes the components and the artifacts required to deploy the components, DAnCE extends the standard OMG D&C deployment plan to specify the server resource configuration options.

As shown in Figure 3, `XMLConfigurationHandler` parses the deployment plan and stores the information as IDL data structures that can transfer information between processes efficiently and enables the rest of DAnCE to avoid the runtime overhead of parsing XML files repeatedly. The IDL data structure output of the `XMLConfigurationHandler` is input to the `ExecutionManager`, which propagates the information to the `DomainApplicationManager` and `NodeApplicationManager`. The `NodeApplicationManager` uses the server resource-related options in the deployment plan to customize the containers in the `NodeApplication` it creates. These containers then use other options in the deployment plan to configure TAO's Real-time CORBA support, including thread pool configurations, priority propagation models, and priority-banded connection models.

ITS components, such as `ItemLocationSensor` and `WorkflowManager`, have stringent QoS requirements since they handle real-time item delivery activities. The server resource configurations for all nodes hosting these components are specified via an MDD tool. Figure 7 shows an example XML document that specifies the server resource configurations defined by a system deployer. The `XMLConfigurationHandler` parses the descriptors produced the MDD tool to notify the `NodeApplicationManager`. To honor all the specified configurations, the component servers hosting these components are configured with server-declared priority model with the highest CORBA priority, thread pools with preset static threads, as well as priority-banded connections.

Resolving Challenge 4: Configuring Common Middleware Services During the Deployment Process. To support the integration of common middleware services into component-based applications, DAnCE provides a meta-programmable *service integration framework* shown in Figure 8. This figure shows how DAnCE uses the service integration framework to integrate various middleware services into a DRE system. At the heart of this service integration framework is the DAnCE *Service Configurator*, which is hosted in each `NodeApplication`. Common middleware services (such as the Naming Service, Event Service, and TAO Real-time Event Service) are configured using standard CORBA interfaces and hence the usage patterns of such middleware services can be formulated easily. For example, when an application uses TAO's Real-time Event Service, it needs to (1) initialize and configure the QoS properties of the event channel, (2) define the semantic behaviors of event publishers and event consumers, and (3) register the event publishers and event consumers through the event channel interfaces.

To configure and deploy middleware services via DAnCE, CIAO encapsulates these common usage patterns and provides a set of reusable service libraries, one for each type of middleware service, *e.g.*, we designed *CIAO Real-time Event Ser-*

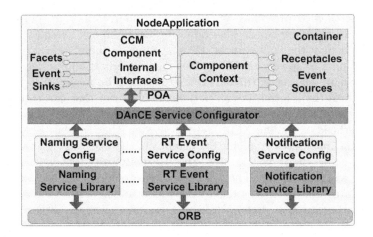

Fig. 8. Configuring Common Middleware Services

vice library for the Real-time Event Service provided by TAO. Each library is a wrapper facade of the middleware service provided by the underlying ORB that shields component developers from tedious and error-prone programming tasks associated with initializing and configuring QoS-enabled common middleware services. These libraries also expose interfaces to the DAnCE Service Configurator to manage the services. For example, the *Real-time Event Service Config* shown in the Figure 8 captures the various usage and configuration options (such as event dispatching threading model, event dispatching priority model and event filtering model) for the CIAO Real-time Event Service library. Our DAnCE Service Configurator is designed to support any CORBA service, even those developed to use the earlier CORBA 2.x object model.

During the deployment process, DAnCE uses the deployment plan to express service configuration properties associated with components and assemblies that inform the `NodeApplicationManager` how to initialize the middleware services with desired configuration settings. The `NodeApplicationManager` then conveys to the `NodeApplication` which components to create and which middleware services they require. In response, the `NodeApplication` triggers the DAnCE Service Configurator to load and configure the corresponding CIAO middleware service libraries automatically.

ITS deployment engineers can use MDD tools [13,14] to model the interactions between the `ItemLocationSensor` and `ConveyorBelt` components and could indicate whether a direct connection or an event channel is needed for communication. Moreover, stringent QoS requirements such as timing constraints and event delivery latency could also be specified in the communication between the two components. If a direct connection is specified, then at deployment time DAnCE makes the `ItemLocationSensor` component with an *event source* port cache the object reference of the *event sink* port of the `ConveyorBelt` component. After the deployment is complete, these two components can communicate directly through a CORBA remote invocation call. If the DRE system deployer specifies the use of CIAO Real-time Event Service, then DAnCE service configurator and its metadata-based configuration mechanisms configures and manages the service and its QoS settings to provide the desired QoS.

4   Related Work

As component middleware becomes more pervasive, there has been an increase in research on technologies, platforms, and tools for deploying components effectively within distributed systems. This section compares our work on DAnCE with other related efforts.

The OpenCCM (`corbaweb.lifl.fr/OpenCCM/`) Distributed Computing Infrastructure (DCI) federates a set of distributed services to form a unified distributed deployment domain for CCM applications. DCI, however, implements the Packaging and Deployment (P&D) model defined in the original CCM specification, which omits key aspects in the component configuration and deployment cycle, including package repository management, server real-time QoS configuration, and middleware service configuration and deployment. We are currently working with the OpenCCM team to enhance their DCI so that it is compliant with the OMG D&C specification and DAnCE.

[15] proposes using an architecture descriptive language (ADL) that allows assembly-level activation of components and describes assembly hierarchically. Although DAnCE is similar, it uses the XML descriptors synthesized by MDD tools to characterize the metadata regarding components to deploy. Likewise, DAnCE descriptors can specify QoS requirements and/or server resource configurations, so its deployment mechanisms are better suited to deploy applications with desired real-time QoS properties.

[16] proposes the use of the Globus Toolkit to deploy CCM components on a computational grid. Unlike DAnCE, this approach does not provide model-driven development (MDD) tools that enable developers to capture various concerns, such as deployment planning and server configuration, visually. Moreover, DAnCE is targeted at DRE systems with stringent real-time QoS requirements, rather than grid applications, which do not provide real-time support.

Proactive [17] is a distributed programming model for deploying object-oriented grid applications. Proactive defines applications as virtual structures and removes references to the physical machines from the functional code written for the applications. The functional code is mapped to the physical machines using XML descriptors. DAnCE is similar since it also separately describes the target environment using XML descriptors, but it goes further to specify component interdependencies and ensure system consistency at deployment time. Moreover, Proactive work focuses on deploying Java applications on Java virtual machines, whereas DAnCE implements the OMG D&C specification, which focuses on deploying DRE systems using language- and platform-independent component middleware written in different languages and running on different operating systems.

5   Concluding Remarks

Component middleware is intended to enhance the quality and productivity of software and software developers by elevating the level of abstraction used to develop distributed systems. Conventional middleware, however, generally lacks mechanisms to handle deployment concerns for distributed real-time and embedded (DRE) systems. This paper describes how we addressed these concerns in the Deployment And Configuration Engine (DAnCE), which is an open-source implementation of the OMG's Deployment and Configuration (D&C) specification targeted for deploying and configuring DRE systems based on Lightweight CORBA Component Model (CCM). DAnCE leverages model-driven development (MDD) tools and QoS-enabled component middleware features to support (1) the efficient storage and retrieval of component implementations, (2) component activation, passivation, and removal semantics within component assemblies, (3) configuring QoS-related client/server resources, and (4) integrating common middleware services into applications.

Our future work on DAnCE will focus on (1) integrating reliable multicast mechanisms in TAO to the various *Manager objects described in Section 3.1 to improve the scalability and reliability of the deployment process, (2) extending DAnCE to support dynamic component assembly reconfiguration, redeployments, and migrations, (3) enhancing DAnCE to provide state synchronization and component redeployment or recovery support for a fault-tolerant middleware infrastructure, such as MEAD [18], and (4) applying specialization techniques (such as partial evaluation and generative programming) to optimize DRE systems using metadata contained in component assemblies.

References

1. Heineman, G.T., Councill, B.T.: Component-Based Software Engineering: Putting the Pieces Together. Addison-Wesley, Reading, Massachusetts (2001)
2. Schmidt, D.C., Schantz, R., Masters, M., Cross, J., Sharp, D., DiPalma, L.: Towards Adaptive and Re ective Middleware for Network-Centric Combat Systems. CrossTalk (2001)
3. Nechypurenko, A., Schmidt, D.C., Lu, T., Deng, G., Gokhale, A.: Applying MDA and Component Middleware to Large-scale Distributed Systems: a Case Study. In: Proceedings of the 1st European Workshop on Model Driven Architecture with Emphasis on Industrial Application, Enschede, Netherlands, IST (2004)
4. Sharma, P., Loyall, J., Heineman, G., Schantz, R., Shapiro, R., Duzan, G.: Component-Based Dynamic QoS Adaptations in Distributed Real-Time and Embedded Systems. In: Proc. of the Intl. Symp. on Dist. Objects and Applications (DOA'04), Agia Napa, Cyprus (2004)
5. Wang, N., Gill, C., Schmidt, D.C., Subramonian, V.: Configuring Real-time Aspects in Component Middleware. In: Proc. of the International Symposium on Distributed Objects and Applications (DOA'04), Agia Napa, Cyprus (2004)
6. Ritter, T., Born, M., Unterschutz, T., Weis, T.: A QoS Metamodel and its Realization in a CORBA Component Infrastructure. In: Proceedings of the 36th Hawaii International Conference on System Sciences, Software Technology Track, Distributed Object and Component-based Software Systems Minitrack, HICSS 2003, Honolulu, HW, HICSS (2003)
7. Sharp, D.C., Roll, W.C.: Model-Based Integration of Reusable Component-Based Avionics System. In: Proc. of the Workshop on Model-Driven Embedded Systems in RTAS 2003. (2003)
8. Object Management Group: Deployment and Configuration Adopted Submission. OMG Document ptc/03-07-08 edn. (2003)
9. Object Management Group: Real-time CORBA Specification. OMG Document formal/02-08-02 edn. (2002)
10. Object Management Group: Light Weight CORBA Component Model Revised Submission. OMG Document realtime/03-05-05 edn. (2003)
11. Schmidt, D.C., Levine, D.L., Mungee, S.: The Design and Performance of Real-Time Object Request Brokers. Computer Communications 21 (1998) 294–324
12. Balasubramanian, K., Krishna, A.S., Turkay, E., Balasubramanian, J., Parsons, J., Gokhale, A., Schmidt, D.C.: Applying Model-Driven Development to Distributed Real-time and Embedded Avionics Systems. International Journal of Embedded Systems special issue on Design and Verification of Real-Time Embedded Software (2005)

13. Balasubramanian, K., Balasubramanian, J., Parsons, J., Gokhale, A., Schmidt, D.C.: A Platform-Independent Component Modeling Language for Distributed Real-time and Embedded Systems. In: Proc. of the 11th IEEE Real-Time and Embedded Technology and Applications Sym., San Francisco, CA (2005)
14. Edwards, G., Deng, G., Schmidt, D.C., Gokhale, A., Natarajan, B.: Model-driven Configuration and Deployment of Component Middleware Publisher/Subscriber Services. In: Proceedings of the Third International Conference on Generative Programming and Component Engineering (GPCE), Vancouver, CA, ACM (2004)
15. Quema, V., Balter, R., Bellissard, L., Feliot, D., Freyssinet, A., Lacourte, S.: Asynchronous, Hierarchical and Scalable Deployment of Component-Based Applications. In: Proc. of the 2nd International Working Conference on Component Deployment (CD 2004), Edinburgh, UK (2004)
16. Lacour, S., Perez, C., Priol, T.: Deploying CORBA Components on a Computational Grid: General Principles and Early Experiments Using the Globus Toolkit. In: Proc. of the 2nd International Working Conference on Component Deployment (CD 2004), Edinburgh, UK (2004)
17. Baude, F., Caromel, D., Huet, F., Mestre, L., Vayssiere, J.: Interactive and Descriptor-based Deployment of Object-Oriented Grid Applications. In: Proc. of the 11th International Symposium on High Performance Distributed Computing (HPDC'02), Edinburgh, UK (2002)
18. Narasimhan, P., Dumitras, T., Paulos, A., Pertet, S., Reverte, C., Slember, J., Srivastava, D.: MEAD: Support for Real-Time Fault-Tolerant CORBA. Concurrency and Computation: Practice and Experience (2005)

Improving Availability in Large, Distributed Component-Based Systems Via Redeployment

Marija Mikic-Rakic[2], Sam Malek[1,3], and Nenad Medvidovic[1]

[1] University of Southern California, Computer Science Department,
Los Angeles, CA, 90089, USA
{malek, neno}@usc.edu
[2] Google Inc., Santa Monica, CA, 90405, USA
marija@google.com
[3] The Boeing Company, 5301 Bolsa Avenue, Huntington Beach,
CA, 92647, USA
sam.malek2@boeing.com

Abstract. In distributed and mobile environments, the connections among the hosts on which a software system is running are often unstable. As a result of connectivity losses, the overall availability of the system decreases. The distribution of software components onto hardware nodes (i.e., the system's deployment architecture) may be ill-suited for the given target hardware en-vironment and may need to be altered to improve the software system's avail-ability. The critical difficulty in achieving this task lies in the fact that deter-mining a software system's deployment that will maximize its availability is an exponentially complex problem. In this paper, we present a fast approx-imative solution for this problem, and assess its performance. In addition to significantly improving availability, our solution, in general, also reduces the overall interaction latency in the system. We evaluate our solution on a large number of automatically generated application scenarios.

1 Introduction

The emergence of mobile devices, such as portable computers, PDAs, and mobile phones, and the advent of the Internet and various wireless networking solutions make computation possible anywhere. Applications involving these mobile devices are highly dependent on the underlying network. Unfortunately, network connectivity fail-ures are not rare: mobile devices face frequent and unpredictable connectivity losses due to their constant location change and lack of network coverage; the costs of wire-less connectivity often also induce user-initiated disconnection; and even the highly reliable WAN and LAN connectivity is unavailable 1.5% to 3.3% of the time [24].

For this reason, highly distributed and mobile systems are challenged by the prob-lem of *disconnected operation* [22], where the system must continue functioning in the temporary absence of the network. This presents a major challenge for software sys-tems that are highly dependent on network connectivity because each local subsystem is usually dependent on the availability of non-local resources. Lack of access to a remote resource can make a particular subsystem, or even the entire system unusable.

A software system's *availability* is commonly defined as the degree to which a sys-tem is operational and accessible when required for use [7]. In the context of highly distributed, mobile environments, where the most common cause of (partial) system inaccessibility is network failure [23], we quantify availability as the ratio of the num-ber of successfully completed inter-component interactions in the system to the total number of attempted interactions over a period of time.

A. Dearle and S. Eisenbach (Eds.): CD 2005, LNCS 3798, pp. 83–98, 2005.
© Springer-Verlag Berlin Heidelberg 2005

In this context, a key observation is that the distribution of software components onto hardware nodes (i.e., a system's software *deployment architecture*, illustrated in Figure 1.) greatly influences the system's availability in the face of connectivity losses. For example, in such cases it is desirable to collocate components that interact frequently. However, the parameters that influence the optimal distribution of a system (e.g., the reliability of network links) may not be known before the system's deployment. For this reason, the (initial) software deployment architecture may be ill-suited for the given target hardware environment. This means that a *redeployment* of the software system may be necessary to improve its availability.

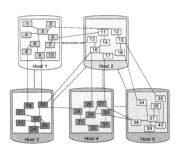

There are several existing techniques that can support various subtasks of redeployment, such as monitoring [4] to assess hardware and software properties of interest, component migration [3] to facilitate redeployment, and dynamic system manipulation [21] to effect the redeployment once the components are migrated to the appropriate hosts. However, the critical difficulty in achieving this task lies in the fact that *determining* a software system's deployment that will maximize its availability (i.e., the *optimal* deployment) is an exponentially complex problem: in the most general case the complexity is k^n, where k is the number of hardware hosts and n the number of software components. Existing approaches that recognize this (e.g., I5 [1]) still assume that all system parameters are known beforehand and that infinite time is available to calculate the optimal deployment.

Fig. 1. A sample deployment architecture with five hardware hosts and 40 software components. Dotted lines represent network connectivity, while solid lines represent interacting components.

Other approaches, such as Coign [6], restrict their solution to two hosts and client-server architectures, thus decreasing the algorithm's complexity, but also the resulting solution's usefulness.

For most practical cases finding the optimal deployment is infeasible: it requires an exponentially-complex "exact" algorithm. This paper presents an approximative algorithm, *Avala*, for increasing a system's availability by estimating the system's redeployment architecture in polynomial time. We provide a detailed assessment of Avala's performance. Since for large systems the optimal redeployment cannot be calculated in a reasonable amount of time, we compare the availability achieved via our solution to the availability of a system's "most likely" deployment. We present two additional algorithms that we have developed to obtain the availability of the most likely deployment. Finally, in addition to significantly improving the overall system availability, we show that Avala, in general, also reduces the overall interaction latency in the system.

The Avala algorithm is part of an integrated solution to increasing a system's availability [13,17,12], which enables the three key redeployment tasks: (1) monitoring the system to gather the data that influences its availability; (2) estimating the redeployment architecture; and (3) effecting that architecture.

The remainder of the paper is organized as follows. Section 2 defines the problem our work is addressing and discusses a set of assumptions in our approach. Section 3 presents an overview of the related work and of our overall redeployment approach. Section 4 describes the exact algorithm and discusses its complexity. Section 5 describes the Avala algorithm for the exponentially complex redeployment problem. Section 6 presents our approach for evaluating Avala, the results of its assessment, and our tool support. Section 7 discusses the characteristics as well as current limitations of the Avala algorithm. The paper concludes with a discussion of future work.

2   The Redeployment Problem

The distribution of software components onto hardware nodes (i.e., a system's software *deployment architecture*) greatly influences the system's availability in the face of connectivity losses. For example, components located on the same host will be able to communicate regardless of the network's status, which is not the case with components distributed across different hosts. However, the reliability of connectivity (i.e., the rate of failure) among the "target" hardware nodes on which the system is deployed is usually not known before the deployment. The frequencies of interaction among software components may also be unknown. Hence, the initial software deployment architecture may be ill-suited for the given target hardware environment. This means that a *redeployment* of the software system may be necessary to improve its availability.

The critical difficulty in achieving this task lies in the fact that determining a software system's deployment architecture that will maximize its availability (referred to as *optimal deployment architecture*) is an exponentially complex problem.

2.1   Problem Definition

In addition to the characteristics of hardware connectivity and software interaction, there are other constraints on a system's redeployment, including: (1) the available memory on each host; (2) the required memory for each software component; and (3) possible restrictions on component locations (e.g., two CPU-intensive components may not be allowed to reside on the same host).

Figure 2. shows a formal model that captures the system properties and constraints, and a formal definition of the problem. The mem_{comp} function captures the required memory for each component. The frequency of interaction between any pair of components is captured via the *freq* relation. Each host's available memory is captured via the mem_{host} function. The reliability of the link between any pair of hosts is captured via the *rel* relation. Using the *loc* relation, deployment of any component can be restricted to a subset of hosts, thus denoting a set of *allowed* hosts for that component. Using the *colloc* relation constraints on collocation of components can be specified.

The definition of the problem contains the criterion function A, which formally describes a system's availability as the ratio of the number of successfully completed interactions in the system to the total number of attempted interactions. Function f represents the exponential number of the system's candidate deployments. To be considered valid, each candidate deployment must satisfy the three conditions. The first condition in the definition states that the sum of memories of the components that are deployed onto a given host may not exceed the available memory on that host. The second condition states that a component may only be deployed onto a host that belongs to a set of allowed hosts for that component, specified via the *loc* relation. Finally, the third condition states that two components must be deployed onto the same host (or on different hosts) if required by the *colloc* relation.

Model

Given:

(1) a set C of n components ($n = |C|$), a relation $freq : C \times C \to \Re$, and a function $mem_{comp} : C \to \Re$

$$freq(c_i, c_j) = \begin{cases} 0 & if \; c_i = c_j \\ frequency \; of \; communication \; between \; c_i \; and \; c_j & if \quad c_i \neq c_j \end{cases}$$

$mem_{comp}(c) = required \; memory \; for \; c$

(2) a set H of k hardware nodes ($k = |H|$), a relation $rel : H \times H \to \Re$, and a function $mem_{host} : H \to \Re$

$$rel(h_i, h_j) = \begin{cases} 1 & if \quad h_i = h_j \\ 0 & if \quad h_i \; is \; not \; connected \; to \; h_j \\ reliability \; of \; the \; link \; between \; h_i \; and \; h_j & if \quad h_i \neq h_j \end{cases}$$

$mem_{host}(h) = available \; memory \; on \; host \; h$

(3) Two relations that restrict locations of software components $loc : C \times H \to \{0,1\}$ $colloc : C \times C \to \{-1,0,1\}$

$$loc(c_i, h_j) = \begin{cases} 1 & if \; c_i \; can \; be \; deployed \; onto \; h_j \\ 0 & if \; c_i \; cannot \; be \; deployed \; onto \; h_j \end{cases}$$

$$colloc(c_i, c_j) = \begin{cases} -1 & if \; c_i \; cannot \; be \; on \; the \; same \; host \; as \; c_j \\ 1 & if \; c_i \; has \; to \; be \; on \; the \; same \; host \; as \; c_j \\ 0 & if \; there \; are \; no \; restrictions \; on \; collocation \; of \; c_i \; and \; c_j \end{cases}$$

Definition

Problem:

Find a function $f : C \to H$ such that the system's overall availability A defined as

$$A = \frac{\sum_{i=1}^{n}\sum_{j=1}^{n}\left(freq(c_i,c_j) * rel(f(c_i), f(c_j))\right)}{\sum_{i=1}^{n}\sum_{j=1}^{n} freq(c_i,c_j)}$$

is maximized, and the following three conditions are satisfied:

(1) $\forall i \in [1,k] \left\{ \forall j \in [1,n] \quad f(c_j) = h_i \; \middle| \; \sum_j mem_{comp}(c_j)) \le mem_{host}(h_i) \right\}$

(2) $\forall j \in [1,n] \qquad loc(c_j, f(c_j)) = 1$

(3) $\forall k \in [1,n] \quad \forall l \in [1,n] \quad (colloc(c_k, c_l) = 1) \Rightarrow (f(c_k) = f(c_l))$

$(colloc(c_k, c_l) = -1) \Rightarrow (f(c_k) \neq f(c_l))$

In the most general case, the number of possible functions f is k^n. However, note that some of these deployments may not satisfy one or more of the above three conditions.

Fig. 2. Formal statement of the problem

2.2   Assumptions

The problem defined in Section 2.1 is an instance of the more general redeployment problem, described in [16]. In this paper, we consider a subset of all possible constraints, and a specific criterion function, which is to maximize the system's availability. Through the *loc* and *colloc* functions, one can include other constraints (e.g., security, CPU, bandwidth), not directly captured in our problem description. However, if multiple resources, such as bandwidth and CPU, are as restrictive as memory in a given system, then capturing them only via the *loc* and *colloc* functions will not be sufficient. In [16] we describe how such cases could be addressed, by introducing additional system parameters into the model and introducing additional constraints that a valid deployment should satisfy. For example, for systems where the network bandwidth and volume of exchanged data severely restrict the number of possible deployments, the formal problem statement would need to include two additional constraint relations and an additional condition: (1) relation *evt_size* to capture the average size of data exchanged between a pair of components; (2) relation *bw* to capture the bandwidth between a pair of hosts; and (3) the following condition:

$$(\forall i \in [1,k] \quad \forall j \in [i+1,k])$$

$$\left(\begin{matrix} (\forall l \in [1,n] \quad \forall m \in [l+1,n]) \\ \left(\begin{matrix} where \; f(c_l) = h_i \wedge f(c_m) = h_j \\ \sum_{l,m} data\_vol(c_l,c_m) \leq effective\_bw(h_i,h_j) \end{matrix}\right) \end{matrix}\right) \begin{matrix} where \\ and \end{matrix} \quad \begin{matrix} data\_vol(c_x,c_y) = freq(c_x,c_y) * evt\_size(c_x,c_y) \\ effective\_bw(h_x,h_y) = rel(h_x,h_y) * bw(h_x,h_y) \end{matrix}$$

This condition states that, for each network link between a pair of hosts, the total volume of data exchanged across that link does not exceed the link's effective bandwidth. The algorithm presented in this paper would need to be altered to ensure the satisfaction of this condition.

Our definition of availability considers all inter-component interactions equally important. For systems in which this may not be the case, the same model and algorithm can still be used: the *freq* relation can be changed to correspond to the product of interaction frequency and importance of data, and the remainder of the model and problem definition would remain unchanged.

The problem presented in Section 2.1 is also based on the assumption that system parameters are stable over a given period of time *T*, during which we want to improve the system's availability.[1] It also relies on the assumption that the time required to perform the system's redeployment is negligible with respect to *T*. Otherwise, the system's parameters would be changing too frequently and the system would undergo continuous redeployments to improve the availability for parameters that change either before or shortly after the redeployment is completed.We believe this to be a reasonable assumption, which is reflective of a number of existing systems (e.g., see [20]).

Finally, our approach relies on the assumption that the given system's deployment architecture is accessible from some central location. We realize that this assumption may not be justified in a class of software systems that are decentralized, and have developed a decentralized solution that is complementary to this work [11]. However, in a centralized system, the algorithm can leverage the availability of global knowledge about system parameters on a central host to run more efficiently than a decentralized algorithm (in terms of required computational and communicational resources). Therefore, when dealing with a centralized system, it is preferable to use a centralized solution instead of a more generally applicable decentralized solution.

3 Background and Related Work

In this section we present a brief overview of disconnected operation approaches, and provide an in-depth look at three approaches that have specifically focused on the system redeployment problem. Additionally, to provide the context for Avala, we present an overview of our overall approach.

3.1 Disconnected Operation

We have performed an extensive survey of existing disconnected operation approaches, and provided a framework for their classification and comparison [18]. The most commonly used techniques for supporting disconnected operation are caching [9], hoarding [10], queueing remote interactions [6], and multi-modal components

---

[1] We do not require that system parameters be constant during *T*, but assume that each parameter can be approximated with its average over *T*, with an error no greater than a given threshold ε [14,17].

[22]. None of these techniques changes the system's deployment architecture. Instead, they strive to improve the system's availability by sacrificing either correctness (in the case of replication) or service delivery time (queueing), or by requiring implementation-level changes to the existing application's code [22].

3.2 Redeployment

I5 [1] proposes the use of the binary integer programming model for generating an optimal deployment of a software application over a given network. I5 is applicable only to systems with very small numbers of software components and target hosts, and to systems whose characteristics, such as frequencies of component interactions, are known at design time and are stable throughout the system's execution.

Coign [6] provides a framework for distributed partitioning of COM applications across the network. Coign employs the lift-to-front minimum-cut graph cutting algorithm to choose a deployment architecture that will result in minimal overall communication time. However, Coign can only handle situations with two-host, client-server applications. Coign recognizes that the problem of distributing an application across three or more hosts is NP hard and does not provide solutions for such cases.

Kichkaylo et al. [8], provide a model, called component placement problem (CPP), for describing a distributed system in terms of network and application properties and constraints, and an AI planning algorithm, called Sekitei, for solving the CPP model. CPP does not provide facilities for specifying the goal, i.e., a criterion function that should be maximized or minimized. Therefore, Sekitei only searches for any valid deployment that satisfies the specified constraints, without considering the quality of a found deployment.

3.3 Our Overall Approach

The Avala algorithm described in this paper is part of an integrated solution for increasing the availability of a distributed system during disconnection [14,15,17,12], without the shortcomings of the existing approaches. For instance, unlike [22] our approach does not require any recoding of the system's existing functionality or human intervention; unlike [9] it does not sacrifice the correctness of computations; in comparison to [6] it minimizes service delivery delays; finally, unlike any of the existing redeployment approaches, our approach scales to very large systems with arbitrary topologies. We directly leverage a software system's *architecture* in accomplishing this task. We support runtime redeployment to increase the software system's availability by (1) monitoring the system, (2) estimating its redeployment architecture, and (3) effecting the estimated redeployment architecture. We provide lightweight facilities for runtime monitoring [17,12] to extract the system's model (recall Figure 2.). The monitoring information is then used by Avala to estimate the improved deployment architecture. Finally, we provide a set of automated deployment facilities [15,12] to effect the estimated architecture.

4   Exact Algorithm

One can ensure that she will find a system's optimal deployment by trying all possible deployments of components onto hosts. The selected deployment is the one that has the maximum availability (referred to as *exact maximum*) and that satisfies the constraints posed by memory and restrictions on the locations of software components. This "exact" algorithm guarantees at least one optimal deployment. The complexity of this algorithm in the general case (i.e., with no restrictions on component locations) is $O(k^n)$, where k is the number of hardware hosts, and n the number of software components. By fixing a subset of m components to selected hosts, the complexity of the exact algorithm reduces to $O(k^{n-m})$. Even with this reduction, this algorithm may be computationally too expensive unless the number of hardware nodes and unfixed software components is very small. For example, even for a relatively small deployment architecture (15 components, 4 hosts), a Java JDK 1.4 implementation of the exact algorithm runs for more than eight hours on a mid-range PC.

5   The Avala Algorithm

Given the complexity of the exact algorithm, we had to devise an approximative algorithm that would significantly reduce this complexity while exhibiting good performance. In this section, we describe and assess the performance of Avala, an approximative algorithm with polynomial time complexity. Avala leverages a greedy approach [2].

Pseudo-code of Avala is provided in Figure 3. Avala incrementally assigns software components to the hardware hosts. At each step of the algorithm, the goal is to select the assignment that will maximally contribute to the availability function. This is achieved by selecting the "best" host and "best" software component at each step.

Avala starts by ranking all hardware nodes and software components. The initial ranking of hardware nodes is done by calculating *initHostRank* for each hardware node i, as follows:

$$initHostRank_i = a * \sum_{j=1}^{k} rel(h_i, h_j) + b * mem_{host}(h_i)$$

where a and b are calibration factors that denote the respective contributions of link reliability and memory to the selection of the "best" host. In Section 6 we discuss how varying a and b influences the algorithm's performance.

The ranking of software components is done by calculating *initCompRank* for each component i, as follows:

$$initCompRank_i = d * \sum_{j=1}^{n} freq(c_i, c_j) + \frac{e}{mem_{comp}(c_i)}$$

where d and e denote the respective contributions of event frequency and memory to the selection of the "best" component. In Section 6 we also discuss how varying d and e influences the algorithm's performance.

After the initial ranking is performed, the host with the highest value of *initHostRank* is selected as the current host h. A component with the highest value of *initCompRank* that satisfies the *mem* and *loc* constraints (conditions 1 and 2 in Figure 2.) is selected and assigned to h. The next software component(s) to be assigned to h are the ones with smallest required memory whose placement on h would maximally contribute to the availability function, i.e., the components with the highest volumes of interaction with the component(s) already assigned (mapped) to h. The selection is performed by calculating the value of *compRank* for each unassigned component as follows:

$$compRank(c_i, h) = d * \sum_{j=1}^{numOfMappedComps} (freq(c_i, mC(j)) * rel(h, f(mC(j)))) + \frac{e}{mem_{comp}(c_i)}$$

where $mC(j)$ is shorthand for $mappedComponents(j)$. The selected component is the one with the highest value of $compRank$ that satisfies memory, loc, and $colloc$ constraints with respect to the current host h and components already assigned. This process repeats until h is full (i.e., there is no component small enough to fit on h).

$$hostRank(h_i) = a * \sum_{j=1}^{numOfMappedHosts} rel(h_i, mappedHost(j)) + b * mem_{host}(h_i)$$

The next host to be selected is the one with the highest memory capacity and highest link quality (i.e., highest value of $hostRank$) with the host(s) already selected:

The process of selecting software components repeats, until all the components have been assigned to a host.

The complexity of the Avala algorithm in the most general case (i.e., when the number of components fixed to a single host is zero, and there are more components than hosts) is $O(n^3)$, derived as follows:

$O(Avala\_algorithm) = O((n-1) * (O(next\_comp) + O(next\_host))) =$
$O((n-1) * (n * O(compRank) + k * O(hostRank)) = O((n-1) * (n * n + k * k)) =$
$O(n^3 + n * k^2) = O(n^3)$, if n>k

Note that if there are few or no constraints on component location, and total available memory on hosts is significantly above the total required memory by the components, some of the hosts will get filled to their capacity, while others may contain few components or even be empty. The uneven distribution of components among hosts results in higher overall availability of the system since it utilizes the maximum reliability for interactions between components residing on the same host. However, it may also result in undesirable effects on the system, such as overloading the CPUs on hosts with large numbers of components, or overloading the used subset of network links. The Avala algorithm currently addresses this concern only via the loc and $colloc$ constraints (e.g., by assigning a UI component to each host). However, as described in Section 2.2, both the problem statement and the algorithm could be modified to take other criteria (e.g., CPU, bandwidth) into consideration.

The contributions of Avala are two fold. By separating the component and host selection process from the remaining algorithm's logic, we can easily extend the algorithm to include other system parameters and constraints. Secondly, by parameterizing the selection process for components and hosts along two separate dimensions (memory and frequency in the case of components, and memory and reliability in the case of hosts) the algorithm can automatically adapt to variations in input parameters.

6 Evaluation

Due to the exponential nature of the deployment problem, evaluating Avala's results against the exact solution is only feasible for very small systems (e.g., less than 15 components and 4 hosts). In these cases, the exact algorithm can also produce the average availability of all the deployments (referred to as *exact average*), thus providing an additional criterion for evaluation. However, we still need to assess how well the Avala algorithm performs for systems with (much) larger numbers of components and hosts. To that end, we use two additional algorithms discussed below.

6.1 Evaluation Criteria

We have developed a stochastic algorithm (called *unbiased* stochastic algorithm) that randomly selects a subset of all possible deployments, and uses the availabilities of these deployments to estimate the average availability of a given system. The obtained average availability corresponds to the system's "most likely" availability. The unbiased stochastic algorithm generates different deployments by randomly assigning each component to a single host from the set of available hosts for that component. If the randomly generated deployment satisfies all the constraints, the availability of the produced deployment architecture is calculated. This process repeats a given number of times, and the average availability (referred to as *unbiased average*) and maximum availability (referred to as *unbiased maximum*) are calculated. The complexity of calculating the availability for each valid deployment is quadratic (recall Figure 2.), resulting in the same complexity of the overall unbiased stochastic algorithm ($O(n^2)$).

In addition to this algorithm, for the sake of completeness we also compare Avala's results against another stochastic algorithm (called *biased* stochastic algorithm) that we have developed and assessed previously [14]. The biased stochastic algorithm randomly orders the hosts and randomly orders the components. Then, going in order, it assigns as many components to a given host as can fit on that host (due to memory constraints), also ensuring that the *loc* and *colloc* constraints are satisfied. Once the host is full, the algorithm proceeds with the same process for the next host in the ordered list of hosts, and the remaining unassigned components in the ordered list of components, until all components have been deployed. This process repeats a given number of times, and the average availability (referred to

Fig. 3. Pseudo-code of the Avala algorithm (left) and its complexity (right)

as *biased average*) and maximum availability (referred to as *biased maximum*) are calculated. The complexity of this algorithm is also polynomial, since we need to calculate the availability for every deployment, and that takes $O(n^2)$ time.

6.2 Testing Environment

To assess Avala's performance, we have leveraged DeSi [15], a visual deployment environment that supports specification, manipulation, visualization, and (re)estimation of deployment architectures for large-scale, highly distributed systems. DeSi provides users with a graphical front-end to input values for numbers of hosts and software components as well as the ranges for available memory on the hosts, required memory for the components, frequency of interaction between components, and reliability of connectivity between hosts. DeSi uses this information to randomly generate a *redeployment problem* by fixing all hardware and software parameters needed as inputs to the algorithms. DeSi provides the ability to invoke different redeployment algorithms and display their results. Finally, the algorithms can be benchmarked a given number of times: DeSi iteratively generates different redeployment problems a specified number of times using the same set of ranges for input data, invokes each one of the algorithms for each problem, and calculates the average results.

DeSi provides a number of additional facilities for visualizing and graphically manipulating a system's deployment architecture, as well as several host- and component-specific views. A discussion of these facilities is outside the scope of this paper, however, and can be found in [15].

6.3 Evaluation Results

We have assessed the performance of the Avala algorithm by comparing it against the exact algorithm and the two stochastic algorithms for systems with small numbers of components and hosts (i.e., less than 13 components, and less than 5 hosts).

In large numbers of randomly generated redeployment problems, the Avala algorithm invariably found a solution that was at least 90% of the optimal (i.e., the *exact maximum*). In Table 1, we present results of 5 different redeployment problems, as well as the average results for 30 different randomly generated problems (using the DeSi's benchmark option and shown in the right-most column).[2]   The   average improvement of availability by Avala over the *exact average* was 34.7%.

Table 1. Comparing the performance of Avala for different architectures with 10 components and 4 hosts

	10 comps 4 hosts 1 iteration	10 comps 4 hosts 1 iteration	10 comps 4 hosts 1 iteration	10 comps 4 hosts 1 iteration	10 comps 4 hosts 1 iteration	10 comps 4 hosts 30 iterations
Unbiased maximum	0.790	0.732	0.636	0.763	0.932	0.742
Unbiased average	0.560	0.558	0.605	0.516	0.581	0.585
Biased maximum	0.621	0.701	0.615	0.679	0.745	0.738
Biased average	0.572	0.551	0.606	0.544	0.633	0.626
Exact maximum	0.895	0.800	0.733	0.985	0.983	0.820
Exact average	0.558	0.555	0.628	0.513	0.580	0.585
Avala	*0.854*	*0.792*	*0.673*	*0.984*	*0.962*	*0.788*
% improvement over the exact average[a]	53.0	42.7	7.2	91.8	65.9	34.7
% improvement over the unbiased average[b]	52.5	41.9	11.2	90.6	65.5	34.7
% of the exact[c]	95.4	99	91.8	99.9	97.9	96.1

a. calculated as 100% * (Avala − exact average) / exact average
b. calculated as 100% * (Avala − unbiased average) / unbiased average
c. calculated as 100% * Avala / exact maximum

---

[2] The highlighted columns in Tables 1 and 2 will be discussed further in Section 7.

For larger problems, where the exact algorithm is infeasible, we have compared the results of Avala against the results of the stochastic algorithms. In [19], we demonstrated that increasing the number of iterations beyond 10,000 does not significantly change the average availability of the two stochastic algorithms. Thus, the stochastic algorithms were executed with 10,000 iterations for larger deployment problems.

Table 2 illustrates the results of 6 different benchmarks where the number of components was varied between 30 and 1000 and number of hosts between 7 and 100. The average relative improvement of availability produced by Avala was 33.9% over the *unbiased average*, 30% over the *unbiased maximum*, 28% over the *biased average*, and 11% over the *biased maximum*. Avala also produced its results quickly. For illustration, it took 38 seconds to solve the largest problem (100 hosts and 1000 components) on a mid-range PC; by comparison, the exact algorithm would require over 10^{1984} *years* to determine the optimal deployment. Solving the same problem on a high-end computer (2.8GHz Pentium 4) reduces Avala's running time over 10-fold.

The following observations have further increased our confidence that Avala is finding nearly-optimal solutions for large systems: (1) for small systems (Table 1) the *unbiased average* was always very close to the *exact average*, denoting that the *unbiased average* precisely calculates the most likely availability; (2) the average improvement over the *unbiased average* for both small and large systems was quite similar (e.g., note

Table 2. Comparing the performance of the Avala algorithm for larger deployment problems

	100 comps 10 hosts 1 iteration	200 comps 20 hosts 1 iteration	1000 comps 100 hosts 1 iteration	100 comps 40 hosts 1 iteration	30 comps 7 hosts 1 iteration	300 comps 70 hosts 30 iterations
Unbiased maximum	0.580	0.562	0.503	0.534	0.602	0.520
Unbiased average	0.521	0.535	0.502	0.527	0.512	0.508
Biased maximum	0.696	0.691	0.527	0.590	0.828	0.610
Biased average	0.574	0.564	0.506	0.539	0.610	0.532
Avala	*0.787*	*.780*	*0.576*	*0.704*	*0.906*	*0.680*
% improvement over the unbiased average[a]	51.1	31.2	14.7	33.6	77.0	33.9

a. calculated as 100% * (Avala – unbiased average) / unbiased average

the rightmost, i.e., benchmark columns of Tables 1 and 2); and (3) Avala's results for small systems were at least 90% of the optimal.

6.4 Calibrating the Avala Algorithm

As described in Section 5, Avala can be fine-tuned by assigning different values to the calibration factors a, b, d, and e. These factors denote the level of contribution of different parameters (link reliability, frequency of interaction, and memory of hosts and components) to the selection of the "best" host or "best" component. There are at least three different possibilities for selecting these factors: (1) predefined, constant values; (2) values selected and varied by a human user; or (3) automatically calculated values. We have implemented a generation facility for these factors that has been demonstrated experimentally to be quite effective. We have observed that, with the increase of the ratio of average host memory to average component memory, better results are obtained if more emphasis is placed on memory factors (i.e., increasing b and e) than on frequency and reliability factors (i.e., decreasing a and d). Experimentally we have obtained the best results for systems where the number of hosts is smaller than the number of components (i.e., $k<n$), calculating the calibration factors as:

$b = e = 0.1 * \text{(average host memory * k) / (average comp memory * n)}$ and $a = d = 1\text{-}b$

The benchmarks shown in Tables 1 and 2 are obtained using the above formulas for the calibration factors. Table 3 shows the benchmark data for the calibration factors using four different, randomly generated systems with varying numbers of components and hosts, and varying ranges for host and component memory. The *"Auto"* value corresponds to the factors calculated using the above formula, while the remaining rows of the table correspond to manually assigned factors. The resulting availability of automatically generated factors was within 1% of the best availability obtained with any other combination of factors.

7   Discussion

Here we discuss the characteristics as well as current limitations of the Avala algorithm, and suggest possible directions for addressing these limitations.

7.1   Interaction Latency

For certain distributed systems, availability may not be the only, or the most crucial property. In fact, networked systems have traditionally focused on minimizing communication latencies as a key goal. Latency is commonly defined as the time taken to deliver a data packet from the source to the receiver [5]. While minimizing latency was not our primary goal in developing Avala, the algorithm's objective does naturally result in significant reductions of component communication latencies. The reason for this is two-fold. First, by

Table 3. Comparing the performance of Avala for different values of calibration factors, including their automatic generation

Value for factors a and c	Value for factors b and e	100 comps 10 hosts avg host mem=85 avg comp mem=5	100 comps 10 hosts avg host mem=165 avg comp mem=11	15 comps 5 hosts avg host mem=60 avg comp mem=11	15 comps 5 hosts avg host mem=70 avg comp mem=11
0.9	0.1	0.739	0.759	0.75	0.85
0.8	0.2	0.745	0.775	0.772	0.86
0.7	0.3	0.739	0.769	0.773	0.858
0.6	0.4	0.737	0.757	0.772	0.856
0.5	0.5	0.732	0.738	0.74	0.853
0.4	0.6	0.722	0.728	0.734	0.837
0.3	0.7	0.699	0.717	0.706	0.837
0.2	0.8	0.672	0.706	0.642	0.837
0.1	0.9	0.66	0.701	0.622	0.832
Auto	Auto	0.744	0.772	0.772	0.861

increasing the overall system availability, some interactions that could not be successfully completed before now can be, thereby effectively reducing their latency from infinity to some finite time. Secondly, by employing the strategy of deploying frequently interacting components on the same host whenever possible, the latencies of those components' interactions are significantly reduced.

In order to compare the average interaction latency of a system's initial deployment to the deployment produced by Avala, we would have to average over all interaction latencies in the system in both deployments. Since in both cases there may be interactions that do not complete successfully due to network disconnections, those interaction latencies will be infinite, thus preventing us from comparing the average latency of the two deployments. For this reason, we will assume that network reliability of all host-to-host links is 1, i.e., that each component interaction successfully completes.

Latency of a single interaction depends on the following parameters: (1) startup latency, which is the constant communication overhead incurred in sending a zero length message [5], (2) network bandwidth of a link through which the interaction is performed, and (3) the size of message exchanged. To calculate the average latency in a given system, we use the following formula:

$$avgLatency = \frac{\sum_{i=1}^{n}\sum_{j=1}^{n}\left(freq(c_i,c_j) * \left(delay(f(c_i),f(c_j)) + \frac{evt\_size(c_i,c_j)}{bw(f(c_i),f(c_j))} \right) \right)}{\sum_{i=1}^{n}\sum_{j=1}^{n} freq(c_i,c_j)}$$

where *delay* represents the startup latency of a given network link between two hosts.[3] We assume that the latency of interaction for two components deployed onto the same host is zero (i.,e., *delay (h,h) =0* and *bw(h,h)=*∞).

We have performed a series of benchmark tests to quantify the effect of Avala's results on average component interaction latency. To that end, we have extended our DeSi environment with random generation of startup latencies within a specified range, and automated calculation of average latencies for both a system's initial deployment and the deployment calculated by Avala.

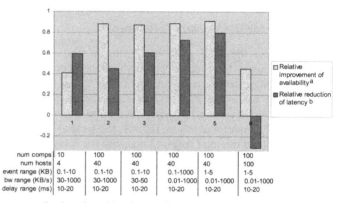

a. calculated as (Avala_availability – initial_availability) /

Figure 4. shows the results of these benchmarks. In most cases, redeployments produced by Avala reduced the average interaction latency by 40% - 80%.

Fig. 4. The effect of redeployment calculated by Avala on average interaction latency. Each result was obtained by averaging over 20 different, randomly generated redeployment problems.

Avala, however, does not *guarantee* interaction latency reduction. In extreme cases, where each host's available memory is limited such that only a very small number of components can be deployed onto the host, the benefit of co-locating components cannot be leveraged. This case is illustrated in last column of Figure 4., where each host could only contain a single component due to memory constraints. Furthermore, since we are not assuming correlation between network reliability and bandwidth (e.g., a highly reliable link may have low bandwidth and vice versa), in some cases Avala may suggest deploying of components between hosts with high reliability and low bandwidth links, thus resulting in increased latency. One way to address this situation is to include bandwidth and event size as selection parameters for the "best" host and "best" component in Avala. We are currently implementing and evaluating this solution and its impact on both system availability and interaction latency.

---

[3] Recall Section 2.2 for definitions of *evt_size* and *bw*.

7.2 Including the Constraints on Component Location

The benchmark results from Section 6.3 assess Avala's performance without using the *loc* and *colloc* constraints. We have also tested Avala with these constraints and have observed that, by introducing a significant number of constraints, the obtained availability starts to decrease. This is primarily due to the fact that the *loc* and *colloc* constraints will render invalid some deployments with otherwise high availabilities. For cases where either the size of the original problem or the reduction in the exact algorithm's complexity induced by the *loc* and *colloc* constraints enable us to invoke the exact algorithm, we have observed that the difference between the *exact maximum* and the availability produced by Avala actually decreases. The reason for this is that, as the system becomes more constrained in terms of component location and collocation, the probability that Avala will divert significantly from the exact solution lessens.

7.3 Reducing the Memory Difference

By reducing the total available memory for hosts and/or increasing the total required memory for components, both the number of valid deployments and the system availability decrease. Again, this is due to the fact that a large number of deployments with otherwise high availabilities become invalid. In Tables 1 and 2 the highlighted columns are illustrative examples that correspond to these types of situations. For the system shown in Table 1, the total available memory for hosts was only 6% greater than the total required memory for components, resulting in 980 valid (out of over 1,000,000 possible) deployments. The relative improvement over the *unbiased average* was 11%, which was substantially lower than in other, less memory constrained systems. At the same time, the achieved availability was still more than 90% of the optimal availability. A similar situation can be observed in Table 2, although in that case the only available comparisons are to the *unbiased* and *biased averages*.

If the reduction of the total available memory for hosts and/or increase in the total required memory for components results in a very small number of valid deployments, our algorithm does not always find a valid deployment. The reason is that Avala initially assigns the component with the highest *initCompRank* to the host with the highest *initHostRank*. If this assignment leads to an invalid solution due to the limited available memory (e.g., just by assigning that component to that host the remaining components cannot be assigned), then our algorithm does not find a valid deployment.

One way to address this situation would be to detect cases when it occurs and try a different initial assignment. The number of different initial assignments is $k*n$, thus increasing the algorithm's complexity to $O(k*n^4)$. However, this still does not guarantee that the algorithm would find a valid deployment. We plan to assess this solution and possibly use additional backtracking techniques to address this limitation of Avala.

8   Conclusions and Future Work

As the distribution, decentralization, and mobility of computing environments grow, so does the probability that (parts of) those environments will need to operate in the face of network disconnections. Our research is guided by the observation that, in these environments, a key determinant of the system's ability to effectively deal with network disconnections is finding the appropriate *deployment architecture*. While the redeployment problem has been identified in the existing literature, its inherent complexity has either been ignored [1], thus making it infeasible for any realistic system, or highly restricted [6], thus reducing the solution's usefulness.

This paper has presented Avala, an efficient algorithm for improving a distributed, component-based system's availability via redeployment. Avala is part of an integrated solution to increasing a system's availability [14,15,17,12]. It has been thoroughly assessed via a series of benchmarks. In addition to significantly improving system availability Avala, in general, also reduces the overall interaction latency in the system. While our experience thus far has been very positive, a number of pertinent questions remain unexplored. Our future work will span issues such as (1) addressing situations in which the system constraints highly restrict the solution space, and (2) expanding our solution to include additional system parameters (e.g., battery power, display size, system software available on a given host, and so on). These issues represent but a small subset of related concerns that are emerging in the domain of distributed, mobile computation and that will increasingly shape the software development of the future.

Acknowledgements

This material is based upon work supported by the National Science Foundation under Grant Numbers CCR-9985441 and ITR-0312780. Effort also partially supported by the Jet Propulsion Laboratory.

References

[1] M. C. Bastarrica, et. al. A Binary Integer Programming Model for Optimal Object Distribution. 2nd *Int'l. Conf. on Principles of Distributed Systems*, Amiens, France, Dec. 1998.

[2] T. H. Cormen, et. al. Introduction to Algorithms. *MIT Press*, Cambridge, MA, 1990.

[3] A. Fuggetta, et. al. Understanding Code Mobility. *IEEE Trans. on Software Engineering*, 1998.

[4] D. Garlan, et al. Using Gauges for Architecture-Based Monitoring and Adaptation. *Working Conf. on Complex and Dynamic Systems Arch.*, Brisbane, Australia, Dec. 2001.

[5] http://www.epcc.ed.ac.uk/HPCinfo/glossary.html

[6] G. Hunt and M. Scott. The Coign Automatic Distributed Partitioning System. *3rd Symposium on Operating System Design and Implementation*, New Orleans, LA, Feb. 1999.

[7] IEEE Standard Computer Dictionary: *IEEE Standard Computer Glossaries*. New York, NY: 1990.

[8] T. Kichkaylo et al. Constrained Component Deployment in Wide-Area Networks Using AI Planning Techniques. *Int'l. Parallel and Distributed Processing Symposium*. April 2003.

[9] J. J. Kistler and M. Satyanarayanan. Disconnected Operation in the Coda File System. *ACM Transactions on Computer Systems*, vol. 10, no. 1, February 1992.

[10] G. H. Kuenning and G. J. Popek. Automated Hoarding for Mobile Computers. Proc. of the 16th *ACM Symp. on Operating Systems Principles*, St. Malo, France, October, 1997.

[11] S. Malek, et. al. A Decentralized Redeployment Algorithm for Improving the Availability of Distributed Systems. In Proc. of *the 3rd Int. Working Conference on Component Deployment (CD 2005)*, Grenoble, France, Nov. 2005.

[12] S. Malek, et. al. Prism-MW: A Style-Aware Architectural Middleware for Resource Constrained, Distributed Systems. *IEEE Trans. on Software Engineering*. Vol. 31, No. 3, March 2005.

[13] N. Medvidovic, et al. Software Architectural Support for Handheld Computing. *IEEE Computer*, September 2003.

[14] M. Mikic-Rakic and N.Medvidovic. Software Architectural Support for Disconnected Operation in Highly Distributed Environments. *CBSE7*, Edinburgh, UK, May 2004.

[15] M. Mikic-Rakic, et. al. A Tailorable Environment for Assessing the Quality of Deployment Architectures in Highly Distributed Settings. *2nd International Working Conference on Component Deploymen (CD 2004)*, Edinburgh, UK, May 2004.

[16] M. Mikic-Rakic, et. al. Improving Availability in Large, Distributed, Component-Based Systems via Redeployment. Technical Report *USC-CSE-2003-515*, 2003.

[17] M. Mikic-Rakic and N. Medvidovic. Support for Disconnected Operation via Architectural Self-Reconfiguration. *Int. Conference on Autonomic Computing (ICAC'04)*, New York, May 2004.

[18] M. Mikic-Rakic and N. Medvidovic. Toward a Framework for Classifying Disconnected Operation Techniques. *ICSE WADS*, Portland, OR, May 2003.

[19] M. Mikic-Rakic and N. Medvidovic. Software Architectural Support for Disconnected Operation in Highly Distributed Environments. *Tech. Report*, USC-CSE-2003-506, 2003.

[20] Multi Router Traffic Grapher. http://scorpion77.cjb.net/mrtg/

[21] P. Oreizy et al. Architecture-Based run-time Software Evolution. *ICSE'98*, Japan, April 1998.

[22] Y. Weinsberg, and I. Ben-Shaul. A Programming Model and System Support for Disconnected-Aware Applications on Resource-Constrained Devices. *ICSE 2002*, Orlando, FL.

[23] J. Weissman. Fault-Tolerant Wide-Area Parallel Computing. *IPDPS 2000 Workshop*, Cancun, Mexico, May 2000.

[24] Y. Zhang, et.al. The Stationarity of Internet Path Properties: Routing, Loss, and Throughput. *Technical Report,* AT&T Center for Internet Research at ICSI, May 2000.

A Decentralized Redeployment Algorithm for Improving the Availability of Distributed Systems

Sam Malek[1,3], Marija Mikic-Rakic[2], and Nenad Medvidovic[1]

[1] University of Southern California, Computer Science Department,
Los Angeles, CA, 90089, USA
{malek, neno}@usc.edu
[2] Google Inc., Santa Monica, CA, 90405, USA
marija@google.com
[3] The Boeing Company, 5301 Bolsa Avenue,
Huntington Beach, CA, 92647, USA
sam.malek2@boeing.com

Abstract. In distributed and mobile environments, the connections among the hosts on which a software system is running are often unstable. As a result of connectivity losses, the overall availability of the system decreases. The distribution of software components onto hardware nodes (i.e., the system's deployment architecture) may be ill-suited for the given target hardware environment and may need to be altered to improve the software system's availability. Determining a software system's deployment that will maximize its availability is an exponentially complex problem. Although several polynomial-time approximative techniques have been developed recently, these techniques rely on the assumption that the system's deployment architecture and its properties are accessible from a central location. For these reasons, the existing techniques are not applicable to an emerging class of decentralized systems marked by the limited system wide knowledge and lack of centralized control. In this paper we present an approximative solution for the redeployment problem that is suitable for decentralized systems and assess its performance.

1 Introduction

Highly distributed and mobile systems are challenged by the problem of *disconnected operation* [25], where the system must continue functioning in the temporary absence of the network. Disconnected operation forces systems executing on each network host to temporarily operate independently from other hosts. This presents a major challenge for software systems that are highly dependent on network connectivity because each local subsystem is usually dependent on the availability of non-local resources. Lack of access to a remote resource can make a particular subsystem, or even the entire system unusable.

A software system's *availability* is commonly defined as the degree to which a system is operational and accessible when required for use [8]. In the context of highly distributed, mobile environments, where the most common cause of (partial) system inac-

A. Dearle and S. Eisenbach (Eds.): CD 2005, LNCS 3798, pp. 99 – 114, 2005.
© Springer-Verlag Berlin Heidelberg 2005

cessibility is network failure [24], we quantify availability as the ratio of the number of successfully completed inter-component interactions in the system to the total number of attempted interactions over a period of time.

The distribution of software components onto hardware nodes (i.e., a system's software *deployment architecture*, illustrated in Figure 1.) greatly influences the system's availability in the face of connectivity losses. For example, in such cases it is desirable to collocate components that interact frequently. However, the parameters that influence the optimal distribution of a system (e.g., network reliability) may not be known before the system's deployment. For this reason, the (initial) software deployment architecture may be ill-suited for the given target hardware environment. This means that a *redeployment* of the software system may be necessary to improve its availability.

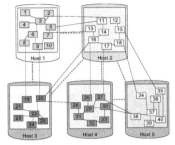

Fig. 1. A sample deployment architecture with five hosts and 40 components

There are several existing techniques that can support various subtasks of redeployment, such as monitoring [4] to assess hardware and software properties of interest, component migration [2] to facilitate redeployment, and dynamic system manipulation [20] to effect the redeployment once the components are migrated to the appropriate hosts. However, one of the critical difficulties in achieving this task lies in the fact that determining a software system's deployment that will maximize its availability (i.e., the *optimal* deployment) is an exponentially complex problem: in the most general case the complexity is k^n, where k is the number of hardware hosts and n the number of software components.

This paper accompanies our work on providing a centralized solution, which is complementary to this paper and requires global knowledge of system parameters and global control of the system's redeployment [18]. Therefore, the centralized solution assumes the existence of a central host that has reliable access to every other host in the system. This assumption has made the centralized solution inapplicable to a wide range of distributed systems (e.g., ad-hoc mobile networks) where such a reliable centralized host does not exist.

In this paper we present an approximative algorithm for increasing a system's availability that scales to the exponentially complex nature of this problem. The algorithm, called DecAp, is decentralized and does not require global knowledge of system properties. We provide a detailed assessment of DecAp's performance through its comparison against several centralized algorithms. We leverage our deployment exploration environment, called DeSi [17], in performing DecAp's performance assessment. DeSi supports quantitative assessment and comparison of different redeployment algorithms as well as active visualization of a system's deployment architecture.

The remainder of the paper is organized as follows. Section 2 defines the problem our work is addressing and discusses a set of assumptions in our approach. Section 3 presents an overview of the related work. Section 4 describes the DecAp algorithm and discusses its complexity. Section 5 discusses DecAp's behavior. Section 6 presents our approach for evaluating DecAp and the results of its assessment. The paper concludes with a discussion of future work.

2   The Redeployment Problem

2.1   Problem Definition

We describe a distributed system as (1) a set of n components with their properties, (2) a set of k hosts with their properties, (3) a set of constraints that a valid deployment architecture must satisfy, (4) the system's initial deployment as a mapping of components to hosts, and (5) a set of system properties that are "visible" from a given host. Figure 2. shows a formal model that captures the above system properties and constraints.

The mem_{comp} function captures the required memory for each component. The frequency of interaction between any pair of components is captured via the $freq$ function. Each host's available memory is captured via the mem_{host} function. The reliability of the link between any pair of hosts is captured via the rel function. Using the loc function, deployment of any component can be restricted to a subset of hosts,

---

(1) A set C of n components ($n = |C|$) and two functions
$freq : C \times C \to \Re$ and $mem_{comp} : C \to \Re$

$$freq(c_i, c_j) = \begin{cases} 0 & if \quad c_i = c_j \\ frequency\ of\ communic.\ between\ c_i\ and\ c_j & if \quad c_i \neq c_j \end{cases}$$

$mem_{comp}(c) = required\ memory\ for\ c$

(2) A set H of k hardware nodes ($k = |H|$) and two functions
$rel : H \times H \to \Re$ and $mem_{host} : H \to \Re$

$$rel(h_i, h_j) = \begin{cases} 1 & if \quad h_i = h_j \\ 0 & if \quad h_i\ is\ not\ connected\ to\ h_j \\ reliability\ of\ the\ link\ between\ h_i\ and\ h_j & if \quad h_i \neq h_j \end{cases}$$

$mem_{host}(h) = available\ memory\ on\ host\ h$

(3) Two functions that restrict locations of software components
$loc : C \times H \to \{0,1\}$ and $colloc : C \times C \to \{-1,0,1\}$

$$loc(c_i, h_j) = \begin{cases} 1 & if \quad c_i\ can\ be\ deployed\ onto\ h_j \\ 0 & if \quad c_i\ cannot\ be\ deployed\ onto\ h_j \end{cases}$$

$$colloc(c_i, c_j) = \begin{cases} -1 & if \quad c_i\ cannot\ be\ on\ the\ same\ host\ as\ c_j \\ 1 & if \quad c_i\ has\ to\ be\ on\ the\ same\ host\ as\ c_j \\ 0 & if \quad there\ are\ no\ restrictions\ on\ collocation\ of\ c_i\ and\ c_j \end{cases}$$

(4) A relation $dep : H \to \mathcal{P}(C)$ where $c_k \in dep(h_i)$ iff c_k is deployed on h_i

(5) A function $aware : H \times H \to \{0,1\}$

$$aware(h_i, h_j) = \begin{cases} 1 & if\ h_i\ and\ h_j\ have\ the\ following\ information: \\ & \forall c_i \in dep(h_i), \forall c_j \in dep(h_j), \forall c_k \in C, \forall h_k \in H \\ & mem_{host}(h_i),\ mem_{host}(h_j),\ dep(h_i),\ dep(h_j), \\ & rel(h_i, h_j),\ mem_{comp}(c_i),\ mem_{comp}(c_j),\ freq(c_i, c_k), \\ & freq(c_j, c_k),\ loc(c_i, h_k),\ loc(c_j, h_k), \\ & colloc(c_i, c_k),\ colloc(c_j, c_k). \\ 0 & if\ h_i\ and\ h_j\ have\ no\ information\ of\ each\ other \end{cases}$$

and a relation $dom : H \to \mathcal{P}(H)$, where $h_k \in dom(h_i)$ iff aware(h_k, h_i) = 1

Fig. 2. Formal redeployment model

---

thus denoting a set of *allowed* hosts for that component. Using the *colloc* function, constraints on collocation of components can be specified. The relation *dep* denotes the current deployment of the system's components on hosts.

The function *aware* and the relation *dom* model the system's decentralized nature. Function *aware* denotes whether two hosts have access to each other's properties and the properties of components that reside on them. Relation *dom* denotes the "domain" of a host h_i, which is the set of all hosts of which h_i is aware. A host's domain corresponds to the host's extent of knowledge about the overall system's parameters. For example, in the centralized approach to the redeployment problem discussed above, the assumption is that at least one host's domain is the entire set of hosts H.

Figure 3. shows a formal definition of the problem we are solving. The criterion function A describes a system's availability as the ratio of the number of successfully completed interactions in the system to the total number of attempted interactions. Function f represents the exponential number of the system's candidate deployments. To be considered valid, each candidate deployment must satisfy the three stated conditions: (1) the sum of memories of the components that are deployed onto a given host may not exceed the available memory on that host; (2) a component

Find a function $f : C \rightarrow H$ such that the system's overall availability A defined as

$$A = \frac{\sum_{i=1}^{n} \sum_{j=1}^{n} (freq(c_i, c_j) * rel(f(c_i), f(c_j)))}{\sum_{i=1}^{n} \sum_{j=1}^{n} freq(c_i, c_j)}$$

is maximized, and the following three conditions are satisfied:

(1) $\forall i \in [1, k] \left\{ \forall j \in [1, n] \quad f(c_j) = h_i \mid \sum_{j} mem_{comp}(c_j)) \leq mem_{host}(h_i) \right\}$

(2) $\forall j \in [1, n] \qquad loc(c_j, f(c_j)) = 1$

(3) $\forall k \in [1, n] \quad \forall l \in [1, n]$
  $\quad if \ (colloc(c_k, c_l) = 1) \Rightarrow (f(c_k) = f(c_l))$
  $\quad if \ (colloc(c_k, c_l) = -1) \Rightarrow (f(c_k) \neq f(c_l))$

In the most general case, the number of possible functions f is k^n. However, note that some of these deployments may not satisfy one or more of the above three conditions.

Fig. 3. Formal statement of problem definition

may only be deployed onto a host that belongs to the set of allowed hosts for that component, specified via the *loc* function; and (3) two components must be deployed onto the same host (or on different hosts) if required by the *colloc* function.

2.2 Assumptions

The problem defined in Figure 3. is an instance of the more general redeployment problem, described in [18]. In this paper, we consider a subset of all possible constraints, and a specific criterion function, which is to maximize the system's availability. Through the *loc* and *colloc* functions, one can include other constraints (e.g., security, CPU, bandwidth), not directly captured in our problem description. However, if multiple resources, such as bandwidth and CPU, are as restrictive as memory in a given system, then capturing them only via the *loc* and *colloc* functions will not be sufficient. In [18] we describe how such cases could be addressed, by introducing additional system parameters into the model and introducing additional constraints that a valid deployment should satisfy.

Our definition of availability considers all inter-component interactions equally important. For systems in which this may not be the case, the same model and algorithm can still be used: the *freq* function can be changed to correspond to the product of interaction frequency and importance, and the remainder of the model and problem definition would remain unchanged.

The problem presented in section 2.1 is also based on the assumption that system parameters are reasonably stable over a given period of time T, during which we want to improve the system's availability.[1] It also relies on the assumption that the time required to perform the system's redeployment is negligible with respect to T. Otherwise,

---

[1] We do not require that system parameters be constant during T, but assume that each parameter can be approximated with its average over the period T, with an error no greater than a given threshold ε [19].

the system's parameters would be changing too frequently and the system would undergo continuous redeployments to improve its availability.

Finally, our approach is based on the assumption that two hosts that are aware of each other will be able to reliably exchange the "meta-level" information (detailed in Section 4) required for the correct functioning of the redeployment algorithm. This can be ensured by employing existing techniques, e.g., delivery guarantee mechanisms [14], or gossip-based protocols [3]. While such techniques may also be used to improve the availability of the system itself, employing them for all *application-level* information exchange will typically be too expensive.

3   Related Work

In this section we present a brief overview of centralized redeployment approaches. We also provide an overview of most commonly used decentralized cooperative algorithms.

3.1   Centralized Deployment Approaches

I5 [1] proposes the use of the binary integer programming model for generating an optimal deployment of a software application over a given network. I5 is applicable only to systems with very small numbers of software components and target hosts, and to systems whose characteristics, such as frequencies of component interactions, are known at design time and are stable throughout the system's execution.

Coign [7] provides a framework for distributed partitioning of COM applications across the network. Coign employs the lift-to-front minimum-cut graph cutting algorithm to choose a deployment architecture that will result in minimal overall communication time. However, Coign can only handle situations with two-host, client-server applications. Coign recognizes that the problem of distributing an application across three or more hosts is NP hard and does not provide solutions for such cases.

Kichkaylo et al. [11], provide a model, called component placement problem (CPP), for describing a distributed system in terms of network and application properties and constraints, and an AI planning algorithm, called Sekitei, for solving the CPP model. CPP does not provide facilities for specifying the goal, i.e., a criterion function that should be maximized or minimized. Therefore, Sekitei only searches for any valid deployment that satisfies the specified constraints, without considering the quality of a found deployment.

Finally, we have developed several algorithms for the centralized version of the redeployment problem [18]. In section 6.2, we briefly describe these algorithms, as they will be used to assess the performance of DecAp.

3.2   Decentralized Cooperative Algorithms

Decentralized cooperative algorithms have been used in distributed systems to achieve higher degrees of fault-tolerance, load balancing, and performance. The emergence of decentralized environments, such as mobile ad-hoc networks and peer-to-peer sensor networks has required decentralized algorithms to enable autonomous agents to coordinate their interactions, make local decisions based on limited information, and cooperate with other agents to achieve the overall system goals. We discuss some of the most common decentralized cooperative approaches.

Voting [12] is a method for coordinating distributed systems. A set of distributed processors works independently on the same task, and then votes on their results to select one correct answer. Decentralized voting [6,10] increases the fault-tolerance in a distributed system by using replicated voters to independently determine the majority result, rather than relying on a central server to tally the results. In the context of the redeployment problem, if each host independently calculates the system's redeployment based on limited information, voting techniques could be employed to decide which one of the redeployments should be effected.

Token Ring [9] is a classic solution to distributed mutual exclusion problems. All hosts are arranged into a set of logical structures called rings. All communication occurs along the channels that define a ring. One or more tokens circulate around the ring. To use a shared resource, a host needs to acquire a token. When the host is finished, it passes the token to the next host. The token ring technique can be used in the context of the decentralized redeployment problem to control the simultaneous component migrations in the system.

Market-Based [13,23] approaches are derived from economics concepts such as trading and auctioning. The most popular market-based solution is the *auction* algorithm, in which each auctioneer agent conducts auctions to sell some items (i.e., provided services or resources) by broadcasting an auction initiation message. A bidding agent interested in an auctioned item sends a bid to the auctioneer agent. The bid is typically calculated using a utility function that determines the bidding agent's interest in the auctioned item. The auctioneer agent determines the winner (typically the highest bidder) and awards it the item. As will be detailed in section 4, DecAp leverages the market-based approach for improving the system's availability.

4 The DecAp Algorithm

DecAp is a decentralized, collaborative auctioning algorithm for improving system-wide availability. Each host in DecAp contains a single autonomous agent. These agents collaborate to improve the overall system's availability. Each agent has access to the monitoring data within its domain of awareness (recall Figure 2.). An agent exchanges messages with other agents that are members of its host domain.

The auctioned items in DecAp are software components. For a component to be ready for auctioning, its relevant parameters must be stable [19]. An agent plays two roles during the redeployment process: (1) auctioneer, in which the agent conducts the auction of its local components, and (2) bidder, in which the agent bids on components auctioned by a remote agent. DecAp extends the classic auction algorithm in two ways: (1) an auctioneer is allowed to participate in auctions it conducts, by setting the minimum bid for the auctioned component; and (2) the auctioneer may adjust the received bids.

To participate in an auction conducted on host h_a, a bidder agent has to reside on one of the hosts that are members of h_a's domain. Each agent can be in one of the following three states: *auctioning*, *bidding*, or *free*. The auctioning process for a single component is as follows. First, the auctioneer announces an auction of a local component c_a. It then receives all the bids from bidders within its domain. Finally, the auctioneer determines the "winner", i.e., the location for c_a within $dom(h_a)$ that results in highest availability. To ensure that the winner is correctly determined, agents participating in this auction cannot participate in other auctions at the same time.

As a result of a single auction, a component can move only to one of the hosts that are inside the domain of the component's auctioneer host. For this reason, multiple auctions of a single component may be required before the "sweet spot" for that component in the given distributed system is found. A component's sweet spot is its deployment location that does not change as a result of future auctions for that component. This is known as the Nash Equilibrium State in market-based literature [13].

DecAp's auctioneer and bidder algorithms use the following two functions:

1. the *contribution* of component c_x to the overall availability of the domain of host h_x when c_x is deployed on h_x, defined as follows:

$$contribution(c_x, h_x) = \sum_{h_i \in dom(h_x)} \sum_{c_j \in dep(h_i)} (rel(h_x, h_i) * freq(c_x, c_j))$$

2. the available memory, (i.e., *freeMemory*) on a given host h , defined as follows:
$$_x$$

$$freeMemory(h_x) = mem_{host}(h_x) - \sum_{c_i \in dep(h_x)} mem_{comp}(c_i)$$

Below we describe both the auctioneer's and the bidder's algorithms and how they are coordinated.

4.1 Auctioneer's Algorithm

The auctioneer's algorithm, performed on auctioneer's host h_a for one of its software components c_a (i.e., $c_a \in dep(h_a)$), consists of the following eight steps, repeating the steps for each component on h_a:

1. If c_a is ready to be auctioned, calculate the minimum bid for c_a as follows: $minBid(c_a) = contribution(c_a, h_a)$
2. If h_a's state is *free*, change it to *auctioning*, send the AUCTION INTENT message to all hosts in $dom(h_a)$, and proceed to step 3. Otherwise, wait for a given time interval and repeat step 2.
3. If all hosts in $dom(h_a)$ respond with an AUCTION ACCEPT message before the specified time-out, continue to step 4. Otherwise, send AUCTION CANCEL message to all hosts in $dom(h_a)$, set h_a's state to *free*, wait for random time interval, and go back to step 2.
4. Broadcast an AUCTION START message to every host in $dom(h_a)$. Include the *minBid* in the message. The *minBid* sets up a threshold for an acceptable bid. It is used by the bidders to determine whether they qualify to participate in the auction or not.
5. When the bids from all the hosts in $dom(h_a)$ are received, or a time-out occurs, adjust the bids from the hosts that do not have enough memory for the auctioned component. When a bidding host does not have enough memory for component c_a, it needs to trade c_a with one of its local components. As will be detailed in section 4.2, each host h_b for which $freeMemory(h_b) < mem_{comp}(c_a)$, in addition to the bid, sends a set of "tradable" components' identifiers $T \subseteq dep(h_b)$ and their contributions (i.e., $\forall c_x \in T \, | \, contribution(c_x, h_b)$). For each host h_b, the auctioneer determines the best candidate component for trade c_t, as a component whose migration from h_b to h_a will have the smallest negative impact on the availability, as follows:

$$c_t = \min\langle \forall c_x \in T \,|\, contribution(c_x, h_b) - contribution(c_x, h_a)\rangle$$

Then, the auctioneer recalculates the bid from host h_b to adjust for the effect of the trade, as follows:

$bid(c_a, h_b) =$

$bid(c_a, h_b) - (freq(c_t, c_a) - rel(h_a, h_b) * freq(c_t, c_a)) - (contribution(c_t, h_b) - contribution(c_t, h_a))$

When adjusting the bids for all the hosts that do not have enough memory is complete, go to step 6.

6. Find the winner host h_w by selecting the highest bidder. If $bid(c_a, h_w) > minBid$, continue to step 7. Otherwise, c_a remains deployed on h_a; skip to step 8.
7. If h_w has enough memory (i.e. $freeMemory (h_w) > mem_{comp}(c_a)$), migrate c_a to h_w. Otherwise, perform the trade by migrating c_a to h_w and migrating c_t to h_a.
8. Broadcast an AUCTION TERMINATION message to every host in $dom(h_a)$ to denote the completion of this auction. Set h_a's state to *free*.

4.2 Bidder's Algorithm

The bidder's algorithm, where $h_b \in dom(h_a)$ is the bidder host, consists of the following eight steps:

1. When an AUCTION INTENT message arrives, if h_b's state is *free*, send the AUCTION ACCEPT message to h_a, set the *state* to *bidding*, and continue to step 2. Otherwise, send the AUCTION REJECT message to h_a.
2. If an AUCTION CANCEL message arrives, set the *state* to *free*, and go back to step 1. If the AUCTION START message arrives from h_a, calculate the bid for c_a as the contribution of c_a to the availability of $dom(h_b)$ if c_a were to be deployed on h_b: $bid(c_a, h_b) = contribution(c_a, h_b)$
3. If $bid(c_a, h_b) < minBid$, h_b does not qualify to place a bid on c_a, skip to step 8. Otherwise create the bid message by including the $bid(c_a, h_b)$. Proceed to step 4.
4. If h_b has enough free memory for c_a (i.e. $freeMemory (h_b) > mem_{comp}(c_a)$), proceed to step 7.
5. Since h_b does not have enough memory for c_a, find the set $T \subseteq dep(h_b)$ of "tradable" components. A component is tradable when it has the adequate memory size for the trade as follows:

$T = \{\forall c_x \in dep(h_b) | mem_{comp}(c_a) \leq$

$(mem_{comp}(c_x) + freeMemory (h_b)) \wedge mem_{comp}(c_x) \leq (mem_{comp}(c_a) + freeMemory(h_a))\}$

6. If T is not empty, append to the bid message both the identifiers of all components $c_x \in T$ and their contributions, $contribution(c_x, h_b)$, and proceed to step 7. Otherwise, when T is empty, a tradable component does not exist and component c_a cannot be deployed onto h_b; skip to step 8.
7. Place the bid by sending the bid reply message to h_a.
8. Upon arrival of the AUCTION TERMINATION message, set h_b's state to *free*.

4.3 Analysis of the Two Algorithms

To ensure that an agent participates in a single auction at a time, we employed a distributed locking mechanism using the *state* variable for each agent as described in steps 2,

3, and 8 of the auctioneer's algorithm, and steps 1, 2, and 8 of the bidder's algorithm. To avoid deadlocks and starvation, each auctioneer waits a random interval of time before the next attempt at starting an auction.

The worst-case time complexity analysis for each of the two algorithms is given below (where k is the number of hosts and n is the number of components). Note that the analysis of agent synchronization time complexity is not provided, since we adopted a well-known distributed locking technique, whose complexity analysis is provided in [22]. We also do not analyze the time complexity of performing the migration of components between hosts, since a detailed analysis is provided in [19].

$$O(auctioneer) = O(step\ 1) + O(step\ 5) + O(step\ 6) = O(k*n) + O(n*k*n) + O(k)$$
$$=O(k*n^2)$$
$$O(bidder) = O(step\ 2) + O(step\ 5) = O(k*n) + O(n) = O(k*n)$$

Finally, the auctioneer's algorithm will be executed several times for each software component. Some of these auctions may occur simultaneously within the entire system, depending on the number of components on each host and the number of hosts within each host's domain. In the worst case (e.g., domain of each host is the entire set of hosts H), the auctioneer's algorithm executes in a sequential manner for each component, resulting in the total complexity of DecAp to be $n*O(auctioneer) = O(k*n^3)$.

5 Discussion

Below we discuss the salient aspects of DecAp's behavior and performance in more detail.

Algorithm's Guarantee to Find a Solution. In [18] we identified situations where the centralized algorithms do not always find a solution (e.g., if the total number of deployments that satisfy all the constraints from Figure 3. is very small). In such situations, DecAp can still find an improved deployment, since it focuses on localized, incremental improvement to the overall availability.

Algorithm's Convergence. DecAp performs a redeployment of components only if it results in the overall system's availability increase. For this reason, each auction guarantees that the system's availability will either increase or remain the same (if the auctioned component remains on the auctioneer host). As will be illustrated in section 6, the algorithm typically converges after only a few auctions for each component, i.e., subsequent auctions do not change the deployment architecture of the system. As soon as the given host becomes the "sweet spot" for all of its components, the auctioneer algorithm on that host assumes the algorithm's convergence with a certain degree of confidence, and extends the period of time before attempting a new auction (i.e., the host's dormant time). If during subsequent auctions the host remains the "sweet spot" for its components, its degree of confidence, and thus the period of dormancy, increase.

Algorithm's Sensitivity to the Level of Awareness. DecAp provides a flexible approach for capturing the level of awareness present at each node, through careful definition of the *aware* function and *dom* relation in our model. DecAp's model does not make any assumptions about what constitutes awareness among two hosts (i.e., when $aware(h_i,h_j)=1$). We simply set a given host's domain (i.e., the *dom* relation) to the set of all the hosts of which it is *aware*. The model can then be instantiated with an imple-

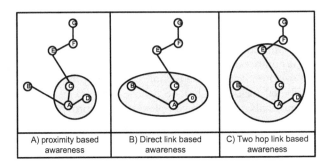

| A) proximity based awareness | B) Direct link based awareness | C) Two hop link based awareness |

Fig. 4. Domain of host A with different policies for determining host awareness

mentation-level definition of awareness. Some commonly used policies in determining aware hosts are: directly connected hosts, proximity of hosts, number of node hops, bandwidth or signal strength, and reliability of links. Figure 4. illustrates the effect of using different policies for determining host awareness. While our algorithm is independent of the policy that constitutes host awareness, the performance of the algorithm is significantly affected by the level of awareness present at each host. We will demonstrate the sensitivity of our algorithm to the level of awareness in the next section.

Location Constraints. In section 2.2 we discussed how using the *loc* and *colloc* functions can be leveraged to capture constraints other than memory. For clarity the algorithm presented in section 4 did not explicitly describe how the location constraints remain satisfied throughout the algorithm's execution. The constraint imposed by the *loc* function is enforced by inviting the hosts to participate in an auction only if they satisfy the *loc* constraint. The constraint imposed by the *colloc* function is enforced as follows: (1) when a component cannot be on the same host as the auctioned component, the auctioneer simply does not invite the host that contains that component to the auction, and (2) when two component have to be on the same host, the components are merged into a single virtual component and therefore always auctioned at the same time. Also note that through the use of *loc* and *colloc*, the complexity of the algorithm is reduced proportionally to the extent of the constraints imposed by the two functions in the given system [18].

Consideration of Additional System Properties. For certain distributed systems, availability may not be the only, or the most crucial property. For example, traditional networked systems have extensively focused on minimizing communication latencies. While minimizing latency was not our primary goal in developing DecAp, we should point out that the algorithm's objective (deploying frequently interacting components on the same host or on hosts with reliable network links) does naturally result in significant reductions of component communication latencies. We are currently trying to quantify the exact impact of DecAp on latency. Another relevant issue is the inclusion of network bandwidth in the system model, and the resulting algorithm. As discussed in section 2.2, in certain situations the location and collocation constraints can be leveraged to capture additional system parameters, including network bandwidth. However, if bandwidth becomes a scarce resource in the system, it will need to be considered separately. Our experience with the centralized redeployment algorithms (see section 6.2) indicates that this parameter can be easily added to the system model and that the resulting change to the algorithms themselves is straightforward.

6 Evaluation

In this section we provide a description of our approach in evaluating the performance of DecAp. We also provide a detailed comparison of DecAp's performance against several centralized algorithms. Note that since DecAp is the first decentralized solution to the redeployment problem of which we are aware, we can only compare its performance against the existing centralized solutions.

6.1 DecAp's Implementation

In order to quickly assess the performance of DecAp on large numbers of redeployment problems, involving large numbers of software components and hardware hosts, we implemented a simulated version of DecAp that runs on a single physical host. The distribution aspect of DecAp is simulated through the use of multiple, autonomous agents. We simulated the decentralization aspect of DecAp through the use of multiple threads and limited visibility among agents. DecAp was implemented in Java and integrated with our deployment exploration environment DeSi. When DeSi's user interface invokes DecAp, a bootstrap thread instantiates an agent object for each host. Each agent class is composed of two inner classes: auctioneer class and bidder class. Both auctioneer and bidder classes have their own threads of execution, which are started once the corresponding agent class is instantiated. Agents in the same domain are given access to each other's class variables. In our implementation of DecAp, we used direct links to denote the awareness level of 1 (recall Figure 4.B). Subsequent levels of awareness correspond to the number of intermediate hosts between a pair of hosts (recall Figure 4.C). Auctioneer and bidder threads synchronize their interactions through message passing. A shared data structure that holds the current deployment of the system is updated as a result of each auction. DeSi's bootstrap class calculates the overall availability of the shared data structure in pre-specified time intervals. The algorithm terminates when the availabilities at two consecutive time intervals are the same, which indicates that the algorithm has converged to a solution.

6.2 Evaluation Criteria

In this section, we briefly describe three centralized algorithms we have developed previously for increasing a system's availability by calculating a new deployment architecture. A detailed explanation and evaluation of these algorithms is given in [18]. These algorithms provide the basis for evaluating DecAp.

Exact Algorithm. This algorithm tries every possible deployment, and selects the one that has maximum availability and satisfies the constraints posed by the memory and restrictions on software component locations (*exact maximum*). This algorithm also finds the average availability of all system deployments (*exact average*). The exact algorithm guarantees at least one optimal deployment (assuming that at least one deployment is possible). The complexity of this algorithm in the general case (i.e., with no restrictions on component locations) is $O(k^n)$, where k is the number of hardware hosts, and n the number of software components. For this reason, executing the exact algorithm is only feasible for very small systems.

Unbiased Stochastic Algorithm. This algorithm generates different deployments by randomly assigning each component to a single host from a set of component's allowable hosts. If the generated deployment satisfies all the constraints, the availability of the produced deployment architecture is calculated. This process repeats a given number of times and the deployment with the best availability is selected (*unbiased maximum*). The average availability of all valid deployments is also calculated (*unbiased average*). The complexity of this algorithm is $O(n^2)$. In [18] we have experimentally shown that *unbiased average* does not significantly deviate from the *exact average* and thus signifies the system's "most likely" availability.

Greedy Algorithm. This algorithm incrementally assigns software components to the hardware hosts. At each step of the algorithm, the goal is to select the assignment that will maximally contribute to the availability function, by selecting the "best" host and "best" software component. Selecting the best hardware host is performed by choosing a host with the highest sum of network reliabilities with other hosts in the system, and the highest memory capacity. Similarly, selecting the best software component is performed by choosing the component with the highest frequency of interaction with other components in the system, and the lowest required memory. Once found, the best component is assigned to the best host, making certain that all the constraints are satisfied. The algorithm proceeds with searching for the next best component among the remaining components, until the best host is full. Next, the algorithm selects the best host among the remaining hosts. This process repeats until every component is assigned to a host. The availability of the resulting deployment (*greedy maximum*) is calculated. The complexity of this algorithm is $O(n^3)$ [18].

6.3 Evaluation Results

Table 1 provides the comparison of DecAp with the three centralized algorithms, in cases where the graph of hosts is fully connected (possibly via unreliable links). Columns 4 and 5 show the results of running the algorithms for 25 different redeployment problems and averaging the results using the benchmarking option of DeSi. De-

Table 1. Comparison of DecAp's performance in deployment architectures with fully connected graph of hosts

| | | 1 | 2 | 3 | 4 | 5 |
		10 comps 4 hosts 1 problem	50 comps 15 hosts 1 problem	250 comps 50 hosts 1 problem	10 comps 4 hosts 25 problems	50 comps 15 hosts 25 problems
1	Exact maximum	0.816	infeasible	infeasible	0.792	infeasible
2	Exact average	0.553	infeasible	infeasible	0.525	infeasible
3	Unbiased maximum	0.756	0.611	0.512	0.699	0.544
4	Unbiased average	0.550	0.558	0.469	0.525	0.508
5	Greedy maximum	0.807	0.734	0.641	0.720	0.729
6	*DecAp Awareness level = 1*	*0.790*	*0.759*	*0.653*	*0.756*	*0.764*
7	% improvement over the unbiased average[a]	43	36	39	44	50

a. calculated as 100% * (DecAp – unbiased average) / unbiased average

Table 2. Comparison of DecAp's performance in deployment architectures with varying levels of disconnected links among hosts

		1	2	3	4	5	6
		50 comps 15 hosts 20% of links missing	50 comps 15 hosts 50% of links missing	50 comps 15 hosts 80% of links missing	100 comps 25 hosts 30% of links missing	100 comps 25 hosts 60% of links missing	100 comps 25 hosts 90% of links missing
1	Original availability	0.427	0.265	0.176	0.385	0.227	0.06
2	Unbiased maximum	0.442	0.319	0.184	0.407	0.258	0.105
3	Unbiased average	0.442	0.284	0.146	0.375	0.219	0.084
4	Greedy maximum	0.604	0.530	0.339	0.590	0.411	0.283
5	DecAp Awareness level = 1	0.644	0.479	0.301	0.613	0.445	0.194
6	DecAp Awareness level = 2	0.747	0.582	0.349	0.618	0.455	0.250
7	DecAp Awareness level = 3	0.747	0.582	0.367	0.618	0.460	0.261
8	% improvement over original availability	74	119	108	60	102	335

cAp provided at least 40% improvement over the system's "most likely" deployment. On average, DecAp produced results that were better than the centralized algorithms' results. However, in certain situations the performance of DecAp could suffer, due to its reliance on the initial deployment. For example, in situations where some of the "best" hosts (recall the above description of the greedy algorithm) in the system do not have any components initially deployed on them, they may not ever be selected as the winners of any of the auctions.

Table 2 provides another comparison of DecAp with centralized algorithms in cases where the graph of hosts is not fully connected (each column is labelled with the percentage of missing host-to-host links). For each problem, the DecAp algorithm was executed three times with different levels of awareness. As the table indicates, the algorithm's performance is negatively affected by the decrease in host inter-connectivity. However, as long as the graph of hosts is con-

Table 3. Demonstration of DecAp's convergence

Iteration Number	10 comps 4 hosts 20% of links missing 1 level of awareness	50 comps 15 hosts 50% of links missing 1 level of awareness	100 comps 25 hosts 70% of links missing 1 level of awareness	250 comps 50 hosts 80% of links missing 2 levels of awareness
Initial Availability	0.450	0.254	0.174	0.099
1	0.776	0.423	0.312	0.219
2	0.881	0.483	0.334	0.231
3	0.910	0.500	0.342	0.243
4	0.933	0.503	0.350	0.248
5	0.974	0.519	0.354	0.250
6	0.974	0.529	0.360	0.253
7	0.974	0.529	0.360	0.253
% first iteration / final solution	79%	79%	86%	86%

nected, increasing the level of awareness improves DecAp's performance significantly. Columns 1-5 show such a scenario, where as a result of increasing the level of awareness, the algorithm outperforms even the centralized algorithms. Column 6 shows another scenario, where as a result of a very high percentage of missing links, "islands" of hosts (i.e. subsets of hosts that are not connected to each other) are created and DecAp is not able to outperform the greedy algorithm. Finally, row 8 shows that DecAp was able to improve the availability by at least 60% over the original availability in the case of a fairly connected architecture, and by at most 335% in the case of a fairly disconnected architecture.

Table 3 shows DecAp's convergence to a solution. Each iteration corresponds to the resulting availability of the overall system after auctioning each one of the components exactly once. Note that the largest gain is achieved in the first iteration of the algorithm, which shows that by just auctioning each component once, we can get a solution that is at least 79% of the final solution. Also note that after the first iteration of the algorithm, most components have found a "sweet spot", which results in no further redeployment of those components. This contributes to the quick convergence of the algorithm, typically around the fifth or sixth iteration. For the largest problem (shown in the last column of Table 3), DecAp's execution time was 9.4s with the maximum auctioneer thread wait of 10ms. However, a variation of DecAp that used thread notification executed the same problem in 0.3s on a mid-range PC.[2]

7 Conclusions and Future Work

As the distribution, decentralization, and mobility of computing environments grow, so does the probability that (parts of) those environments will need to operate in the face of network disconnections. Our research is guided by the observation that, in these environments, a key determinant of the system's ability to effectively deal with network disconnections is finding the appropriate *deployment architecture*. While the redeployment problem addressed by our work has been identified in the existing literature, its inherent complexity has either been ignored [1], thus making it infeasible for any realistic system, or highly restricted [7], thus reducing the solution's usefulness. Furthermore, the existing solutions are not applicable to an emerging class of decentralized systems marked by the limited system knowledge and lack of centralized control.

This paper has presented an efficient decentralized algorithm for improving a distributed, mobile, component-based system's availability via redeployment. The algorithm is currently being integrated into an existing middleware platform [15] with built-in capabilities for system monitoring and redeployment [19]. The algorithm has been thoroughly assessed via a series of benchmarks. While our experience thus far has been very positive, a number of pertinent questions remain unexplored. In addition to assessing the performance of DecAp in a truly distributed environment, our future work will span issues such as (1) extending the algorithm to identify "good" hosts in the system even when they initially do not have any deployed components, (2) expanding our solution to include additional system parameters (e.g., battery power, display size, system software available on a given host, and so on), and (3) leveraging techniques such as simulated annealing [21] to further improve the algorithm's performance. These issues represent but a small subset of related concerns that are emerging in the domain of distributed, mobile computation and that will increasingly shape the software development of the future.

---

[2] Since we only wanted to illustrate the execution time of the algorithm's logic, and not that of agents' synchronization, to obtain this result we leveraged the thread notification technique instead of the random thread wait times described in Section 4. Note that employing thread notification is possible only in a single-processor simulation of the algorithm.

Acknowledgements

This material is based upon work supported by the National Science Foundation under Grant Numbers CCR-9985441 and ITR-0312780. Effort also partially supported by the Jet Propulsion Laboratory.

References

1. M. C. Bastarrica, et al. A Binary Integer Programming Model for Optimal Object Distribution. *2nd Int'l. Conf. on Principles of Distributed Systems*, Amiens, France, Dec. 1998.
2. A. Fuggetta, G. P. Picco, and G. Vigna. Understanding Code Mobility. *IEEE Trans. on Software Engineering*, May 1998.
3. A. J. Ganesh, A. Kermarrec, L. Massoulie. Peer-to-Peer Membership Management for Gossip-Based Protocols, *IEEE Transactions on Computers*, Vol. 52, pp. 139-149, Feb. 2003.
4. D. Garlan, et al. Using Gauges for Architecture-Based Monitoring and Adaptation. *Working Conf. on Complex and Dynamic Systems Arch.*, Brisbane, Australia, Dec. 2001.
5. D. K. Gifford, Weighted Voting for Replicated Data. In Proceedings of the *7th Symposium on Operating System Principles*, New York, 1979, pp. 150-162.
6. B. Hardekopf, et. al. A Decentralized Voting Algorithm for Increasing Dependability in Distributed Systems. *5th World Multi- Conference on Systemic, Cybernetics and Informatics (SCI2001)*, 2001.
7. G. Hunt and M. Scott. The Coign Automatic Distributed Partitioning System. *3rd Symposium on Operating System Design and Implementation*, New Orleans, LA, Feb. 1999.
8. IEEE Standard Computer Dictionary: *A Compilation of IEEE Standard Computer Glossaries* New York, NY: 1990.
9. W. Jia, J. Kaiser, E. Nett. An Efficient and Reliable Group Multicast Protocol. *Second International Symposium on Autonomous Decentralized Systems*. Phoenix, Arizona., April 1995.
10. B. Johnson. Design and Analysis of Fault Tolerant Digital Systems, *Addison-Wesley*, 1989.
11. T. Kichkaylo et al. Constrained Component Deployment in Wide-Area Networks Using AI Planning Techniques. *Int'l. Parallel and Distributed Processing Symposium*. April 2003.
12. R. Kieckhafer, C. Walter, A. Finn, P. Thambidurai. The MAFT Architecture for Distributed Fault Tolerance. *IEEE Transactions On Computers*, Vol. 37, No. 4, April 1988, pp. 398-405.
13. D. Kreps. Game Theory and Economic Modeling. *Clarendon Press*, Oxford, 1990.
14. E. A. Lee. Embedded software. *Advances in Computers, 56,* 2002.
15. S. Malek, M. Mikic-Rakic and N. Medvidovic. Prism-MW: A Style-Aware Architectural Middleware for Resource Constrained, Distributed Systems. *IEEE Trans. on Software Engineering.* Vol. 31, No. 3, March 2005.
16. N. Medvidovic, et. al. Software Architectural Support for Handheld Computing. *IEEE Computer*, September 2003.
17. M. Mikic-Rakic et. al. A Tailorable Environment for Assessing the Quality of Deployment Architectures in Highly Distributed Settings. *2nd International Working Conference on Component Deployment (CD 2004)*, Edinburgh, UK, May 2004.
18. M. Mikic-Rakic, et. al. Improving Availability in Large, Distributed, Component-Based Systems via Redeployment. In Proceeding of *the 3rd International Working Conference on Component Deployment (CD 2005)*, Grenoble, France, Nov. 2005.

19. M. Mikic-Rakic and N. Medvidovic. Software Architectural Support for Disconnected Operation in Highly Distributed Environments. *International Symposium on Component-based Software Engineering (CBSE7)*, Edinburgh, UK, May 2003.
20. P. Oreizy et al. Architecture-Based run-time Software Evolution. *ICSE'98*, Kyoto, Japan, April 1998.
21. S. Russell and P. Norvig. Artificial Intelligence: A Modern Approach. *Prentice Hall,* Englewood Cliffs, NJ, 1995.
22. A. Tanenbaum. Computer Networks. *Prentice Hall*, Englewood Cliffs, New Jersey.
23. C. A. Waldpurger, et. al. Spawn. A Distributed Computational Economy. *IEEE Trans. On Software Engineering*, February 1992
24. J. Weissman. Fault-Tolerant Wide-Area Parallel Computing. *IPDPS 2000 Workshop*, Cancun, Mexico, May 2000.
25. Y. Weinsberg, and I. Ben-Shaul. A Programming Model and System Support for Disconnected- Aware Applications on Resource-Constrained Devices. *ICSE 2002*, Orlando, FL.

Propagative Deployment of Hierarchical Components in a Dynamic Network

Didier Hoareau and Yves Mahéo

Valoria Laboratory– University of South Brittany, France
{Didier.Hoareau, Yves.Maheo}@univ-ubs.fr

Abstract. This paper addresses the distribution and the deployment of hierarchical components on heterogeneous dynamic networks. Such networks may include fixed and mobile resource-constrained devices and are characterized by the volatility of their hosts and connections, which may lead to their fragmentation. We propose a propagative, hierarchically-controlled deployment process for such networks and an ADL extension allowing the specification of this context-aware deployment.

1 Introduction

The component-based approach becomes widely reckoned to be relevant for developing complex distributed applications and many component models and their associated technologies are now available. Some of the proposed models (*e.g.* Koala [11], Darwin [6] or Sofa [9]), known as hierarchical models, wake up the interest of software architects. In such models, a component –that is then called a composite component– can be itself an assembly of components, recursive inclusion ending with primitive components that encapsulate computing code.

Besides, the distributed platforms that are susceptible of being the target of complex distributed applications, have evolved in a few years from homogeneous networks of workstations to networks of heterogeneous hosts that may comprise mobile and resource-constrained devices. Among these platforms, dynamic networks represent common but challenging environments. What we call a dynamic network is a network that is characterised by its heterogeneity (e.g. hosts do not all provide similar hardware and software resources), and its dynamism (e.g. hosts may become unaccessible because of their mobility or their volatility). A major consequence of this dynamism is that the target platform cannot be considered as a fully connected network. It is rather described as a partitioned network, viewed as a collection of independent islands. An island is equivalent to a connected graph of hosts that can communicate together, while no communication is possible between two islands. In addition, the configuration of the islands may change dynamically.

This paper describes a distribution scheme of hierarchical components and its associated deployment process that targets the abovementioned dynamic networks. Because of the very constrained environment in which the application is to be deployed, we can hardly envisage a permanent access to the services offered by the application or an optimal use of the resources. The emphasis is put on finding a distribution scheme and

A. Dearle and S. Eisenbach (Eds.): CD 2005, LNCS 3798, pp. 115–118, 2005.

some deployment mechanisms (focusing on the instantiation and the activation phases) that achieve a minimal availability while taking account of the environment.

2   Distributed Hierarchical Component Model for Dynamic Networks

In order to support network disconnections we propose a distributed hierarchical component model which allows an application to run in a degraded mode, avoiding that the entire application becomes unusable. We introduce the notion of *active interface* to the component model. Our runtime support detects network disconnections and deactivates some components' interfaces accordingly. The underlying distribution scheme of the model is based on the replication of composite components. This replication allows the interfaces of a composite to be easily accessible on a set of hosts. Only the membrane, that contains architectural information, is replicated, thus reducing consistency maintenance problems. Each primitive component is localized on a single host, which reflects the semantics of the architecture descriptor in which each reference to a component corresponds one (possibly statefull) component. Further details about the distribution and the support of this distributed hierarchical component model can be found in [5].

3   Context-Aware Deployment Specification

When considering the deployment of distributed components, the key issue is to build a mapping between the component instances and the hosts of the target platform. This task implies to have some knowledge not only about the identity of the hosts involved in the deployment phase, but about the characteristics of each of them as well. However, at design-time, the designer is unlikely to know where to deploy each component regarding resource availability. This motivates the need to differ this task at runtime. We propose to add a deployment aspect to an existing architecture description language (such as [2, 3]).This will allow the description of the resource properties that must be satisfied by a machine for hosting a specific component.

We follow the approach of [4] to specify the deployment of the hierarchy of components in a constraint-based declarative way (see figure 1). The architecture descriptors of the components are augmented with deployment descriptors in which constraints on the resources required by components and on their possible locations can be specified. It is not mandatory to give explicit names or addresses to target machines: the placement of components are mainly driven by constraints on the resources the target host(s) should satisfy. The choice of the machine that will host a component will be made automatically at runtime (during the deployment).

When the deployment is triggered, all the constraints listed in the deployment descriptor may not be satisfied immediately. The dynamism of the network makes the situation even more difficult as it may occur that the set of hosts that would satisfy globally the deployment constraints are never connected together at the same time, precluding any deployment.

```
<component name="DocumentSearch">      <resourceconstraint>             <locationconstraint>
  <component name="DocumentFinder">      <memory free="200" unit="MB"      <operator name="alldiff">
    <deploymentcontext>                    operator="min" />             <arg varname="this.DocumentSearch.x"/>
      <locationconstraint>               </resourceconstraint>            <arg varname="this.DocumentBuffer.y"/>
        <target varname="x"/>            <locationconstraint>             </operator>
      </locationconstraint>                <target varname="y"/>         </locationconstraint>
    </deploymentcontext>                 </locationconstraint>            <deploymentcontext>
  </component>                         </deploymentcontext>              </component>
  <component name="DocumentBuffer">   </component>
    <deploymentcontext>               <deploymentcontext>
```

Fig. 1. Deployment descriptor

4 Propagative Deployment

The deployment process we propose is a *propagative* one: it allows an application to be activated progressively, that is, part of its provided services can be put at disposal even if some machines that are required for the "not yet" installed components are not available. As soon as these machines become connected (or accessible) or some required resources appear (or become available), the deployment will go along. Thanks to our distributed hierarchical component model and the dynamic activation of interfaces, the application can run in a degraded manner even if some of its parts are not yet started.

The main issue of such a deployment is to ensure the unicity of the component instantiations imposed by the architecture descriptor. Indeed on one hand, since we cannot predict which machines will be connected at any time, we cannot select one to be responsible for the instantiation decisions of the entire application. On the other hand, if we let each machine make an instantiation decision, we cannot guarantee that in two different islands contradictory instantiations may not be performed.

Ensuring consistent instantiations comes down to establishing a distributed consensus across several islands. We use the results of [8] where the authors identify *conditions* for which there exists an asynchronous protocol that solves the consensus problem despite the occurrence of crashes. It is thus possible to elect a machine responsible for the instantiation of a component within an island composed of a *majority* of machines. When an applicant machine is elected and when an instantiation is made, the deployment descriptor is updated with this information. As in the work described in [10], the scalability of our proposition is ensured by the distributed and hierarchical organisation of the control: each composite component of the hierarchy is represented by a machine.

We propose to alleviate the risk that the consensus algorithm may not terminate (*e.g.* the number of hosts within an island may not be sufficient) by taking advantage of network changes to make the consensus evolve. We detect network changes (*e.g.* a machine is newly connected) and possibly react to these changes (*e.g.* make a newly connected machine participate to the consensus). Moreover, in order to avoid that a machine responsible for a composite component makes instantiation decisions in a non-majority island, a reelection mechanism is triggered after comparing the different versions of the deployment descriptors.

5 Conclusion

This paper has presented a support for deploying and executing an application built with hierarchical components on an heterogeneous and dynamic network. The main contribution of this work is that it attempts to take into account a challenging distributed target platform characterized by the heterogeneity and the volatility of the hosts, volatility that may result in the fragmentation of the network.

The propagative deployment presented in this paper is based on a constraint-based language for the description of the placement of the components according to resource requirements. Our distributed component model has been implemented using Julia, a Java implementation of the Fractal component model [1]. The standard Fractal ADL has been extended thanks to the addition of new modules. We use D-Raje [7], a framework developed in our team, dedicated to the observation of distributed system resources in Java. We can thus detect network changes and exploit them in the deployment process.

The main direction of our future work consists in the extension of our propagative deployment in order to define an autonomic deployment in which decisions about the placement of components could be reconsidered.

References

[1] E. Bruneton, T. Coupaye, M. Leclercq, V. Quéma, and J.-B. Stefani. An Open Component Model and its Support in Java. In Proc. of the Int. Symposium on Component-based Software Engineering, Edinburgh, Scotland, May 2004.

[2] Acme: Acme Extensions to xArch. School of Computer Science Web Site: http://www-2.cs.cmu.edu/ acme/pub/xAcme/, 2001.

[3] E. Dashofy, A. van der Hoek, and R. Taylor. An Infrastructure for the Rapid Development of XML-based Architecture Description Languages. In Proceedings of the Int. Conference on Software Engineering, pages 266–276, Orlando, Florida, USA, May 2002.

[4] A. Dearle, G. Kirby, and A. McCarthy. A framework for constraint-based deployment and autonomic management of distributed applications. In Proc. of the Int. Conference on Autonomic Computing, 2004.

[5] D. Hoareau and Y. Mahéo. Distribution of a Hierarchical Component in a Non-Connected Environment. In Proc. of the 31th Euromicro Conference - Component-Based Software Engineering Track, Porto, Portugal, September 2005.

[6] J. Magee, N. Dulay, S. Eisenbach, and J. Kramer. Specifying Distributed Software Architectures. In Proc. of the 5th European Software Engineering Conference, Sitges, Spain, September 1995.

[7] Y. Mahéo, F. Guidec, and L. Courtrai. A Java Middleware Platform for Resource-Aware Distributed Applications. In 2nd Int. Symposium on Parallel and Distributed Computing, pages 96–103, Ljubljana, Slovenia, October 2003.

[8] A. Mostéfaoui, S. Rajsbaum, M. Raynal, and M. Roy. Condition-based consensus solvability: a hierarchy of conditions and efficient protocols. Distributed Computing, 17(1), 2004.

[9] F. Plasil, D. Balek, and R. Janecek. SOFA/DCUP: Architecture for Component Trading and Dynamic Updating. In Proc. of the 4th Int. Conference on Configurable Distributed Systems, Annapolis, Maryland, US, may 1998.

[10] V. Quéma, R. Balter, L. Bellissard, D. Féliot, A. Freyssinet, and S. Lacourte. Asynchronous, hierarchical and scalable deployment of component-based applications. In Proc. of the 2nd Int. Working Conference on Component Deployment, Edinburgh, Scotland, May 2004.

[11] R. C. van Ommering. Koala, a Component Model for Consumer Electronics Product Software. In Proc. of the ESPRIT ARES Workshop, Las Palmas de Gran Canaria, Spain, February 1998.

Modelling Deployment Using Feature Descriptions and State Models for Component-Based Software Product Families*

Slinger Jansen and Sjaak Brinkkemper

Institute of Information and Computing Sciences,
Utrecht University
{slinger.jansen, s.brinkkemper}@cs.uu.nl

Abstract. Products within a product family are composed of different component configurations where components have different variable features and a large amount of dependency relationships with each other. The deployment of such products can be error prone and highly complex if the dependencies between components and the possible features a component can supply are not managed explicitly. This paper presents a method that uses the knowledge available about components to ensure correct, complete, and consistent deployment of configurations of interrelated components. The method provided allows the user to perform analysis on the deployment before the deployment is performed, thus allowing error prevention before making any changes to the system. The method and model are discussed and presented to provide an alternative to current component deployment techniques.

1 Component Deployment Issues

The deployment of enterprise application software is a complex task. This complexity is caused by the enormous scale of the undertaking. An application will consist of many (software) components that depend on each other to function correctly. On top of that, these components will evolve over time to answer the changing needs and configurations of customers. As a consequence, deployment of these applications takes a significant amount of effort and is a time consuming and error-prone process.

Software components are units of independent production, acquisition, and deployment [1]. Software deployment can be seen as the process of copying, installing, adapting, and activating a software component [2]. Usually the only way to find out whether a deployment has been successful is by running the software component. This leads to frustrating and complex deployment processes for both the software vendor and the system manager. There are many reasons why components that have been deployed onto a system cannot be activated and run. The factors that increase complexity during the steps of building, copying, installing, adapting, and activating a component are numerous.

To begin with, there are relationships amongst components. Components can explicitly require or exclude a specific revision of a component. Some components allow for

---

* This research was supported by NWO/Jacquard grant 638.001.202.

A. Dearle and S. Eisenbach (Eds.): CD 2005, LNCS 3798, pp. 119–133, 2005.

only one version of the component to be deployed onto one system, placing a restriction on the components that are to be deployed onto that system. If such relationships are not respected the deployments will result in missing components and inconsistent component sets. Secondly, deployments are also complex due to the fact that components can be instantiated in different shapes and forms, due to variability [3]. A component that supports variability can have different features that are offered to the user, which are bound and finalized at different times during the deployment of that component. The binding time of a component can be at different stages of the component deployment, such as build-time or run-time. Thirdly, the order in which components are deployed can determine whether the deployment process of a set of components is successful. Components require other components during the deployment process and these can be removed when the system has a limited set of resources. Also, when components exclude each other and different deployment orderings are possible, the possibility arises that one of these orders does not ensure correct deployment. The above holds especially for component based product families [4], where many different variants of one system are derived by combining components in different ways.

A components' lifecycle consists of different states, such as *source*, *built*, *deployed*, and *running*. Many parts of the process of a component going through these phases have been automated to do such things as COTS (Components Off The Shelf) evaluation, automated builds, automatic distribution, automatic deployment, and automated testing. Current component lifecycle management systems, however, do not support different component (lifecycle) types, variability, component evolution, and are not feature driven. One of the main reasons for initiating this research is that the current tools for component deployment [5] do not take into account both variability, different types of distribution (source, binary, packaged), and different binding times.

There are tools that can manage the lifecycle of components, such as Nix [6], the Software Dock [2], and Sofa [7]. These systems have downsides however. To begin with, Nix is a technology based on an open source environment that can guarantee consistency between components and allows for concurrent installations of components. The biggest downside of Nix is that it requires a system manager to "stop the world", i.e., to adjust all the components the system uses to include a component description and reinstall the system. The Software Dock can be used to deploy software using the XML based Deployable Software Description [8] for describing the software. The Software Dock does not support the complete lifecycle of a software component. It does, however, focus on the complete deployment process of software, including such states as *activate*. Finally, SOFA is a corba based component model that uses the OMG Deployment and Configuration specification [9], and is also focussed on the deployment of generic components. Sofa, as well as Software Dock, only assumes a very simple lifecycle with four states being *source*, *built*, *deployed*, and *running*. Of these three component tools, only Nix focusses on variable features provided by different instantiations of components, and only Nix discusses the opportunities for a transparent configuration environment [10]. Software component developers often use their own specific deployment tools or custom build checks to see whether the system on which the component is deployed satisfies all requirements for consistent and correct deployment [11]. The developer therefore must develop its own models and formalisations to ensure a correct component deployment.

The situation described above calls for a generic modelling technique that can handle the complex issues that are introduced by the use of variable components that can be instantiated in different versions and forms on one system. Such functionality, of which none of previously evaluated systems above provide it [5], requires a central knowledge base that stores the variables that initialize the different varieties of component instances and a categorization of such knowledge. This paper presents a modelling technique that can support the deployment of a component in different versions and variants, and still guarantee consistency and correctness. The modelling technique is based on a central storing of the restrictions and knowledge about component features and the system, thus allowing all components to use such information for correct build, release, testing, deployment, and activation of software.

The rest of this paper is structured as follows. Section 2 proposes two types of describing the properties of a software component and its relationships to other software components. Section 3 describes how the knowledge can be used to create an instantiation tree of component instantiations by using the provided algorithm, thus enabling the user to reason about deployment of software components. The algorithm is clarified with an example. Finally, we discuss the proposed methods and models in Section 4 and provide some insight into our future work and the conclusions reached throughout this research in Sections 5 and 5.

2   Component Descriptions

Currently used component models generally do not support consistent and complete deployment. Most models used by conventional technology [5] such as InstallShield and RPM-Update, focus on the artefacts that make up a component. Next to that these technologies perform some very general dependency resolution and only support the "Requires Always" relationship. These tools often have some scripting capabilities that can be used to check whether the right resources are available, if required components for the deployment processes are available, and to perform some pre- and post-installation checking of the artefacts. These qualities, however, are underemphasized.

The model proposed here is based on three viewpoints. To begin with, a component is not merely a set of artefacts. A component has a context that describes the relationships to the components, hardware, and configuration information that affect the component upon and after deployment. A component also has internal variability, influencing that context, which is bound at different times. Secondly, if a component model supports variability, component features must be communicated to the user. This allows for the user to select these features at different stages of the deployment, changing the context as the component is built, activated, copied, and run. Thirdly, components are available in different revisions. When relationships amongst components can be specified with a specific version number, many deployment problems can be averted. Most deployment tools, including Nix [12] and RPM-Update, already have advanced versioning and dependency resolution mechanisms.

To summarize there are four factors that make a the deployment of a software component with internal variability complex. Each of these factors is handled by the presented model using specific modeling techniques and model extensions. These are as follows:

- **States** - Components can exist on a system in different incarnations simultanaously. These incarnations, such as a *source* incarnation or *installed* incarnation, have relationships to eachother. States enable the modeling of the complete build and deployment process, by describing such relationships as "to build this component the source is required first". The introduction of states leads from Figure 1(a) to 1(b).
- **Revisions** - Components are generally available in different revisions. Different revisions have different states, thus leading to a seperate set of states for each component revision. Such revisions are modelled in Figure 1(c).
- **Features** - A component can have variable internal functionality, depending on parameters that have been bound at several times during the deployment process. Such points in time are known as binding times. These features can be modelled using a feature description language. In the model provided, each revision of the component source leads to a new feature description, since the code and thus the variability options might have changed. In Figure 1(d) this is displayed by the addition of feature trees per revision.
- **Relationships** - Component states have explicit and implicit relationships to eachother, such as the *built* state of an e-mail client requires both an instance of a *source* state that an e-mail client (explicit) and an instance of a running build tool state with a c++ compiler feature (implicit). These relationships can be further classified into "requires always" and "requires once" dependencies. An example of a "requires always" is that a *running* state instance requires a library at all time during the existence of the instance. An example of a "requires once" relationship is when a build instance requires the compiler only during its instantiation.

To support the presented techniques a component description describes the component name, revisons, the revision's states, and the revision's feature diagram. This

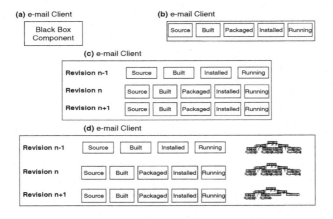

Fig. 1. Expanding Model for Software Components

definition shows that a component has one or more revisions. Each revision consists of a set of component states, a feature diagram, and a number of feature restrictions expressed by feature logic. The component states describe the shape or form in which a component can be present on a system. Examples include *built, activated,* and *running*. Component states can have relationships, such as *e-Mail client running always requires e-Mail client installed* or *e-Mail client built requires once a running build tool*. In the following sections these component states are described further. The feature diagram is used to describe the features a revision of a component supplies to the user and is defined using a feature description language (FDL) [13]. The feature restrictions describe whether features exclude or require each other. Figure 1 does not show feature constraints. These constraints are, however, an important part of our model. Features and FDL will also be explained further in the following sections.

2.1   Component States and Instantiations

The introduction of component states has many reasons. To begin with, component states force a developer to manage component relationships, restrictions, and deployment environment from the moment the component is created. Component states allow for a more detailed specification of component requirements. Some tools, such as Nix and SOFA, already include state models with the states *source, built, installed,* and finally *running*. Also, component states enable the component developer to specify and manage the process of how to create a component state instance.

A component state can generally be seen as a portable encapsulation format for a collection of artefacts, relationships to other component states, and a number of state instantiations. A state instantiation is a list consisting of actions and requirements that upon fulfilment of all the requirements performs the list of actions to reach the requested component state. In the presented model component states belong to one revision. A revision of the component can thus have a set of component states in which it can reside. The component state definition describes the component state's name, it's instantiation list, and it's relationships to other component states. The component state has relationships to other component states *Requires Always* and *Excludes*. These requirements are actually expressed as a combination of a component state and provided feature(s). This allows for a component state to have a relationship with a component state with a specific feature, such as *excludes(eMailClientRunning, Pop3)* which can be interpreted as "this component state cannot exist on a system concurrently with the eMailClientRunning state instance that provides the Pop3 feature".

Once the developer is forced to consider component states many possibilities arise. To begin with, the processes of automated building, testing, and deployment can all be performed using the same component state model. Secondly, since the developer can describe any type of component [14] the component model described here can be used to manage different component types, such as Corba or Java components, using the same model. Thirdly, since component state instances are portable, component state instances can be distributed amongst different systems. The model allows for derivation of component dependencies, and can therefore be used to create complete packages of component state instances to be delivered to customers. Finally, a component state model allows developers to model and reason about component updates. Component states can have relationships with component states from other revisions, thus enabling modelling of complex patch or update processes. Such processes are, after all, nodes in the instantiation tree, which represents the full update process.

Previously some criticism was expressed toward a four component state model. The main reason for this is that evidence was found, during case studies at a number of software vendors, that there is a need for more states. The software vendor Planon [15], for instance, has a component state model with seven states, being *source, built, packaged, packaged with license, installed, activated* and *running*. Another software vendor we encountered applies six states, being the same ones as Planon but without the *packaged with license*. This software vendor builds plug-ins for Autocad for which the software vendor actually adjusts the component state model. The software vendor first unpacks Autocad from its installation package, then binds some variabilities, and then packages Autocad with their plug-in. Clearly, a component state is added to the Autocad state model as well.

A component state description is only a description and does not have any effect on a system. To create a state instance on a system, a component instantiation is required. A component state instantiation consists of a list of actions and a list of component state instances that are required to execute the instantiation and create an instance. The component instantiation consists of a *Requires Once* list and an action list. The *requires once* list shows what component states and features are required once the instantiation is activated. The *built* instantiation will generally require a compiler and a component state instance of *source*. The actions are specified as a tuple of *(precondition, action, postcondition)*. These actions usually are operations on artefacts, such as copy or edit actions.

To clarify the concepts of component state description, component state instantiation, and component state instance the following example is used. Figure 2 displays a compilation component, its feature tree, and the binding time of the feature. The feature tree can be interpreted as follows. The compilation tool has one main feature, that is bound as soon as the component is instantiated, called "build". The compilation tool also has two features that mutually exclude each other (one-of). The next section provides more information on the feature descriptions at hand. When executed, the compilation tool can build either C++ and Java code. The user binds this feature at run-time, i.e., when a developer wishes to compile his Java code, he will state at start-up time that the code to be compiled is written in Java. The R stands for *running* and corresponds to the *running* component state. It is necessary to remind the reader that the figure does not show anything about the state of the system. The system can contain just the knowledge

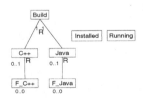

Fig. 2. Compilation Component Example

about this component, but also multiple instances of this components' states, such as two installed versions and one running.

For this example a system containing an installed version of this compilation tool is used. That implies that the component state *installed* has been instantiated on the system once. This component state instance can be used to create a *running* instance. The relationship for the build tool is "Compilation Tool Revision 1: State Running Always Requires Compilation Tool Revision 1: State Installed". The fact that it is a *Requires Always* relationship can be derived from the fact that it is the state that requires another state, and not an instantiation that requires another state. The *Requires Always* relationship describes that as long as a component state instance is present on a system, the required component must be present too.

Once the presence of the *installed* state instance has been confirmed, we must check for feature bindings. In this case that means a choice must be made between Java or C++. Once the right language has been chosen the instantiation of the component state can be performed. As mentioned before, it is well possible to instantiate a state multiple times, to do a parallel compilation of different source files, for instance. The aim of the algorithm described in Section 3 is to create an instantiation tree of component state instances, instantiations, and features. An instantiation tree for this component revision is quite simple, since no instances from other components are required and the component only has one revision. It will consist of two nodes, with the node "Compilation Tool Revision 1: Running" depending on "Compilation Tool Revision 1: Installed".

2.2   Feature Diagrams

To express variability we use the varied feature description language (VFDL). VFDL is a succinct, natural, and non-redundant language [16] that can be used to express features of components or products within a product family that contain any number of other components. The VFDL describes *and*, *or*, *mutex*, *xor*, and *requires* feature relationships. The *and* relationship is described by using a variation point that states that each of the features must be selected, by stating "S..S", where S equals the number of available features. An *xor* relationship can be described by introducing a variation point with two children stating "1..1", which means that one and only one feature can be selected. In case an *or* relationship must be represented a variation point is introduced stating "1..S", where S is the number of nodes and 1 means that at least one must be chosen. An *optional* relationship is described by adding a variation point is added stating "0..1" and using F_node is added that can either be chosen or be ignored. If two features exclude each other, they share a top variation point (using "1..1"), and each feature is optional.

The advantages of using a feature description language to express variability are numerous. FDL allows us to describe complex composition relationships, such as *one-of*, *optional*, and *more-of*, for features. If we then annotate these features with component state requirements it enables the creation of large component compositions. This is best clarified with an example of an e-Mail client that can both support the IMAP and Pop3 protocols (see Figure 3 for its feature tree). The binding time of these features is at install time. This means that one or both of these protocols can be installed. If these features have requires relationships with an IMAP and Pop3 component, it becomes

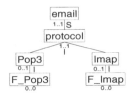

Fig. 3. e-Mail Client Feature Tree

possible to deploy (and build) only the minimal required set, which is useful for space restricted systems such as mobile phones. If a user chooses the IMAP protocol, only the IMAP component needs to be deployed onto his system.

Another advantage of using FDL to describe our feature model is the fact that there are many tools available to perform calculations and operations on the feature descriptions. More specifically, the techniques developed by van der Storm [17] allow for automatic composition of components using feature trees. Many of his techniques are reused here.

To satisfy the research goal of also incorporating binding times, each relationship between two features, such as *one-of* and *more-of* is annotated with a binding time. Binding times are directly related to component states in our model so each of these relationships is annotated with a pointer to a component state. Next to that, features have two lists of requirements attached to them, being *requires once* and *Requires Always*. Features can thus require component state instances and other features.

3   Instantiation Trees

One application of using feature descriptions and component state models is the creation of instantiation trees. An instantiation tree can model a number of instantiation sequences to reach a certain state or feature. This section describes algorithm 1, which creates an instantiation tree from a number of component descriptions and component state instances.

The algorithm uses some functions that are explained here. The function *returnFeatureBindings(State)* returns all features than can possibly be bound by instantiating the component state *State*. In the example shown in Figure 3 the function will return Pop3 and IMAP if called *returnFeatureBindings(Installed)*, which means that these features must be selected at install time. The function *returnFeatureList(RequestedFeatures, State)* returns a subset of the *RequestedFeatures* with a binding time that lies before the component state *State* or is bound during the instantiation of the component state *State*. The *alreadyInstantiated(State, Features)* function checks whether a component state instance already exists on the system with the features supplied in *Features*. Not all features need to be specified, since quite often the requirement relationship is with one feature only. An example is when someone requests an e-mail client with the Pop3 protocol. That person at that point does not care whether the IMAP protocol is also included or not.

The *featureSetConsistent(Features, N, State)* function applies the techniques of van der Storm [17]. *featureSetConsistent* checks whether the feature collection *Features* and the feature tree of the component the state *State* can return a consistent feature binding. van der Storms technique returns an empty set if it's impossible to bind these features, an empty list if this feature binding is correct, and a list of unbound features is returned if there are still features left unbound. In the case of an empty set the function *featureSetConsistent(Features, N, State)* returns a dead node, meaning that this branch can never be reached. In the case of an empty list the features can be bound correctly, implying that the component can be instantiated with these feature bindings. Finally, when a set of unbound features is returned, the function checks whether these feature bindings are relevant yet. If they should be bound first, this is returned to the tree. If not, these are simply discarded. The function thus returns a changed node in two cases, and an unchanged node in one case. The first parameter is a list that contains the features that have been required up to now. The reason for that is that otherwise it would be possible to get a conflict, even though this conflict is one that will occur in the future. The algorithm leaves room for improvement here, but the current interface excludes conflicts because all features that can be bound must be bound by the user anyway. The full algorithm is shown in algorithm 1. The main idea is that a new node

---

Algorithm 1 createTree(State, RequestedFeatures)

---

new List RequiresOnce = {}, RequiresOnceCurrentInstantiation = {}
new List RequiresAlways = State.RequiresAlways, new Node N
new FeatureList StateBoundFeatures = returnFeatureBindings(State)
new FeatureList FeaturesUpToNow = returnFeatureList(RequestedFeatures, State)
if alreadyInstantiated(State, StateBoundFeatures $\cap$ RequestedFeatures) **then**
    Return N
end if
if StateBoundFeatures $\neq$ {} **then**
    if N $\neq$ FeatureSetConsistent(FeaturesUpToNow, N, State) **then**
        return N
    end if
    for all CurrentFeature $\in$ StateBoundFeatures **do**
        RequiresOnce = RequiresOnce $\cup$ CurrentFeature.RequiresOnce
        RequiresAlways = RequiresAlways $\cup$ CurrentFeature.RequiresAlways
    end for
end if
$i = 0, j = 0$
for all (RAState, RAFeatureList) $\in$ RequiresAlways, $i + +$ **do**
    N.RAChild[i] = createTree(RAState, RAFeatureList $\cup$ RequestedFeatures)
end for
for all Instantiation $\in$ State.InstantiationList, $j + +$ **do**
    RequiresOnceCurrentInstantiation = Instantiation.RequiresOnce $\cup$ RequiresOnce
    for all (ROState, ROFeatureList) $\in$ RequiresOnceCurrentInstantiation **do**
        N.Instantiation[j].ROChild = createTree(ROState, ROFeatureList $\cup$ RequestedFeatures)
    end for
end for

---

is created each time this function is called. This node will have two types of children being *require always* children and the more elaborate "Instantiation" children. Each instantiation will then again have a number of children, which are nodes that are created once the algorithm is called for the state instances that are *required (once)* for that instantiation.

The tree will expand until an instantiation tree is created that shows for each node what component states must be instantiated first before that node can be created. There are some prerequisites, however. Some branches will end because the right features have not been bound. If there is no sequence available due to the fact that insufficient feature bindings have been specified the user will need to add more features. Also, if the current system contains no first component instances a problem is encountered, simply because the tree building cannot end. Another problem is when a component state diagram includes a circular dependency, this will lead to an endless tree. Thus, there cannot be circular dependencies.

3.1   An Example: Instantiating the e-Mail Client

The aim of the following example is to clarify the workings of algorithm 1. In Figure 4 a number of components are shown. The components are an e-Mail client, a Pop3 protocol implementation component, an IMAP protocol implementation component, a binary patch component for the e-Mail client, and a compilation tool that can compile Java and C++ source files. The e-Mail component is the focal point of our example and to instantiate the e-Mail client with certain features, all these other components are required.

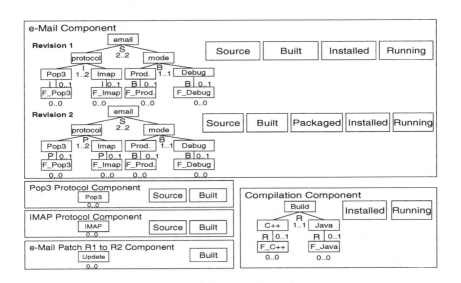

Fig. 4. Component Definition Examples

The following example is based on a system that contains two source state instances (revisions 1 and 2) of the e-Mail client, a source instance of the Pop3 and IMAP protocol implementation, an *installed* instance of the compilation tool, and a *built* state instance of the update component. The component knowledge in Figure 4 will now be used to create an instantiation tree for the state *running* of the second revision of the e-Mail client component with the feature IMAP.

The example begins with the top node, being "ECR2: Running with IMAP". In the table for state dependencies is found that the *running* instance cannot exist without the *installed* instance of the second revision of the e-Mail client. The second node, thus becomes the *installed* node. This node requires the *packaged* instance of the e-mail client. At this point the tree building has been straightforward. However, the IMAP feature inclusion now causes there to be two requirements at instantiation time, being the *built* instance of the e-Mail client and the *built* state instance of the IMAP protocol implementation. The *built* state of the second revision of the e-Mail client can be reached in two ways, being through the source of the second revision (ECR2: Source) or through the *built* state of the first revision in combination with the patch. The first instantiation thus depends on the compilation tool with the Java feature and the source code of the second revision. The second instantiation depends on the patch and *built* state of the first revision of the e-Mail client component. The final instantiation tree can be found in figure 5.

To illustrate the following section, some practical uses of the tree are explained here. To begin with, different instantiation sequences can be derived using the instantiation tree. It is possible, for instance, to first satisfy the right subtree of the instantiation of "ECR2: Packaged" and then decide which of the two instantiations must be used for the left side. An example instantiation sequence for "ECR2: Running" thus consists of

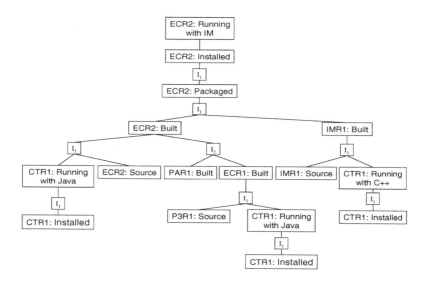

Fig. 5. Instantiation Tree for Component State ECR2: Running With Pop3

Table 1. Requires Relationships Between Instantiations and Instances

Ins No.	Instantiation	Component State with Feature(s)
		Requires Once
1	ecR1: Instantiation Build	ecR1: State Source
1	ecR1: Instantiation Install	ecR1: State Built
1	ecR1: Instantiation Build	btR1: State Running with Java
1	ecR1: Feature Pop3	p3R1: State Built
1	ecR1: Feature IMAP	imR1: State Built
1	ecR2: Instantiation Build	ecR2: State Source
1	ecR2: Instantiation Package	ecR2: State Built
1	ecR2: Instantiation Build	btR1: State Running with Java
1	ecR2: Instantiation Install	ecR2: State Package
1	ecR2: Feature Pop3	p3R1: State Built
1	ecR2: Feature IMAP	imR1: State Built
2	ecR2: Feature Pop3	p3R1: State Built
2	ecR2: Feature IMAP	imR1: State Built
2	ecR2: Instantiation Build	ecR1: State Built
2	ecR2: Instantiation Build	upR1: State Built
1	p3R1: Instantiation Install	p3R1: State Source
1	p3R1: Instantiation Install	btR1: State Running with Java
1	imR1: Instantiation Install	imR1: State Source
1	imR1: Instantiation Install	btR1: State Running with C++

"CTR1: Running with Java (to build ECR2: built)", "ECR2: Built", "CTR1: Running with C++ (to build IMR1: built)", "ECR2: Packaged", "ECR2: Installed", and finally "ECR2: Running w IM". In the following section is demonstrated that it's possible to perform some calculations using the properties and prerequisites for state instantiations.

4   Discussion

The main advantage of the presented models, besides correct and consistent deployment, is the possibility of "what-if" questions. The presented models enable analysis on the deployment of a component *before* the deployment of a component state instance, its dependent features, and state instances. The what-if questions are answered using a number of properties of the instantiation trees. **Excludes relationships** are specific to one state instance instead of components, allowing for components that normally exclude eachother to still reside on a system simultaneauosly. The **tree depth** and instantiation descriptions can be used to evaluate deployment effort. Finally, during the building of the tree, **users can be queried** about what options they have left open, to reduce both the number of possible configurations and to give the user insight into the instantiation order building process.

There is a large advantage of dividing excludes amongst states instead of full components, since it imposes a minor restriction compared to full component exclusion. The example presented in section 3, displays that many components are only required once during the deployment process of others. This allows for removal (of the patch, for instance) after a certain state has been reached. To support this, the *requiredConcurrently* sets have been introduced as a property of the instantiation tree. These are sets of component state instances that must be present on a system concurrently during the deployment of a component state instance. When two component state instances are in a *requiredConcurrently* set they cannot exclude each other.

Another advantage of the instantiation trees is that the depth of the tree can be used to estimate the effort a deployment costs. The example instantiation tree in figure 5 has two instantiations below the "ECR2: Built" state instance. The branch on the left has less children thus indicating less steps to a final deployment. This tool must be used with care, however. When an instantiation sequence is shorter, that does not necessarily mean it takes less deployment effort. Another indirect advantage of composing these instantiation trees is that during the composition of such a tree, when unbound features are encountered these can be communicated back to the user. The user can then bind the feature to see what the results are of that action. The user can then again remove the feature if it is not to his liking, before actually executing the instantiation sequence.

There are clear links between the methods applied here and the practices of product lifecycle engineering. This research can be seen as a first step in creating a software product lifecycle management system that can facilitate and support the processes of development, release, delivery, and deployment. The following steps in this process are a distribution architecture and a knowledge management framework. The closeness between software product management and product data management is further confirmed by Crnkovic et al. [18].

The main downside of the presented models and methods is that the data entered by the component developers is crucial for the correct functioning of the deployment algorithms, since "garbage in results into garbage out". As discussed in the previous section, however, there are many possibilities for adding information to the software knowledge base. To begin with, automatic feedback can be used to report back to a supplier of a component after the deployment of that component [19]. This feedback can then be used to test for excludes on external products that a software vendor can never discover independently.

Feature descriptions are rather misused here, since they are generally used to describe high-level application requirements and features [13]. The framework, however, uses feature descriptions to model the binding times of features, the requirements of components, and the relationships between the features. We firmly believe that feature descriptions form the solution to many of the complexities related to component configuration and deployment. Feature descriptions can be used to model binding times and show the relationships between features and other required instances. Feature logic and restrictions allow for complex relations to be modelled and simplified, thus enabling algorithms such as shown in algorithm 1. The final question that needs to be answered is whether a software knowledge base really improves the processes of release, delivery, and deployment. There are four facts that point to that direction.

- **Product data management** improves the release and delivery of other products [20]. Since software production processes share many similarities with other production processes [18], software release, delivery, and deployment can also be improved.

- Since the current trend in the software market is **mass customisation**, much of the information gathered in the development stages of the product can be reused at later stages during implementation at the customer and customisation phases.
- **Case studies** [19] [15] show that centrally storing knowledge leads to reduced delivery effort.
- The ability to present **"what-if" questions** to a local software knowledge base that is connected to multiple component sources can increase the reliability of the component deployment process. These questions enable a system manager to more explicitly predict what changes can be made to a system and what features can be provided within a certain configuration of components.

These facts show that managing knowledge about software explicitly and making it available to all involved parties improves release, delivery, and deployment processes.

5   Future Work and Conclusions

Currently the models have been implemented in Prolog, however, to fully apply the models in an industrial setting, a new implementation technology must be chosen with the support of cross platform compilers. We are hoping to apply the tools in a practical situation in the context of a case study. To avoid reinventing the wheel and to standardize the models, the applicability and feasibility of the OMG specifications for reusable assets [21] and IT portfolio management [22] must be evaluated for the current models. The current algorithm blindly builds trees that can explode in complexity quite quickly. There are many opportunities for reuse and further research is required in that area to reduce the complexity of these instantiation trees. Also, the representation of the software component knowledge must be compared to other methods [8] to store and share software component knowledge.

This paper establishes a relationship between component state models and feature descriptions enabling reasoning about the deployment of a component or component set without actually deploying the software. An algorithm is provided that can build instantiation instantiation trees to determine the deployment order of components. These trees can be used to answer "what-if" questions about the deployment of a component or set of components. The research has shown that both feature descriptions and a component state model can be used to create a software knowledge base that stores information about components and their context. The knowledge used to achieve this, however, relies on information provided by developers and users of the components.

Acknowledgements. The authors thank Vedran Bilanovic and the Trace team for their many inspiring ideas that contributed to this paper. Also, the anonymous reviewers did a great job in reviewing this paper and giving highly constructive criticism. Finally, The authors thank Tijs van der Storm for providing the Prolog implementation of FDL to BDD conversion and partial evaluation functions that made the prototype implementation so much quicker.

References

1. Szyperski, C.: Component Software: Beyond Object-Oriented Programming. Addison-Wesley Longman Publishing Co., Inc. (2002)
2. Hall, R.S., Heimbigner, D., Wolf, A.L.: A cooperative approach to support software deployment using the software dock. In: ICSE. (1999)
3. Jaring, M., Bosch, J.: Representing variability in software product lines: A case study. In: Second Product Line Conference (SPLC-2),San Diego CA, August 19-22. (2002)
4. Bosch, J., Högström, M.: Product instantiation in software product lines: A case study. In: LNCS. Volume 2177. (2001) 147
5. Jansen, S., Brinkkemper, S., Ballintijn, G.: A process framework and typology for software product updaters. In: Ninth European Conference on Software Maintenance and Reengineering, IEEE (2005) 265–274
6. Dolstra, E., Visser, E., de Jonge, M.: Imposing a memory management discipline on software deployment. In: IEEE Workshop on Software Engineering (ICSE'04), IEEE (2004)
7. Hnetynka, P.: Component model for unified deployment of distributed component-based software. In: Tech. Report No. 2004/4, Charles University, Prague. (2004)
8. Hall, R., Heimbigner, D., Wolf, A.: Specifying the deployable software description format in xml. In: Technical Report CU-SERL-207-99, University of Colorado SERL. (1999)
9. Object Management Group: Deployment and Configuration of Component-based Distributed Applications Specification. In: OMG document ptc03-07-08. (2003)
10. Dolstra, E., Florijn, G., de Jonge, M., Visser, E.: Capturing timeline variability with transparent configuration environments. In Bosch, J., Knauber, P., eds.: IEEE Workshop on Software Variability Management (SVM'03), Portland, Oregon, IEEE (2003)
11. Carzaniga, A., Fuggetta, A., Hall, R., van der Hoek, A., Heimbigner, D., Wolf, A.: A characterization framework for software deployment technologies. In: Technical Report CU-CS-857-98, Dept. of Computer Science, University of Colorado. (1998)
12. Dolstra, E., de Jonge, M., Visser, E.: Nix: A safe and policy-free system for software deployment. In Damon, L., ed.: 18th Large Installation System Administration Conference (LISA '04), Atlanta, Georgia, USA, USENIX (2004) 79–92
13. Kang, K., Cohen, S., Hess, J., Novak, W., Peterson, A.: Feature-oriented domain analysis feasibility study. Technical Report CMU/SEI-90-TR-21, Pittsburgh, PA (1990)
14. Clegg, S.: Evolution in extensible component-based systems. In: Master Thesis. (2003)
15. Jansen, S.: Software Release and Deployment at Planon: a case study report. In: Technical Report CWI, SEN-E0504. (2005)
16. Bontemps, Y., Heymans, P., Schobbens, P.Y., Trigaux, J.C.: Semantics of feature diagrams. In Männistö, T., Bosch, J., eds.: Proc. of Workshop on Software Variability Management for Product Derivation (Towards Tool Support), Boston (2004)
17. van der Storm, T.: Variability and component composition. In: Software Reuse: Methods, Techniques and Tools: 8th International Conference (ICSR-8). LNCS, Springer (2004)
18. Ivica Crnkovic, U.A., Dahlqvist, A.P.: Implementing and integrating product data management and software configuration management, Artech House Publishers (2003)
19. Jansen, S., Brinkkemper, S., Ballintijn, G., van Nieuwland, A.: Integrated development and maintenance of software products to support efficient updating of customer configurations: A case study in mass market erp software. In: Proceedings of the 21st International Conference on Software Maintenance, IEEE (2005)
20. Helms, R.W.: Product data management as enabler for concurrent engineering, ph.d. dissertation. In: Eindhoven University of Technology press. (2002)
21. Object Management Group: Reusable Asset Specification. (2004)
22. Object Management Group: IT Portfolio Management Specification. (2004)

J2EE Packaging, Deployment and Reconfiguration Using a General Component Model

Takoua Abdellatif[1,2], Jakub Kornaś[2], and Jean-Bernard Stefani[2]

[1] Bull SA
[2] LSR-IMAG laboratory (CNRS, INPG, UJF) - INRIA - Sardes project
INRIA Rhône-Alpes, 655 av. de l'Europe, F-38334 Saint-Ismier Cedex, France
Firstname.Lastname@inrialpes.fr

Abstract. This paper describes a case study of enhancing the deployment process in J2EE application servers (AS), and more precisely the services building such servers and the applications executing on the servers. We show how, by following a component-based approach to the design of the server, we address the versioning and licensing issues raised by the fact that a J2EE server is built out of heterogeneous, third-party software.

As a proof of concept, we present a re-engineered version of the JOnAS J2EE server implemented using Fractal, a component model providing flexible control capabilities and hierarchical composition. We describe how Fractal packaging together with a JOnAS-specific deployment system are used to deploy and reconfigure our Fractal-based version of the JOnAS server. Finally, we show how the same model and packaging can be used to deploy applications executing on the server.

1 Introduction

J2EE [1] application servers are complex, service-oriented architectures. Existing open-source solutions usually implement services as wrappers of legacy code. For example, the JOnAS [2] application server[1] contains a Web service wrapping either Tomcat [3] or Jetty [4], a transaction service that wraps JOTM [5], etc. Since services are developed by third parties, it is necessary to allow deploying and updating them independently. Indeed, the application server must both allow choosing between different licenses at deployment time, and allow services to be updated when a new version is available.

Service update issues are not handled by current J2EE specifications. The JSR88 [6] focuses on the deployment of applications, but not on the deployment of the middleware. JSR77 [7] defines an information model that must be exposed to managers in charge of monitoring and controlling the system. This model does not contain the necessary information for dynamically updating services.

---

[1] JOnAS is an open-source application server freely available under an LGPL license at http://jonas.objectweb.org

A. Dearle and S. Eisenbach (Eds.): CD 2005, LNCS 3798, pp. 134–148, 2005.

This lack of specification regarding the middleware management (e.g. licensing, versioning) is currently left to the server providers.

Updating a service code at runtime (i.e. without stopping the server) involves three main tasks: (i) isolation of services as independent packages, (ii) deployment and redeployment of services, and (iii) handling service dependencies and state at runtime. Regarding the packaging part, the main issue is to handle the dependency between the different packages and the compatibility between code versions they contain. Regarding the deployment and redeployment part, each service needs to have an independent life cycle, in particular it must be deployable independently from other services. Finally, handling the running service state implies taking into account the service's stateful data and dependencies between the updated service and other running services.

Issues raised in point (iii) necessitate reconsidering the middleware architecture. Indeed, service dependencies must be explicit so that when a service is updated, the behavior of dependent services can be controlled. This has been the purpose of previous work [8] on JOnAS, which led to`the JonasALaCarte prototype. JonasALaCarte adopts a component-based architecture, implemented using the Fractal [9] component model. Fractal allows building hierarchical architectures (using composite components), where components communicate through explicit bindings. JonasALaCarte uses Fractal components to wrap services, thus making them independent units of configuration and deployment with an independent lifecycle.

This paper focuses on points (i) and (ii), i.e. the packaging and deployment parts. We show that we can adopt the same component model (Fractal) to implement the service packaging and the deployment infrastructure. Service packages are represented by Fractal components and dependencies between packages are expressed using Fractal bindings. Moreover, the deployment infrastructure is implemented using Fractal components, which allows dynamically plugging various deployment policies adapted to the deployment environment (e.g. centralized, clusters, grids, etc.).

Furthermore, we show that our deployment tool and packaging model is also applicable to J2EE applications. Unifying the packaging and deployment process thanks to the Fractal component model allows for abstracting the management tasks (packaging, deployment and system adaptation) to a configuration of Fractal components. Regarding existent solutions in open source application servers, our management solution is uniform: we use the same model for the packaging and the AS execution at runtime. Moreover, we adopt the same package structure for the middleware services and the J2EE applications.

The main innovative aspects of our work are that: we allow for versioning and redeployment of services building the JOnAS J2EE server, we solve the possible licensing issues by packaging each JOnAS service independently, we use a uniform component model from the package level, through the AS level, to the application level, and finally, in our solution, dependencies between JOnAS services are made explicit and map on package dependencies.

The rest of the paper is structured as follows: in section 2 we briefly introduce the Fractal component model and Fractal packaging. Section 3 describes the drawbacks of JOnAS in terms of deployment and presents how, by re-engineering JOnAS, we have obtained JonasALaCarte, a Fractal-based version of the server. Sections 4 and 5 present how components building the JonasALaCarte are packaged, deployed and redeployed. In section 6 we describe the related work before concluding the article in section 7.

2   Fractal Component Model

In this section we briefly describe the Fractal component model: the principles underlying the model, the Fractal ADL (architecture description language) and Fractal packaging.

2.1   Fractal Principles

Fractal [10] is a general component model. It distinguishes two types of components: *primitive* and *composite*. Primitive components are standard Java classes that conform to certain coding conventions. Composite components encapsulate a group of primitive and/or composite components.

A Fractal component is made of two parts: a *controller part*, which exposes the component's interfaces and comprises controller and interceptor objects, and a *content part*, which can be either a standard Java class in case of a primitive component, or other components (called subcomponents), in case of a composite component.

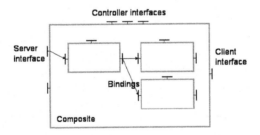

Fig. 1. An example Fractal architecture

Similar to other component models, Fractal distinguishes *server interfaces*, which correspond to provided services, and *client interfaces*, which correspond to required services. Moreover, Fractal supports both primitive bindings (i.e. Java references) and composite bindings which are built out of a set of primitive bindings and binding components (stubs, skeletons, adapters, etc).

Figure 1 illustrates the different constructs in a typical Fractal component architecture. The gray boxes denote the controller part of the components. Arrows correspond to bindings; the interfaces appearing on the top of a component represent the controllers, the interfaces on the left are server interfaces and on the right are client interfaces.

The construction of a system with Fractal component yields a dynamically adaptable system where the component is the unit of configuration, deployment and reconfiguration. The system architecture, written in ADL, is expressed in terms of the component model, exhibiting bindings between components and containment relationships. These properties are specific to Fractal, compared to other component models, as explained more in detail in [10]. For these reasons we chose to build our new AS, as well as the deployment system itself, using Fractal.

2.2   Fractal ADL

Fractal Architecture Description Language (ADL) is a mean to define architectures of Fractal applications. It is XML-based, and each description of the Fractal architecture is stored in a .fractal file. A sample ADL description of a Fractal component is represented in figure 2. This example corresponds to an ADL description of a component named WebContainer. This component has four client (required) interfaces, named jmx, security, jprop and lmgr, implemented by the following Java interfaces: JmxServiceItf, SecurityServiceItf, JProperty and LManager. The WebContainer component also has one server (provided) interface, named service and implemented by a Java interface ServiceItf. Finally, the implementation of this component's functional (content) part is provided by a Java class called WebContainerWrapper. WebContainer can be bound to other components, it can also be a subcomponent of some other component.

```
<definition name="WebContainer">
  <interface name="jmx" role="client" signature="JmxServiceItf"/>
  <interface name="security" role="client" signature="SecurityServiceItf"/>
  <interface name="jprop" role="client" signature="JProperty"/>
  <interface name="lmgr" role="client" signature="LManager"/>
  <interface name="service" role="server" signature="ServiceItf"/>
  <content class="WebContainerWrapper"/>
</definition>
```

Fig. 2. WebContainer.fractal: A sample ADL description of a Fractal component

Fractal ADL has been designed to be open and extensible: it is made of several units, where each unit defines syntax for one architectural aspect (like interface, binding, attribute etc). Developers are free to define their own units. At deployment time, an ADL description of the application is parsed by a factory tool. This factory tool can also be extended to take into account added units.

2.3   Fractal Packaging

Fractal packages are used to deploy Fractal applications. These packages are stored in package repositories, which can be of various kinds, such as file systems, databases etc. Each Fractal package `A.far` is a Fractal component `A` in a serialized form, which is described by a Fractal ADL definition `A.fractal` contained in the package itself. Such a definition of packages unifies the package and component concepts, in the sense that a package is just a special form of a component. All the properties of Fractal packages are deduced from this identity relation: for example, Fractal packages can contain sub-packages, just like Fractal components can contain subcomponents. Figure 3 illustrates an example of Fractal packages, including their metadata.

```
package JonasALaCArte.far
   JonasALaCarte.fractal:
      <definition name="JonasALaCarte" version="1.0">
         <component name="WebContainer" definition="WebContainer"/>
         ...
      </definition>
   ow_jonasbootstrap.jar
   ... other, non ADL files ...

package WebContainer.far
   WebContainer.fractal:
      <definition name="WebContainer" version="1.0">
         <interface name="jmx" role="client"
            signature="JmxServiceItf"/>
         <interface name="security" role="client"
            signature="SecurityServiceItf"/>
         ...
      </definition>
   catalina.jar
   tomcat-coyote.jar
   ... other, non ADL files ...

package JMX.far
   JMX.fractal:
      <definition name="JMX" version="1.0">
         <interface name="service" role="server"
            signature="JmxServiceItf"/>
         ...
      </definition>
   jmx.jar
   ... other, non ADL files ...
```

Fig. 3. An example of Fractal package files

Dependencies between Fractal components can only be of two sorts: dependencies through component encapsulation, and dependencies through component interfaces. These two dependency types give two dependency types between Fractal packages : (i) a containment dependency gives a strong dependency between two packages (in the example presented in figure 3, the containment of `WebContainer` inside `JonasALaCarte`, gives a strong dependency between package `JonasALaCarte.far` and package `WebContainer.far`) (ii) a dependency through interfaces gives a loose dependency between packages (in the example presented in figure 3, the client interface `jmx` gives a loose dependency between package `WebContainer.far` and any package that provides the `JmxServiceItf` interface), which in the example presented in figure 3 is the `JMX.far` package.

3   Re-engineering JOnAS Using Fractal

In this section we first briefly describe the JOnAS J2EE server. Then we outline the drawbacks of the existing implementation of JOnAS focusing mainly on deployment, licensing and updates issues. Finally we present our re-engineered, Fractal-based version of the server which we call JonasALaCarte. In the next two sections we explain how this re-engineering work allows us to address all the deployment-related issues of the "standard" server.

3.1   The JOnAS Server

JOnAS is an open source J2EE application server. It is developed within the ObjectWeb Consortium [11]. The server's role is to host J2EE-compliant applications by providing them with an execution environment that offers a well-defined set of non-functional services (persistency, transactions, security, etc.). To achieve that, the server integrates various software from different providers, such as the Apache Software Foundation [12], the ObjectWeb consortium etc. This heterogeneous software builds the services that offer non-functional properties to the J2EE applications. Even though each software providing different non-functional aspect could be considered as an independent component with explicitly defined relations to other components, JOnAS does not employ a component-based approach in its design. On the contrary, JOnAS is a monolithic block of code in the sense that the relations between the third-party "components" integrated by the server are not explicit - they are hard-coded in JOnAS' classes. Such an approach has major drawbacks in terms of both architecture and deployment. In terms of software architecture, the non-component-based approach makes the internals of JOnAS difficult to understand and the server difficult to manage at runtime. In terms of deployment, it does not allow the redeployment of only parts of the server - since JOnAS services are not components, they cannot have a life cycle independent of the life cycle of the server. Therefore, it is impossible to, for example, redeploy JOnAS services independently. Moreover, it is impossible to address the licensing issues raised by the fact that for certain third-party components it can be illegal to package and distribute them together with other third-party components. To address these issues we have re-engineered the JOnAS server to obtain a component-based version of it.

3.2   Fractalized JOnAS

JonasALaCarte [8] is our re-engineered, component-based version of the JOnAS server. In our re-engineering work we have adopted the Fractal component model.

As a result of our re-engineering work, all JOnAS services and management entities became Fractal components. As illustrated in figure 4, each instance of the JonasALaCarte server is therefore a composite component encapsulating a set of interacting services (primitive components). The latter are bound using Fractal bindings. The first advantage of such an approach, compared to traditional JOnAS server, is that the architecture of the server is explicit - connections between services are well defined, services building the server can be managed thanks to the control interfaces of the components that wrap these services. Second advantage is that components building the server can be packaged, deployed and redeployed independently. Note, however, that for most of these components it is impossible to have two versions of them running in a single application server. This is due to the way these components are implemented.

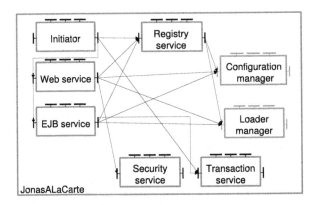

Fig. 4. Architecture of the JonasALaCarte J2EE servers

We have implemented a JSR77 lifecycle controller of each deployable Fractal component (in our case the services and the management components) as a Fractal controller. Figure 5 presents the JSR77 automate. When a Fractal component is deployed, its state is set to `Starting`. Each service component asks the `Loader Manager` for its class loader, performs some initialization operations and starts. If the service starting succeeds, its lifecycle controller is positioned to the `Running` state; otherwise the latter is set to `Failed`. To stop a service its state is set to `Stopping` and the service performs some state storage and clean-up. If these operations succeed, the service sets its state to `Stopped`, otherwise it is set within a configurable time-out to `Failed`.

4   Packaging

In this section we describe how Fractal packaging applies in the context of the Fractalized JOnAS server.

Fractalized JOnAS services are fractal components, therefore packages used for storage and deployment of these services are Fractal packages (serialized forms of Fractal components).

As stated in section 2.3, package-level dependencies between services building the server are the same as runtime-level dependencies, and are therefore

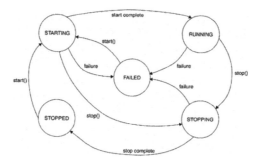

Fig. 5. JSR77 component lifecycle automate

expressed in the same ADL file. However, this file is enriched with versioning information needed by the package-management system. This information is used to solve package dependency and compatibility issues.

In addition to the `.fractal` file, each package contains also the `.jar` files that provide the actual code needed by the services at execution.

As can be seen, dependencies between packages correspond to the runtime dependencies between services building the server. Therefore, the `WebContainer-1.0.far` package depends on any package providing the `JmxServiceItf` interface, any package providing the `SecurityServiceItf` interface etc. These package dependencies are resolved by the JonasALaCarte deployment mechanism.

```
package WebContainer-1.0.far
   WebContainer.fractal:
      <definition name="org.objectweb.jonasALaCarte.WebContainer"
         version="1.0">
         <interface name="jmx" role="client"
           signature="org.objectweb.jonas.jmx.JmxServiceItf"
           compatibility="[1.0, *]"/>
         <interface name="security" role="client"
           signature="org.objectweb.jonas.security.SecurityServiceItf"
           compatibility="[1.0, *]"/>
         <interface name="jprop" role="client"
           signature="org.objectweb.jonasALaCarte.configurator.JProperty"
           compatibility="[1.0, *]"/>
         <interface name="lmgr" role="client"
           signature="org.objectweb.jonasALaCarte.loaderManager.LManager"
           compatibility="[1.0, *]"/>
         <interface name="service" role="server"
           signature="org.objectweb.jonas.service.ServiceItf"/>
         <content
         class="org.objectweb.jonas.web.wrapper.catalina55.WebContainerWrapper"/>
         ... the rest of the ADL file
      </definition>
   catalina.jar
   tomcat-coyote.jar
   ... other, non ADL files ...
```

Fig. 6. The content, including metadata, of the `WebContainer-1.0.far` package

The J2EE modules (WARs, EARs, RARs and EJBJars), as defined in JSR88 are wrapped as Fractal components. The ADL files in the .far archives describe the module version and the dependencies between the module and the services where it will be deployed. The deployment manager checks the code version compatibility. On the other hand, we express in ADLs, the dependencies between the modules themselves. For example, it is possible that two EARs archives need to share the same RARs. Note that JSR88 specification does not address the dependency between modules. We offer this feature thanks to our packaging structure without breaking the specification. Again, adopting the same package structure for both applications and middleware allows using the same APIs and management tools.

Since packages are only units of code distribution, they do not provide information on how the code contained in a package should be loaded at runtime, that is information relative to class loading. This is important in the context of JOnAS, since the server employs a rather complex class-loading hierarchy, allowing for example for run-time versioning of code. We believe that this class loading hierarchy is orthogonal to the code packaging - it is the deployment tool's role to have enough knowledge and means to create class loader hierarchies for the packages it obtains from package repositories. Thus, as will be explained in the next section, our deployment tool creates a proper class loader hierarchy for JOnAS.

5   Deployment and Updates

This section describes how Fractal packages containing the JOnAS services are deployed by our deployment tool and how JOnAS services can be redeployed without the need to redeploy the whole server. The first part of this section describes the architecture of the JonasALaCarte deployment tool, the second part outlines the properties of this deployment tool and finally the third part presents a redeployment use case.

5.1   Architecture

As illustrated in figure 7, our deployment tool is built of the following components: The Deployment Manager, the Repository and the Loader Manager. The role of the Deployment Manager is to parse the package meta-data, to identify the dependencies between the packages and check package availability and version compatibility. If no problem (lack of necessary packages, package incompatibility, etc.) is detected, the deployment manager extracts the content of .far packages (middleware or application ones) and asks the Repository component to store locally the content of these packages. Various storage policies can be implemented. In our current implementation, the Repository component stores the contents of packages in a folder structure equivalent to the one defined by JOnAS. It is possible to have other storage semantics or other storage support like data bases for persistence. The deployment manager asks the Initiator

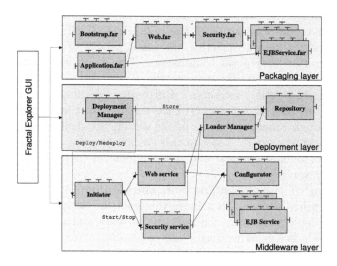

Fig. 7. Uniform Fractal-based representation of packages, the deployment infrastructure and the middleware

component to deploy services. The latter invokes then the *start* interfaces on the different service components.

The `Initiator` component polls the service lifecycle states and sends a notification to the deployment manager if a service deployment fails. As a future work we plan to implement some repair deployment policies as Fractal components. Note that currently the same protocol is used for the deployment of J2EE applications [13].

5.2   Properties

Our deployment architecture has three main properties:

Separation of deployment policies from deployment mechanisms by adopting a component-based architecture. In our context, the deployment policies define (i) how packages are stored, (ii) how dependencies between packages are handled, and (iii) how class loaders are created. Implementing these three concerns using separate components communicating through well defined interfaces allows modifying the behavior of each component independently from the others. For example, our existing implementation of the `Loader Manager` component creates a class loader hierarchy equivalent to the one used in JOnAS [14]. Another possible implementation could use Module Loader [15] as a class loading mechanism, and thus allow for the usage of any of the module loader's search policies. Finally, an implementation of the `Loader Manager` could map directly the packaged components, based on their metadata, on the namespaces provided by class loaders as we explain it in [16].

Unification of the packaging and the deployment tools by adopting the component model used to build the middleware itself. Adopting the same component model allows abstracting the management of the different phases to the configuration of Fractal components. This unification allows for using the same API to monitor and manage the application server lifecycle steps: from packaging to runtime execution. Currently, we enhanced the fractal explorer tool [17] to offer a common GUI for these steps. Figure 8 illustrates the navigation through Fractal packages of the server, the deployment components and the middleware services. Later in this section we explain in detail how this GUI tool allows for management and redeployment of components building the JonasALaCarte server.

Unification of the packaging and the deployment of J2EE applications and middleware. To achieve this goal, we adopt the same package structure and deployment tool for both middleware and applications. Indeed, the middleware services as well as J2EE applications are packaged as Fractal packages (.fars).

5.3   Redeployment Use Case

The `Deployment Manager` allows for redeployment of services. For that it obtains the new `far` from the package repository, asks the `Initiator` to store the `far`'s content locally and calls the *deploy* interface of the `Initiator` component. The `Initiator` calls *redeploy* interface of the service. The service is then stopped together with all the services that use it. The service component subject to redeployment asks the `Loader Manager` for its new class loader and restarts.

The redeployment of JonasALaCarte services can be performed using the Fractal Explorer tool that we have extended for our needs. Figure 8 illustrates an example of redeploying the `WebContainer` component. Figure 8a presents the initial state of the redeployment operation. On the left we can see all the subcomponents of the JonasALaCarte composite component, including the `WebContainer` component. We can also see the `redeployment-controller`, a Fractal controller specific to JonasALaCarte, responsible for initiating the redeployment of services. In figure 8b we see that the administrator chose the `WebContainer` component for redeployment. At this stage, the deployment manager queries the (possibly remote) package repository for the available versions of .`far` files containing the `WebContainer` component. As can be seen in figure 8c, two versions of this component are available and the administrator decides to deploy the "2.0" version of the component. This example shows how we achieve our goal of being capable to redeploy the services building the JOnAS server. Moreover, since services are packaged independently, we also solve the possible licensing issues. It has to be mentioned that redeployment of the `WebContainer` also involves the redeployment of all `war` and `ear` files.

In the use case described above we do not address the state preservation issue. The capacity to provide such state preservation depends on the properties of legacy software building the server.

(a)   (b)

(c)

Fig. 8. Example of JonasALaCarte service redeployment using Fractal Explorer

6   Related Work

The related work can be divided into two types of systems: the J2EE application servers and the generic, "Module" systems for Java.

6.1   J2EE Servers

In JBoss [18], the architecture of the AS is completely based on JMX. A JMX agent represents the middleware kernel. The services are implemented as MBeans and are deployed using the MLet service. In JBoss, some tools are built on top of JMX to express the dependencies between MBeans and thus between services. JBoss adopts different packaging structures for the application deployment modules (JARs, RARs, EARs) and the service deployment modules (SARs). Consequently, there is no uniform package structure for the middleware and the application parts. MBeans architecture unit is not exploited for the packaging and the deployment. Regarding JBoss, JonasALaCarte is based on a uniform model, the Fractal component model, for the packaging, the deployment and the middleware architecture. Furthermore, we are not aware of the dynamic versioning feature in JBoss, which we provide in JonasALaCarte.

Geronimo [19] developers are aware of the JMX limitation to uniform the complexity of the system. In fact, relation betweens the MBeans and the communication between them are not in the scope of the JMX model. Geronimo adopts instead an IoC [20] kernel based architecture. Inversion of Control, also called dependency injection, is a pattern supported by IoC containers and frameworks to achieve separation of concerns. Components inside the container can isolate dependencies and have these dependencies injected into them during execution/deployment. Components inside Geronimo are called GBeans and are the manageable units in Geronimo. The deployment process is separated into the user part (the modules creation) and the execution part (the configurations creation). During deployment, one or more modules are packaged together into a configuration. Internally, Geronimo sees only configurations, as packaged deployment of one or more GBeans. Like Fractal ADLs in JonasALaCarte, a Geronimo deployment plan is the Geronimo-specific meta-data. Like in Geronimo, our packaging and deployment tools aim at unifying the complex system by adopting the same structure of the deployment modules and deployment plans for the middleware and the J2EE applications. However, in JonasALaCarte, we adopt the same model for the packaging, the deployment tools and the middleware implementation itself. The administrator handles the packages, the management units and the middleware as Fractal components.

6.2 "Module" Systems

OSGi [21] allows the deployment of Java applications packaged in a form of *bundles* and runtime updates of those bundles. A bundle contains jar files and metadata describing those files (versioning etc.). The OSGi platform's role is to manage the lifecycle of bundles (deployment, activation, updates etc.). One of the contributions brought by the OSGi to Java community is taking jar versioning into account. The main drawback of OSGi compared to Fractal, and therefore to our solution, is that it does not provide an explicit notion of application's architecture. Moreover, OSGi services are not hierarchical and provide no control interfaces.

MJ [22] is a module system for Java. Its primary goal is to solve the issue of unexpected interactions between software components raised by large Java systems. To achieve it, MJ uses multiple class loaders but provides a high-level interface to manage these class loaders. However, MJ does not address the issue of redeployment of modules. With regards to MJ, our solution focuses mainly on the packaging, deployment and updates of services building such large Java systems, and J2EE servers in particular. The unexpected interactions between services do not occur in JonasALaCarte since we reuse the runtime separation of services provided by the standard hierarchy of JOnAS class loaders.

7   Conclusion

In this paper we addressed the issue of service versioning and licensing in the context of J2EE application servers. We presented the use case of updating the Web container service in JOnAS J2EE server at runtime. To allow redeployment, services are packaged independently and a middleware deployment tool is used to instantiate them. Furthermore, we reconsidered the architecture of the JOnAS application server since updating a service requires that each service has a lifecycle independent from the lifecycle of the application server. We selected the Fractal component model for the redesign and the reimplementation of the JOnAS application server and its management units. This choice was driven by the fact that construction of a system with the Fractal component model yields a dynamically adaptable system where the components are units of configuration, deployment and reconfiguration.

We illustrated that by adopting a component-based approach to package the services, to build the deployment tool and to architecture the middleware itself we achieve our versioning goal in a flexible and practical way. By flexibility we understand the ability to change the deployment policies, the class loading strategies or the package storage backends by replacing the correspondent component with a new component implementing the new policy. Our solution is practical because by unifying the implementation of the packages, the deployment tool and the middleware, the management tasks from packaging to the middleware monitoring and adaptation are abstracted to the configuration of Fractal components. The manager deals with the same API for the administration of the application server in its different phases: from packaging to the dynamic adaptation at execution time. We illustrated in this paper how an administrator can navigate through the same graphical interface (Fractal Explorer) to explore a service package, to perform a redeployment operation and to check the success of the service redeployment.

Currently, we implemented the packaging and the deployment infrastructure for the middleware services. In future, we plan to apply our solution to the packaging and the deployment of the J2EE applications, as we explained in this paper. We also aim at unifying the management of the J2EE middleware and the applications. Finally, we plan to enhance the deployment process by developing new deployment policies, such as transactions, security and failure recovery, as Fractal components.

References

1. J2EE: Java 2 Platform, Enterprise Edition (2002) http://java.sun.com/j2ee/docs.html.
2. JOnAS: Java Open Application Server (2005) http://jonas.objectweb.org/.
3. Apache Tomcat (2005) http://jakarta.apache.org/tomcat/.
4. Jetty Java HTTP Servlet Server (2005) http://jetty.mortbay.org/jetty/.
5. Java Open Transaction Manager (2005) http://jotm.objectweb.org/.

6. J2EE Deployment Specification (JSR88) (2005) http://jcp.org/jsr/detail/88.jsp.
7. J2EE Management Specification (JSR77) (2005) http://jcp.org/jsr/detail/77.jsp.
8. Abdellatif, T.: Enhancing the Management of a J2EE Application Server using a Component-Based Architecture. In: Proceeding of the 31st EUROMICRO Conference (EUROMICRO'2005), Porto, Portugal (2005)
9. Bruneton, E., Coupaye, T., Stefani, J.B.: The Fractal Composition Framework (2002) http://www.objectweb.org.
10. Bruneton, E., Coupaye, T., Leclercq, M., Quéma, V., Stefani, J.B.: An Open Component Model and its Support in Java. In: Proceedings of the International Symposium on Component-based Software Engineering (CBSE'2004), Edinburgh, Scotland (2004)
11. The ObjectWeb Consortium (2005) http://objectweb.org.
12. The Apache Software Foundation (2005) http://apache.org.
13. Exertier, F. J2ee deployment: The jonas case study. CoRR **cs.NI/0411054** (2004)
14. JOnAS class loader hierarchy (2004) http://jonas.objectweb.org/current/doc/.
15. Hall, R.S. A Policy-Driven Class Loader to Support Deployment in Extensible Frameworks. In: Proceedings of the International Conference on Component Deployment (CD'2004), Edinburgh, Scotland (2004)
16. Kornas, J., Leclercq, M., Quema, V., Stefani, J.B.: Support for evolutionary changes in Java applications (2004) http://sardes.inrialpes.fr/papers/kornas04cl.pdf.
17. The Fractal Project (2005) http://fractal. objectweb.org.
18. Fleury, M., Lindfors, J.: JMX-Managing J2EE with Java Management Extensions. Sams, The JBoss Group (2002)
19. Mulder, A.: Apache Geronimo Development and Deployment. Pearson Education (2004)
20. The PicoContainer project (2004) http://www.picocontainer.org/.
21. Open Services Gateway Initiative, OSGi service gateway specification, Release 3 (2003) http://www.osgi.org.
22. Corwin, J., Bacon, D.F., Grove, D., Murthy, C.: Mj: a rational module system for java and its applications. In: Conference on Object-Oriented Programming Systems Languages and Applications (OOPSLA'2003), Anaheim, California, USA (2003)

A Model of Dynamic Binding in .NET

Alex Buckley

Imperial College London
a.buckley@imperial.ac.uk

Abstract. Millions of programmers use ECMA CLI-compliant languages like VB.NET and C#. The resulting bytecode can be executed on several CLI implementations, such as those from Microsoft and the open-source Mono organisation. While assemblies are the standard unit of deployment, no standard exists for the process of finding and loading assemblies at run-time. The process is typically complex, and varies between CLI implementations. Unlike other linking stages, such as verification, it is visible to programmers and can be a source of confusion.

We offer a framework that describes how assemblies are resolved, loaded and used in CLI implementations. We strive for implementation-independence and note how implementations from different organisations vary in behaviour. We describe the reflection features available for dynamic loading, and give C# examples that exercise the features modelled in the framework.

1   Introduction and Motivation

Traditional language mechanisms for modular development - packages in Ada, modules in Modula-2, namespaces and classes in C++ - have no role at run-time. A compiler typically employs a static linker to emit a monolithic executable file, so the compilation environment automatically becomes the entire execution environment. Few (or no) dynamic checks are needed to resolve external dependencies. In contrast, the basic unit of development in Java and C# - the class - maintains its discrete identity throughout compilation and execution. A Java Virtual Machine or Microsoft's .NET Common Language Runtime (CLR) can start with the bytecode for just one class, then lazily load and link classes from the execution environment as necessary for continued execution.

Class loading tends to be highly configurable, unlike later linking stages such as verification. UNIX offered the `dlopen` C-language interface and most OO languages offer an API for dynamic class loading in their reflection libraries. Java has the familiar `CLASSPATH` mechanism for identifying class locations, and custom classloaders can be installed into the JVM.

Matters are complicated in a CLI implementation [7] because classes are not deployed as standalone units. Instead, classes are encapsulated inside assemblies. An assembly enumerates classes it provides and also the names of other assemblies whose classes it uses. Assembly resolution consists of converting a bytecode's reference to an assembly name into a physical location where a suitable assembly exists. Because an assembly's identity incorporates version and

A. Dearle and S. Eisenbach (Eds.): CD 2005, LNCS 3798, pp. 149–163, 2005.

security information, resolving an assembly is more complex than (and indeed, a pre-requisite to) finding a class inside an assembly.[1]

Different CLI implementations have different rules for assembly resolution. Also, the process of loading an assembly from a given location is implementation-specific. We use the term *binding* for the combined resolution and loading process.

Microsoft's CLI implementation, the Common Language Runtime (CLR) [15], provides a user-configurable, network-aware system for binding called "Fusion". For resolution, it supports a hierarchy of policies that can modify the requested version of an assembly. This allows security and performance patches to be used without rebuilding an assembly's manifest (akin to recompiling source code). It can also resolve references to assemblies compiled for other platforms, such as the .NET Compact Framework. For loading, it supports downloading of code from remote machines and, as a last resort, on-demand installation where the user is asked to provide an assembly.

Fusion's behaviour is typically explained in verbose official technical documentation. Recently, "blogs" written by Microsoft employees [3,19] [20,11,17] have explained areas of poorly documented behaviour in the current CLR release (v1.1), and given detailed information about the next CLR release (v2.0). Programmer understanding is significantly enhanced by this new channel, but there is no single place where dynamic loading is explained in full detail from 'top to bottom'. One must piece together information from around the Internet in order to explain a program's exact assembly and classloading behaviour.

An alternative CLI implementation is Mono [4]. Its functionality is a subset of the CLR's, including for assembly binding, so documentation is shorter and easier to understand. However, its binding process is subtly different from Fusion's. Other CLI implementations, such as Microsoft's .NET Compact Framework for mobile devices, also exhibit different behaviour from Fusion.

We wish to unify the rules that govern assembly binding in CLI implementations. We present a model that describes, at one level, how assemblies are bound (*i.e.* resolved and loaded), and at another level, how loaded assemblies are used when evaluating bytecode instructions. Assembly binding is interleaved with bytecode evaluation as in all current CLI implementations.[2] The model is parameterised by resolution and loading policies, so we specialise it for the Microsoft CLR v1.1 and Mono v1.1.

2   The Assembly Model

2.1   Assembly Structure

In the COM and Java environments, a file that contains code has only one identifier: its filename. "DLL hell" [8] arises because multiple DLL files, each containing

---

[1] We do not consider, in this paper, the resolution of classes in an assembly or of members in a class.

[2] The CLI specification allows resolution to take place when an application is installed, but we do not know of any implementation that takes such an eager approach.

different code, share the same filename and are placed in a shared location on disk. An application's dependency is resolved to a filename, but there is no guarantee that the DLL file with that filename is what the application was tested against. Java applications face a similar problem, even without a standard location in the filesystem for classes.

In contrast, the CLI specification[7] gives an assembly a logical identity quite different from its filename. We call this identity an *assembly name*, and reflection APIs in CLI-compliant languages typically make it a first-class value. It contains a display name, a version number (consisting of major, minor, revision and build numbers), a cultural identifier (for internationalisation) and a public key. It is convenient to just consider the presence of a security value in an assembly name, rather than the public key per se.

$AssemblyName\ \alpha : AN =$
$DisplayName : id, Version : int \times int \times int \times int, Culture : id, Security :$
$id, Retargetable : bool$

Binding maps an assembly name to an assembly definition. All elements in an assembly name are potentially used during binding, *e.g.* if the culture is present, it can be used to choose a directory on disk where an assembly definition might be found. The security value plays the most important role because it determines whether an assembly name is a *strong name*. A non-null security value indicates that the assembly has been signed by a private key. A verification procedure can use the security value to detect unauthorised changes to the assembly, but we do not consider verification further since it happens after binding. However, whether or not an assembly name is strong significantly affects binding, so this definition will be useful:

$$StrongName(\alpha) \equiv Key(\alpha) \neq \epsilon$$

An *assembly definition* consists of an assembly name, assembly dependencies and class definitions. Bytecode refers to assemblies by their display name, so the dependencies map display names to full assembly names. We assume that bytecode is encapsulated in class definitions of some type $ClassDef$. An assembly definition knows the location of the file that it was loaded from; this is used in type-casting and reflection operations.

$AssemblyDefinition\ \delta : AD =$
$Name : AN, Refs : id \longrightarrow AN, Code : id \longrightarrow ClassDef, Loc : id$

The CLI specification defines an assembly as comprised of modules (that contain bytecode) and other resource files. An assembly's module and resource files may be placed in a single physical file or left as independent files. However, modules and the physical layout of an assembly play no role in binding[3], so we ignore them in our model. This keeps the definition of the $Code$ element simple.

---

[3] Partition I, §9.6: "... rather than establishing relationships between individual modules and referenced assemblies, every reference is resolved through the current assembly. This allows each assembly to have absolute control over how references are resolved."

2.2   Assembly Environment

Most CLI implementations (though not the CLI specification itself) support a standard location on disk where assemblies can be placed, typically if they have a strong name. At load-time, this location is typically checked before others, and thus provides the default environment from which assemblies come. In the CLR and Mono, the environment is provided by the Global Assembly Cache (GAC).

$Environment\ \Delta : Env = AN \longrightarrow AD$

We introduce the *extended environment* to represent both the filesystem of the machine executing the code, and a URL-addressable space of machines that have assemblies available for download. Given a list of paths, the extended environment tries each in turn until an assembly definition is found; it returns ϵ if the list is exhausted without finding an assembly.

$Extended\ Environment\ EE : ExtEnv = id^* \longrightarrow AD$

3   Assembly-Oriented Execution

3.1   State

We wish to show how assembly identity, resolution and loading affect execution. We distinguish the state of the executing program from the state of the runtime system itself. Program state P is a pair whose elements are an instruction stack and an operand stack.

$Program\ state\ P : I^* \times V^*$

A CLI instruction I is parameterised by a display name and a member descriptor, M. The display name must have a corresponding entry in the $Refs$ element of the enclosing assembly. A member descriptor is simply a class and a field/method signature. Values come from a type V with which we are not concerned.

The runtime system's state is represented by three elements: an environment (defined in section 2), a heap and a stack.

The runtime system's heap stores assembly definitions loaded from the environment and extended environment. The CLR's heap is divided into two parts, called *contexts*.[4] Contexts stop a programmer circumventing the system's binding policies. The Mono system does not support contexts at present.

An assembly loaded by the CLR itself is placed in the first context. This happens when a bytecode instruction is jitted and the instruction's display name is resolved. Assemblies loaded directly from a filename are placed in the second context. This happens when a programmer uses the reflection API provided by the core assemblies in the CLR and Mono. With a heap consisting of a pair of mappings from assembly name to definition, we write H_x for $H \downarrow_1$.

$Heap\ H : (AN \longrightarrow AD) \times (AN \longrightarrow AD)$

---

[4] In fact, there is a third heap context, but its role is not important in our current model.

In a CLI implementation, the heap of loaded assemblies is part of an appdomain, which is a logical unit of isolation in a process. As we do not model the ability of a program to dynamically create and destroy appdomains, there is exactly one appdomain per executing application. Therefore, we do not need to qualify our heap of assemblies with an appdomain.

We need to track the call stack of assemblies at each dynamic program point. This is because the references of the currently executing assembly is consulted when resolving a reference to another assembly.[5] In addition, the context of the currently executing assembly is important when resolving an assembly reference. The stack starts with the assembly that the operating system considers is the entrypoint for an application.

$$Stack\ S : (AN \times \{1, 2\})^*$$

3.2   Evaluation

Evaluation is performed by a small-step operational semantics that evolves the state of the runtime system (δ, H, S) and the program state (P).

$$\Delta, H, S, P \longrightarrow \Delta', H', S', P'$$

The rules are shown in fig. 1. The bytecode instruction on the program's instruction stack can be evaluated if it depends on an assembly already loaded into the system heap. (Rules EXEC-INSTR, EXEC-INSTR-CALL, EXEC-INSTR-CAST) Details of the evaluation are not important, so we abstract it into this judgement which evolves the program state given an assembly definition needed by the instruction:

$$\delta, P \longrightarrow P'$$

We are forced to differentiate the call instruction from other instructions because we need to add the called assembly's name to the system stack, and modify the program's instruction stream with the body of the called method. We assume a *lookup* function that can find a member M in an assembly.

A binding step can take place to resolve and load an assembly that an instruction is dependent on. (Rule EXEC-BIND) It uses the binding rules that evolve an environment and heap with an assembly definition for assembly name α, returning the name of the actual assembly loaded:

$$\Delta, H, \alpha \longrightarrow \Delta', H', \alpha'$$

The execution is stuck if binding fails to find an assembly definition, *i.e.* α' is ϵ.

Heap Contexts in Evaluation. To evaluate a bytecode instruction, a definition must be available for the assembly it refers to. As per the CLI specification, we take the display name N mentioned in an instruction and look it up in the references of the currently executing assembly T, obtaining a full assembly name α. In the CLR,

---

[5] CLI Specification Partition 1 §9.6.

$$P[-] \;=\; (-::is \;,\; v::vs)$$

$$I[-] \;=\; ldfld\,[-]M \;|\; stfld\,[-]M \;|\; new\,[-]M$$

(EXEC-INSTR)
$$\frac{Refs(H_x(T))(N) = \alpha \qquad y = context(\alpha, H, x) \qquad Code(H_y(\alpha)), P[I[N]] \longrightarrow P'}{\Delta, H, (T, x) :: Ts, P[I[N]] \longrightarrow \Delta, H, (T, x) :: Ts, P'}$$

(EXEC-INSTR-CALL)
$$\frac{Refs(H_x(T))(N) = \alpha \qquad y = context(\alpha, H, x) \qquad lookup(H_y(\alpha), M) = e}{\Delta, H, (T, x) :: Ts, P[call\,[N]M] \longrightarrow \Delta, H, (\alpha, y) :: (T, x) :: Ts, P[e]}$$

(EXEC-INSTR-CAST)
$$\frac{\begin{array}{c} Refs(H_x(T))(N) = \alpha \qquad y = context(\alpha, H, x) \\ type(v) = (\alpha', C') \qquad z = context(\alpha', H, x) \\ Loc(H_y(\alpha)) = Loc(H_z(\alpha')) \\ Code(H_y(\alpha)), P[cast\,C'\,to\,C] \longrightarrow P' \end{array}}{\Delta, H, (T, x) :: Ts, P[castclass\,[N]C] \longrightarrow \Delta, H, (T, x) :: Ts, P'}$$

$$E[-] \;=\; I[-] \;|\; castclass\,[-]M \;|\; call\,[-]M$$

(EXEC-BIND)
$$\frac{Refs(H_x(T))(N) = \alpha \qquad \Delta, H_1, \alpha \longrightarrow \Delta', H_1', \alpha'}{\Delta, H, (T, x) :: Ts, P[E[N]] \longrightarrow \Delta', (H \cup_1 H_1'), (T, x) :: Ts, P[E[N]]}$$

(EXEC-RUN)
$$\frac{\Delta, H, S, P[E[N]] \longrightarrow \Delta', H', S, P[E[N]] \qquad \Delta', H', S, P[E[N]] \longrightarrow \Delta', H'', S, P'}{\Delta, H, S, P[E[N]] \longrightarrow \Delta', H'', S, P'}$$

$$H \cup_1 H' \equiv (H_1[y \mapsto H'(y) | y \in dom(H')], H_2)$$

Fig. 1. Execution and Loading

which heap context to look up this assembly name α in depends on which context the currently executing assembly is loaded in. An assembly loaded in the first context can only "see" assemblies also loaded in the first context; an assembly loaded in the second context can see assemblies in both contexts, preferring the second. This policy is justified by the first context being where assemblies are "officially" loaded and the second context being where expert programmers place their own assemblies. (Mono only has one context, so the issue does not arise.)

$$context^{CLR}(\alpha, H, x) = \begin{cases} x \; if \; \alpha \in dom(H_x) \\ 1 \; if \; x = 2 \;\wedge\; \alpha \notin dom(H_2), \in dom(H_1) \end{cases}$$

$$context^{Mono}(\alpha, H, x) = x$$

Casting. Casting is complicated because assemblies play the same role as class-loaders in Java, *i.e.* scoping a class such that a type is an (assembly name,class name) pair. Ensuring that the same classes from different assemblies are not confused is an important defence against attacks. Therefore, in the CLR, the source and target classes must be defined in the same *assembly file on disk*.

In addition, the heap context in which an assembly is loaded provides another level of qualification for a class, *i.e.* a type in the CLR is a (context id,assembly name,class name) triple. The same assembly definition can be loaded into multiple contexts, but casting an object across contexts would give rise to the same problems as casting it across classloaders. Therefore, the assembly definitions containing the source and target classes must be in the same context.

The EXEC-INSTR-CAST rule first obtains the full assembly name α referred to by the `castclass` instruction. We assume that the object to be cast is accessible via the top value v on the program state's value stack, and that the auxiliary function *type* returns an (assembly name,class name) pair representing the object's type. The assemblies named by α and α' must be loaded, potentially in different contexts. We check that the two loaded assemblies were loaded from identical paths, as required by the CLR. If so, then the success of the cast is for the program to determine; we assume a notional *cast* operator that checks subclassing using the class definitions provided from an assembly definition:

$$Code(H_y(\alpha)), P[cast\ C'\ to\ C] \longrightarrow P'$$

4   Assembly Binding

The binding rules in fig. 2 take a logical assembly name and return an assembly definition plus a name. If the assembly is not already loaded in the heap, then they use a name resolver η, a location resolver $\odot$, a assembly installer $\oplus$, and a name matcher $\sim$.

A name resolver performs a logical-to-logical mapping, applying versioning policy to an assembly name in order to obtain a more refined assembly name. A location resolver performs a logical-to-physical mapping, taking an assembly name and applying a "probing" policy that describes where to search for an assembly definition. If the location resolver fails to provide a location where a suitable assembly can be found, then an on-demand (*i.e.* "just-in-time") assembly installation operation is tried, via $\oplus$.

If the extended environment is able to find an assembly, or an assembly is installed on-demand, then the binding rules return the heap augmented with the assembly definition, plus the name of the assembly that was actually loaded. CLI implementations require that the loaded name matches the name of the desired assembly (*i.e.* produced by the name resolver), according to $\sim$.

$Name\ Resolver\ \eta : AN \longrightarrow AN$
$Location\ Resolver\ \odot : AN \times E \longrightarrow id^*$
$Installer\ \oplus : AN \times E \longrightarrow E$
$Name\ Matcher\ \sim: AN \times AN \longrightarrow bool$

$$
\begin{array}{ll}
\text{(Bind-Already-Loaded)} & \text{(Bind-Available)} \\
& \alpha \notin dom(H) \\
\dfrac{\alpha \in dom(H)}{\Delta, H, \alpha \longrightarrow \Delta, H, \alpha} & \dfrac{\eta(\alpha) = \alpha' \quad EE(\Delta \odot \alpha') = \delta \quad \alpha' \sim Name(\delta)}{\Delta, H, \alpha \longrightarrow \Delta, H[\alpha \mapsto \delta], Name(\delta)}
\end{array}
$$

$$
\text{(Bind-Install-On-Demand)}
$$
$$
\alpha \notin dom(H)
$$
$$
\dfrac{\eta(\alpha) = \alpha' \quad EE(\Delta \odot \alpha') = \epsilon \quad \Delta \oplus \alpha' = \Delta' \quad \alpha' \sim Name(\Delta'(\alpha))}{\Delta, H, \alpha \longrightarrow \Delta', H[\alpha \mapsto \Delta'(\alpha)], Name(\Delta'(\alpha'))}
$$

$$
\text{(Bind-Unavailable)}
$$
$$
\dfrac{\alpha \notin dom(H) \quad \eta(\alpha) = \alpha' \quad EE(\Delta \odot \alpha') = \epsilon \quad \Delta \oplus \alpha' = \Delta}{\Delta, H, \alpha \longrightarrow \Delta, H, \epsilon}
$$

Fig. 2. Binding

We introduce an *application context* that stores facts about the runtime environment for use by the name and location resolvers.

$$
\begin{aligned}
\textit{Application Context } \Gamma : &(RuntimeVersion : int \times int \times int \times int, \\
&Mapping : AN \longrightarrow (AN \times id), AppPath : id)
\end{aligned}
$$

We define a Binding Framework $BF = (\Gamma, \Delta, \eta, \odot, \oplus, \sim)$. A binding framework is instantiated for a specific combination of CLI implementation and user application. The CLI implementation supplies the environment Δ, which is a single directory for the CLR and one or more directories for Mono. The CLI implementation also supplies $\Gamma_{RuntimeVersion}, \eta, \odot, \oplus$ and $\sim$. The user application supplies its location on disk $\Gamma_{AppPath}$, which is independent of any CLI implementation. $\Gamma_{Mapping}$ is discussed in the next section.

Instantiating the binding framework several times allows modelling of "side-by-side execution", where several CLI implementations can be installed on the same machine, each with its own core assemblies. The operating system chooses which implementation is suitable for executing a given application, which provides further information necessary for its execution.

4.1   Name Resolution

A name resolver η maps a logical assembly name to another logical assembly name, according to three policies: servicing, unification and retargeting. Fig. 3 shows name resolvers for the CLR and Mono.

Servicing policy. To allow assemblies to be *serviced* (*i.e.* upgraded for security and performance reasons without modifying calling applications), the CLR supports policies for redirecting references to strongly-named assemblies. (A reference to a non-strongly-named assembly cannot be serviced.)

$$
\eta^{CLR}(\alpha) = \begin{cases} \alpha \\ \quad if \quad \neg StrongName(\alpha) \\[2ex] \Gamma_{Mapping}(\alpha) \downarrow_1 \\ \quad if \quad StrongName(\alpha) \quad \wedge \quad \neg Core^{CLR}(\alpha) \\[2ex] \alpha[Version \mapsto \Gamma_{RuntimeVersion}] \\ \quad if \quad StrongName(\alpha) \quad \wedge \quad Core^{CLR}(\alpha) \quad \wedge \quad \neg Retargetable(\alpha) \\[2ex] \alpha[Version \mapsto \Gamma_{RuntimeVersion}, Security \mapsto \text{`}b77a5c561934e089'] \\ \quad if \quad StrongName(\alpha) \quad \wedge \quad Core^{CLR}(\alpha) \quad \wedge \quad Retargetable(\alpha) \end{cases}
$$

$$
\eta^{Mono}(\alpha) = \begin{cases} \alpha \\ \quad if \quad \neg Core^{Mono}(\alpha) \\[2ex] \alpha[Version \mapsto \Gamma_{RuntimeVersion}] \\ \quad if \quad Core^{Mono}(\alpha) \end{cases}
$$

$$
Core^{CLR}(\alpha) \equiv \\
DisplayName(\alpha) \in \{mscorlib, System.Windows.Forms, ...\} \\
Core^{Mono}(\alpha) \equiv StrongName(\alpha) \quad \wedge \quad DisplayName(\alpha) \in \{mscorlib\}
$$

Fig. 3. Name Resolution

First, each application can supply a policy file for redirecting one version of a given assembly to another. Second, "publisher policies" can redirect requests for assemblies in the GAC. Third, a machine-wide redirection policy is applied after the application and publisher policies. We represent the union of these policies as a mapping from assembly name to assembly name in $\Gamma_{Mapping}$ (using the first element of the range). In contrast, Mono does not currently support redirection policies, so its $\Gamma_{Mapping}$ is empty.

Unification policy. A CLI-compliant virtual machine, such as the CLR, is often developed by different individuals from those who program the core assemblies that accompany the VM.[6] It is often practical to test a VM only with the exact framework assemblies that will accompany it.

The CLR and Mono both impose a restriction that some core assemblies (the exact set differs) must be the same version as that of the runtime execution system itself.

Retargeting policy. As well as the CLR, Microsoft produces a CLI implementation for mobile devices called the .NET Compact Framework. An application compiled *for the CLR* will not run on a mobile device equipped with just the .NET Compact Framework, even if the developer is careful to use only assemblies available in the

---

[6] In Java, the java.lang.* class hierarchy.

Compact Framework. This is because the core assemblies that accompany the CLR have different strong names from the assemblies in the Compact Framework [16].

However, an application compiled *for the .NET Compact Framework* will run on the CLR. This is possible because the generated assembly references the Compact Framework's assemblies by their strong names, as usual, but each reference features a *retargetable* flag. The .NET Compact Framework's runtime ignores this flag and resolves the core assemblies as usual. The CLR reacts to it by rewriting the retargetable assembly names to the relevant core assembly names; the version number is unified and the key token is set to a standard value that indicates a core assembly to Fusion. This is Microsoft-specific behaviour; the Mono runtime will halt on failing to resolve the strong names of the Compact Framework assemblies referenced by the application.

4.2 Location Resolution

A location resolver $\odot$ supplies a list of physical filenames for the extended environment to try to obtain an assembly from. Fig. 4 shows location resolvers for the CLR and Mono.

Given an assembly name, the CLR's location resolver prefers to search the environment first if the assembly's name is a strongname. The next possible location is a "codebase" from the application context, specifically the second element of the $\Gamma_{Mapping}$ entry for the target assembly name. The codebase's location is final in the sense that no alternative paths are tried if it is specified. If a codebase is not specified, then various locations in the filesystem are suggested, using the path of the

$$\Delta \odot^{CLR} \alpha = \begin{cases} \Delta, L \\ \quad if\ StrongName(\alpha)\ \wedge\ \Gamma_{Mapping}(\alpha) \downarrow_2 = L \\ \\ \Delta, Locs(\alpha) \\ \quad if\ StrongName(\alpha)\ \wedge\ \Gamma_{Mapping}(\alpha) \downarrow_2 = \epsilon \\ \\ L \\ \quad if\ \neg StrongName(\alpha)\ \wedge\ \Gamma_{Mapping}(\alpha) \downarrow_2 = L \\ \quad \wedge\ L = \Gamma_{AppPath} +''/'' + x\ for\ some\ x \\ \\ Locs(\alpha) \\ \quad if\ \neg StrongName(\alpha)\ \wedge\ \Gamma_{Mapping}(\alpha) \downarrow_2 = \epsilon \end{cases}$$

$$\begin{aligned} Locs(\alpha) = &(\Gamma_{AppPath} + ''/'' + DisplayName(\alpha) + ''.dll''), \\ &(\Gamma_{AppPath} + ''/'' + DisplayName(\alpha) + ''/'' + DisplayName(\alpha) + ''.dll''), \\ &(\Gamma_{AppPath} + ''/'' + Culture(\alpha) + ''/'' + DisplayName(\alpha) + ''.dll''), \\ &(\Gamma_{AppPath} + ''/'' + Culture(\alpha) + ''/'' + DisplayName(\alpha) + ''/'' + \\ &DisplayName(\alpha) + ''.dll'') \end{aligned}$$

$$\Delta \odot^{Mono} \alpha = (\Gamma_{AppPath} +''/'' + DisplayName(\alpha) +''.dll''), \Delta$$

Fig. 4. Location Resolution

$$\Delta \oplus^{CLR} \alpha = \Delta' \text{ for some } \Delta' \supseteq \Delta \text{ where } \Delta'(\alpha) \neq \epsilon \implies \Delta(\alpha) = \epsilon$$

$$\Delta \oplus^{Mono} \alpha = \Delta$$

Fig. 5. Software Installation

currently executing application (which is not necessarily that of the currently executing assembly). The extended environment will "probe" each of these locations in turn.

When performing location resolution for an assembly name that is not a strong-name, the environment is not used. If a codebase is available, it must come from the same location as the executing application. Otherwise, the filesystem is tried as before.

The location resolver for Mono is quite different. It tries the application's local directory first before the environment. (It also searches a `CLASSPATH`-style directory list before the environment, but we do not show this.)

4.3   Name Matching

The CLR and Mono require an exact match between desired and loaded assembly versions:

$$\alpha \sim^{CLR,Mono} \alpha' \equiv$$
$$StrongName(\alpha) \Longleftrightarrow StrongName(\alpha') \land$$
$$Version(\alpha) = a.b.c.d \Longleftrightarrow Version(\alpha') = a.b.c.d$$

4.4   Install-on-Demand

If both the environment and the extended environment fail to supply an assembly, the $\oplus$ function tries to perform an "install-on-demand" operation. Unlike the extended environment, which is queried at a specific location (*e.g.* a URL), the installer is required to return an assembly given just its name.

In the CLR, we suppose that the end user is asked to supply an assembly, *e.g.* on a CD. Because the supplied assembly is totally free, we pass the old environment to $\oplus$ to see that if it does grow, then a truly new assembly is available in the new environment. This approach allows us to accept that the installation can fail, leaving the environment unchanged and propagating (through binding rule BIND-UNAVAILABLE) a loading failure.

Mono does not support on-demand installation, so returns an unchanged environment.

4.5   Dynamic Loading Through Reflection

As stated in section 2, assemblies can be loaded using a reflection API. This is widely used by developers building applications that support plug-ins. Among the many reflection methods provided by the CLR's core assemblies, we consider Load and LoadFrom. Mono's core assemblies provide Load only. The full method signatures are shown in fig. 6.

The Load method takes a strong name α from the program state's value stack, and defers to the standard binding rules in fig. 2 to resolve and load it. It is as if a strongname α has been found in an assembly's metadata, *i.e.* Load's behaviour is that of EXEC-BIND in fig. 1.

$LOAD \equiv call[mscorlib]System.Reflection.Assembly :: Load$
$LOADFROM \equiv call[mscorlib]System.Reflection.Assembly :: LoadFrom$

$$\boxed{P[-,-] \;=\; (-:: is \;,- :: vs)}$$

(EXEC-INSTR-CALLLOAD)
$$\frac{\Delta, H_1, \alpha \longrightarrow \Delta', H_1', \alpha'}{\Delta, H, (T, x) :: Ts, P[LOAD, \alpha] \Longrightarrow \Delta', (H \cup_1 H_1'), (T, x) :: Ts, P[\epsilon, \alpha']}$$

(EXEC-INSTR-CALLLOAD2)
$$\frac{IsDisplayName(N) \qquad EE(\Delta \odot N) = \delta \qquad \Delta, H_1, Name(\delta) \longrightarrow \Delta', H_1', \alpha}{\Delta, H, (T, x) :: Ts, P[LOAD, N] \Longrightarrow \Delta', (H \cup_1 H_1'), (T, x) :: Ts, P[\epsilon, \alpha]}$$

(EXEC-INSTR-CALLLOAD3)
$$\frac{IsDisplayName(N) \qquad EE(\Delta \odot N) = \delta \qquad \Delta, H_1, Name(\delta) \longrightarrow \Delta, H_1, \epsilon}{\Delta, H, (T, x) :: Ts, P[LOAD, N] \Longrightarrow \Delta, (H \cup_1 [Name(\delta) \mapsto \delta]), (T, x) :: Ts, P[\epsilon, Name(\delta)]}$$

(EXEC-INSTR-CALLLOADFROM)
$$\frac{\begin{array}{c} EE(L) = \delta \qquad \Delta, H_1, DisplayName(Name(\delta)) \Longrightarrow \Delta', H_1', \alpha \\ \alpha \neq \epsilon \;\wedge\; Loc(\delta) = Loc(H_1'(\alpha)) \end{array}}{\Delta, H, S, P[LOADFROM, L] \Longrightarrow \Delta', (H \cup_1 H_1'), S, P[\epsilon, \alpha]}$$

(EXEC-INSTR-CALLLOADFROM2)
$$\frac{\begin{array}{c} EE(L) = \delta \qquad \Delta, H_1, DisplayName(Name(\delta)) \Longrightarrow \Delta', H_1', \alpha \\ \alpha = \epsilon \;\vee\; Loc(\delta) \neq Loc(H_1'(\alpha)) \end{array}}{\Delta, H, S, P[LOADFROM, L] \Longrightarrow \Delta, (H \cup_2 [Name(\delta) \mapsto \delta]), S, P[\epsilon, Name(\delta)]}$$

$H \cup_1 H'$ as before
$$H \cup_2 [\alpha \mapsto \delta] \equiv \begin{cases} H & if \; \alpha \in dom(H_2) \\ (H_1, H_2[\alpha \mapsto \delta]) & otherwise \end{cases}$$

Fig. 6. Dynamic loading through reflection

Load can also take a display name N, *e.g.* "Calc". In this case, it probes the local directory first. If Calc.dll is found and does not have a strongname, then that file is bound to immediately. But if the file has a strongname, then that strongname is used to initiate the standard binding process. If this process succeeds, the assembly it finds is Load's result, rather than the local Calc.dll. If the process fails, then Load return the local Calc.dll assembly. The interesting case is when Calc.dll is not present locally, because then there is no strongname available to attempt to bind with - *even if a suitable Calc assembly is in the GAC*. The formal system is stuck in this case, reflecting that no assembly would be returned by Load.

The LoadFrom method is complex too. It takes a location L from the program state's value stack, and loads the file at that location, *e.g.* c:\app\Calc.dll. It then initiates the standard binding process with the *display name* embedded in that file, *i.e.* Calc. If this process returns an identical assembly definition from the heap's first context - *i.e.* an assembly in that context was already loaded from c:\app\Calc.dll - then that assembly in the first context is LoadFrom's result. The file just loaded from c:\app\Calc.dll is ignored and the second heap context is unchanged. However, if the standard process fails to find an exact match for Calc in the first context - perhaps one exists, but loaded from d:\libs\Calc.dll - then the assembly from c:\app\Calc.dll is bound in the second context.

5 Related and Further Work

Classloading in Java has received significant attention[5,13,14,18], and [10] presents it in an abstract setting. However, relatively little work focuses on the CLI platform. [6] unifies dynamic linking in Java and the CLI, but abstracts the assembly binding process to a very high level. [8] and [9] offer a formal model of a well-formed GAC, where assembly addition and removal do not break existing dependencies. Our work is clearly complementary to this, as we show how the GAC is used in the wider assembly binding process. Our $\oplus$ operator would ideally maintain a stronger safety property concerning evolution of the GAC[9].

We have described and formalised how assemblies are resolved and loaded by common CLI implementations. Most programmers assume that an assembly's strong name is its sole identity once loaded, but we show how the CLR, during execution, considers an assembly's identity to have more elements. Namely, it considers where an assembly was loaded from (*i.e.* a disk or URL-based location) and where it was loaded to (*i.e.* its heap context). These elements are necessary because the CLR exposes reflective assembly loading operations that can load arbitrary assemblies. While merely loading such assemblies is harmless, it is essential to avoid using their classes if the assembly's identity masquerades as one of the core assemblies. We plan to state formally that binding is "safe" in the current CLR in that it never leads to a heap where a non-core assembly is mistaken for a core assembly. The Mono system avoids the problem at present by not offering reflective loading capabilities.

A weakness of the current model is that name resolution produces a very precise answer, *i.e.* a single assembly name. This does not accurately model the .NET Compact Framework or, indeed, more flexible future schemes for choosing an assembly to load[1,2]. The .NET Compact Framework does not support servicing policies that redirect an assembly's desired version, so applications cannot be directed to use later, better code. However, the Compact Framework's binding rules permit the loader to provide version $a.b.c.x$ of an assembly when a reference is made to version $a.b.c.d$, *i.e.* the last element of the version number can "float". The binding rules also permit *any* version of an assembly to be loaded when the reference mentions version 0.0.0.0.

In our model, this equates to the name resolver producing $a.b.c.*$ for the desired version to locate. We could modify name resolution to produce a constraint on permitted names, rather than a specific name. Location resolution would then need to iterate through the files found in the extended environment to choose the "best" one matching the constraint. The name matcher would have the following definition:

$$\alpha \sim^{CompactFramework} \alpha' \equiv$$
$$StrongName(\alpha) \Longleftrightarrow StrongName(\alpha') \wedge$$
$$((Version(\alpha) = a.b.c._{-} \Longleftrightarrow Version(\alpha') = a.b.c._{-}) \vee Version(\alpha) = 0.0.0.0)$$

The CLR v2.0 will be released in late 2005 and makes some small changes to unification policy[19], so we will need a new name resolver. More interesting are Microsoft's plans for binding in Longhorn[12], where assemblies are typed and servicing policy is affected by the types of referencing and referenced assemblies. A feature called "interim roll-back" is also planned, where assemblies installed in the environment are temporarily hidden due to flaws being found in them. Our model can handle the new servicing policy (at name resolution) and rollback policy (at location resolution). More challenging is to state whether syntactic or semantic compatibility is assured by these new features.

References

1. Alex Buckley and Sophia Drossopoulou. Flexible Dynamic Linking. In *ECOOP Workshop on Formal Techniques for Java Programs (FTfJP 2004)*, Oslo, Norway, June 2004.
2. Alex Buckley, Michelle Murray, Susan Eisenbach, and Sophia Drossopoulou. Flexible Bytecode for Linking in .NET. In *First Workshop on Bytecode Semantics, Verification, Analysis and Transformation (BYTECODE 2005)*, ENTCS, Edinburgh, Scotland, March 2005. Elsevier BV.
3. Suzanne Cook. .NET CLR Loader Notes. `http://blogs.msdn.com/suzcook`, 2005.
4. Miguel de Icaza. Mono. `http://www.mono-project.com/`, 2005.
5. Drew Dean. The Security of Static Typing with Dynamic Linking. In *Proceedings of the Fourth ACM Conference on Computer and Communications Security*, Zurich, Switzerland, April 1997.
6. Sophia Drossopoulou, Giovanni Lagorio, and Susan Eisenbach. Flexible Models for Dynamic Linking. In Pierpaolo Degano, editor, *Proceedings of the 12th European Symposium on Programming (ESOP 2003)*, volume 2618 of *LNCS*, pages 38–53. Springer-Verlag, April 2003.
7. ECMA. *Standard ECMA-335: Common Language Infrastructure*. ECMA International, December 2002. `http://www.ecma-international.org/publications/standards/Ecma-335.htm`.
8. S. Eisenbach, V. Jurisic, and C. Sadler. Feeling the way through DLL Hell. In *Proceedings of the First Workshop on Unanticipated Software Evolution (USE 2002)*, Malaga, Spain, June 2002.

9. S. Eisenbach, V. Jurisic, and C. Sadler. Managing the Evolution of .NET Programs. In *6th IFIP International Conference on Formal Methods for Open Object-based Distributed Systems (FMOODS 2003)*, volume 2884 of *LNCS*, pages 185–198, Paris, France, November 2003. Springer-Verlag.
10. Sonia Fagorzi, Elena Zucca, and Davide Ancona. Modeling Multiple Class Loaders by a Calculus for Dynamic Linking. In *Proceedings of the ACM Symposium on Applied Computing (SAC-2004)*, Nicosia, Cyprus, March 2004.
11. Shawn Farkas. .NET Security Blog. http://blogs.msdn.com/shawnfa, 2005.
12. Cathi Gero and Jeffrey Richter. The Future of Assembly Versioning. http://www.theserverside.net/articles/showarticle.tss?id=AssemblyVersioning, 2004.
13. T. Jensen, D. Le Metayer, and T. Thorn. Security and Dynamic Class Loading in Java: A Formalisation. In *Proceedings of the IEEE International Conference on Computer Languages*, pages 4–15, Chicago, IL, USA, 1998.
14. Sheng Liang and Gilad Bracha. Dynamic Class Loading in the Java Virtual Machine. In *Proceedings of the 13th ACM SIGPLAN Conference on Object-Oriented Programming, Systems, Languages & Applications (OOPSLA'98)*, Vancouver, BC, Canada, October 1998.
15. Eric Meijer and John Gough. *Technical Overview of the Common Language Runtime*. Microsoft, 2000.
16. Daniel Moth. http://www.danielmoth.com/Blog, 2004.
17. Steven Pratschner. .NET CF WebLog. http://blogs.msdn.com/stevenpr, 2005.
18. Zhenyu Qian, Allen Goldberg, and Alessandro Coglio. A Formal Specification of Java Class Loading. In *Proceedings of the 15th ACM SIGPLAN Conference on Object-Oriented Programming, Systems, Languages & Applications (OOPSLA 2000)*, pages 325–336, Minneapolis, MN, USA, 2000.
19. Alan Shi. The Fusion Weblog. http://blogs.msdn.com/alanshi, 2005.
20. Junfeng Zhang. .NET Framework Notes. http://blogs.msdn.com/junfeng, 2005.

A   Examples

C# examples that demonstrate heap contexts and assembly identity can be found at http://slurp.doc.ic.ac.uk/pubs/dynamicbindingindotnet-examples.pdf

Reuse Frequency as Metric for Dependency Resolver Selection

Karl Pauls[1] and Till G. Bay[2]

[1] Freie Universität Berlin,
Fachbereich Mathematik und Informatik,
Takustr. 9, D-14195 Berlin, Germany
pauls@inf.fu-berlin.de
[2] Eidgenössische Technische Hochschule Zürich,
Chair of Software Engineering,
ETH Zentrum, CH-8092 Zürich, Switzerland
bay@inf.ethz.ch

Abstract. The demand for component and service discovery engines to use in extensible applications is surging. No one so far has devoted much effort to metrics that aid selecting among different resolvers of the same dependency. This paper defines the Reuse Frequency: a metric that relates components or services to each other and measures their relative importance. Additionally, the ComponentGraph is presented that builds the averaged dependency graph of entities augmented with their popularity and the likelihood of each possible dependency resolver. The Reuse Frequency targets all scenarios where entities have dependencies on each other and a metric for the measurement of their relative importance is needed; the target implementation environment of the ComponentGraph is the Open Service Gateway Initiative framework, but the concepts are applicable to component or service repositories in general.

1 Introduction

Modern applications and software solutions increasingly center around loosely coupled and extensible architectures. Component or Service orientation is applied in almost all areas of application development including distributed systems, ubiquitous computing, embedded systems, and client-side applications. The concept of a component is broad, ranging from simple class files to plugins and other units of modularization. In general, component models and systems employing component-oriented approaches all define a concept similar to a component, e.g., an independently deployable executable unit of composition that is subject to composition by third parties [1].

The ability to compose a component is related to the component model's ability to express dependencies on other components. Dependencies describe prerequisites of a component. Component dependencies may exist at the deployment unit level, such as a dependency on a resource like a library, or they may exist at the instance level, such as a dependency on a service provided by

A. Dearle and S. Eisenbach (Eds.): CD 2005, LNCS 3798, pp. 164–176, 2005.

another component. As a consequence, deploying a component requires deploying the transitive closure of all its dependencies. In practice, if a component has dependencies, then it cannot be used until the transitive closure of all its dependencies is satisfied. This raises the issue of how to locate the resources required to resolve the dependencies [2].

The demand for component discovery engines to use in extensible applications is surging. Several partial solutions already exist, focusing on the discovery of components and the satisfaction of the transitive closure of their dependencies, but no one so far has devoted much effort to metrics that can aid in the selection among different resolvers of the same dependency. More specific, extensible applications face the situation where they can easily discover new extensions or services to make use of and resolve dependencies of chosen components but are unable to provide suggestions in a scenario where several components provide the same required resources, let alone making sound decisions automatically. To date, two approaches predominate: Namely, presenting the user with a list of possibilities together with a working (i.e., not necessarily optimal) suggestion of transitive closure resolving components or the definition of fixed sets of components by a specific provider. Both solutions however, present a problem when it comes to selection between multiple resolvers or resource providers respectively. Subsequently, a metric for weighing individual solutions, which could be called their popularity, becomes interesting. If one considers component dependencies as references to resolving resources (i.e., links), then this issue has much in common with measuring of the relative importance of web pages. Consequently, it is interesting to investigate whether the ideas from the web page popularity measurement domain are useful and/or applicable for component and service measurement.

To this end, this paper defines the Reuse Frequency of a component. The Reuse Frequency is a metric that relates components to each other and measures their relative importance. It is based on the topology of all possible dependency resolving graphs of a given repository. The main idea is that if a component A has a dependency to a component B, then A regards B as important enough to deserve being considered by and maybe deployed to an extensible system. In other words, the Reuse Frequency can be used as an order relation between possible extensions when presented to the end-user. It facilitates reasoning about the structure of entities in a component repository. Additionally, a tool is presented that builds the averaged dependency graph of entities in a repository, augmented with their popularity and the likelihood of each possible dependency resolver for each dependency of an entity, called the ComponentGraph. The Component-Graph allows reasoning about the structure of a given repository and shows the average relative importance of its entities.

Applying the Reuse Frequency to components enables to weight different dependency resolving transitive closures among each other, while their visualization via the ComponentGraph enables reasoning about overall coherence. The Reuse Frequency targets all scenarios where entities depend on each other and a metric for measuring their relative importance is needed. The target implementation environment of the ComponentGraph is the Open Service Gateway Initiative framework, but the concepts are applicable to component repositories in general. This paper derives and defines the Reuse Frequency in the next section, then the ComponentGraph is presented in detail; this is followed by usage scenarios and related work. The paper finishes with future work and conclusions.

2   Reuse Frequency

The usage of the term "component" in this paper is intended to be vague. In general, the meaning of component for this paper is an independently deployable executable unit of composition. An important advantage of Component Based Software Engineering is reuse. By reusing existing solutions to problems one can reduce time to market. Components capture solutions in a way that reuse is easier. Subsequently, it makes sense to measure the relative importance of a component by means of how often it is reused.

To this end, components may provide both service interfaces and resources to other components. Two levels of dependencies exist: deployment and instance. Deployment-level dependencies are on provided resources, such as libraries (e.g., Java packages), whereas instance-level dependencies are on component service interfaces. In the simplest case, the static structure of a set of resolved components is similar to web pages that link to each other. A dependency from one component on another is like a link from one web page to another. Consequently, it is interesting to investigate how techniques from web search engines can be applied in order to determine the popularity of a component. Fortunately, the ranking mechanism from one of the most popular web search engines is known: Google's PageRank.

2.1   PageRank Explained

Google's PageRank is a method to measure the relative importance of web pages. The main principles of PageRank are explained in a paper written by the two founders of Google [3]. The algorithm has most likely changed since that time but the basis remains the same. It is based on the topology of web pages i.e., a graph-like structure where entities are connected with arbitrary other entities by means of links. The general idea is to take only this structure into account when measuring the popularity of a page.

If page A has a link to page B, then page A "thinks" that page B is important enough to deserve being cited and maybe visited by visitors of page A [4]. In other words, a link from A to B increases the PageRank of B. Furthermore, the individual importance of a specific site is propagated to all sites it links to – hence, the higher the PageRank of page A, the higher the increase of the PageRank of page B. Furthermore, the propagated popularity of a page is split among all outgoing links i.e., the fewer pages A has links to other sites besides page B, the more the PageRank of B increases. These two properties of the PageRank algorithm add up to an interesting overall attribute of it – namely,

the more important the sites that link to a specific site and the more exclusive
the links are the higher is the importance of the site. The algorithm is iterative
and is defined as follows:

Definition 1. *PageRank*
Let A1, A2, ..., An: be n pages linking to page B. Let PR(Ak) be the PageRank
of page Ak, N(Ak) the number of outward links within page Ak, and d a damping
factor between 0 and 1, generally equal to 0.85. Then the PageRank of page B is
computed from the PageRank of all pages Ak in the following way:

$$PR(B) = (1-d) + d \ x \ (\ PR(A1) \ / \ N(A1) \ + \ ... \ + \ PR(An) \ / \ N(An) \ )$$

In other words: a page's PageRank = 0.15 + 0.85 * (a "share" of the PageRank of
every page that links to it) where "share" = the linking page's PageRank divided
by the number of outbound links on the page.

The algorithm appears simple at first sight, but the iterative approach adds
complexity. In order to calculate the PageRank of a specific site, the PageRank of
all pages linking to it must have been computed. This is addressed by assuming
an initial value of one. The damping factor is needed to prevent that the iteration
goes on forever. If it is too low the values will just drain away and converge to
zero. If it is too high the iteration may never settle hence, the proposed value
0.85 (out of the original paper) seems to be the most authoritative. Between 40
and 50 iterations are normally sufficient to let the individual values settle. In
practice, the convergence is obtained after several tens of iterations; depending
on the total number of pages.

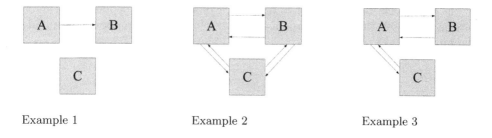

Example 1   Example 2   Example 3

Fig. 1. PageRank Examples

As a small set of examples (for more see [5]) consider the structure of pages
in Figure 1. In Example 1, site A has a link on page B while page C is not
connected. Once we apply the algorithm with an initial value for each page we
end up with: PR(A) = 0.15, PR(B) = 1, and PR(C) = 0.15 After a few iterations
the ranks have changed: PR(A) = 0.15, PR(B) = 0.2775, and PR(C) = 0.15.
This is where the values settle and we are done. The second example shows a
scenario where all sites are linking to each other. It is quite obvious that in a
situation like this the PageRank of the sites ends up being one, no matter how

many iterations. Finally, example 3 shows page A linking to both B and C. B and C are also linked to A. After the first iteration the results are: $PR(A) = 1.85$, $PR(B) = 0.575$, and $PR(C) = 0.575$. The results settle at: $PR(A) = 1.459459$, $PR(B) = 0.7702703$, and $PR(C) = 0.7702703$. In both cases page A ends up with a much larger proportion of the PageRank than the other two pages. This is because pages B and C are passing PageRank to A exclusively.

In summary, Google's PageRank lends itself well to calculate the relative importance of a page inside a fixed static set of pages. After the calculation shown in the examples the acquired values have to be normlized and scaled. The specific details of the normalizing and scaling (i.e., to/by which values) is up to the provider and not further explained by the authors [3]. In general, this must be decided based on the specific scenario. The next section derives the Reuse Frequency of a component and explains why the simple PageRank is not enough to capture dependencies among components.

2.2   Deriving the Reuse Frequency

As stated above, Google's PageRank lends itself well as a metric to measure relative importance of an entity in a static graph. Unfortunately, this is not the case in a component scenario. While it is possible to resolve the transitive closure of dependencies before execution, instance-level dependencies allow the possibility of dynamically extensible systems. To support extensible systems, a resource discovery service should not only provide support prior to runtime, but during runtime so that extensible systems can integrate new components dynamically. More importantly, a link is a fixed connection between two pages. A dependency of a component is the explicit need of a resource that is needed by the component in order for it to function. Consequently, a dependency can be satisfied by more than one component in case that several components provide the same resource.

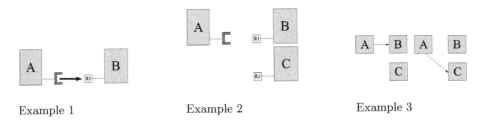

Example 1   Example 2   Example 3

Fig. 2. Multiple Resolver Dependency Graph Examples

Selecting a possible resolution of component dependencies actually shows a possible graph instance but not necessarily the one used at any given time. Since we assume an arbitrary framework, it is up to the specific framework to decide how it resolves a dependency in the case that multiple components export the same dependency satisfying resource. Subsequently, the links in the overall dependency graph are actually more, if such multiple exporters exist. Selecting any given resolution would give different metrics. Consider a situation similar to the examples shown in Figure 2. In Example 1, we see component A that depends on resource R1 which can be provided by the component B. Example 2 then displays the multiple resolver scenario. A's dependency on R1 could be resolved by either B or C. This effectively, leads to the situation where two possible graph instances exist (i.e., Example 3).

Assuming one would apply PageRank to this scenario two different outputs are possible. On the one hand, $PR(A) = 0.15$, $PR(B) = 0.2775$, and $PR(C) = 0.15$ on the other hand, $PR(A) = 0.15$, $PR(B) = 0.2775$, and $PR(C) = 0.2775$. To remedy this issue, we propose to define the Reuse Frequency as follows:

Definition 2. *Reuse Frequency*
Let CS be a set of components. Let DG1,...DGn be all possible resolution graphs of CS. Let the component rank CR(Ci, DGk) be the PR(Ci) in the graph DGk. Let N(C,CS) be the number of DGs for the C in CS. Then the Reuse Frequency of a component C is computed from the CR of C in all DGi in the following way:

$$RF(C) = CR(C,DG1) + CR(C, DG2) + ... + CR(C, DGn) / N(C,CR)$$

In other words: the Reuse Frequency of a component C out of a repository R is the average of all component ranks of C in every possible resolving context out of R.

Consider Example 2 from Figure 2 again. Firstly, we need to calculate the possible resolution graphs of the components A, B, and C. Example 3 shows the two possible graphs DG1 and DG2. Subsequently, we can build the component ranks: $CR(A,DG1) = 0.15$, $CR(B,DG1) = 0.2775$, $CR(C,DG1) = 0.15$, $CR(A,DG2) = 0.15$, $CR(B,DG2) = 0.15$, $CR(C,DG2) = 0.2775$. It follows that the Reuse Frequencies are: $RF(A) = 0.15$, $RF(B) = 0,214$, $RF(C) = 0,214$. The two components B and C end up with a higher Reuse Frequency than A. This is due to both of them being a resolver in one graph or the other. Note that nevertheless, their RF is less than their PR would be in case they are resolvers but higher than their PR in the case they were not.

In general, the Reuse Frequency gives a better estimation of the relative importance than the PageRank due to the nature of component dependencies. However, when locating components a resource discovery service should support at least two different ways to search components: by what a component provides and by what it requires. Subsequently, the question remains whether the Reuse Frequency can be applied in both scenarios. In the definition given here, the metric clearly targets the scenario where it is beneficial to prefer components that are more important (i.e., have a higher likeliness to be reused). This can be cumbersome when what one actually wants is to determine those components that will make the most out of the already installed components (i.e., by what a component provides). Consequently, the Reuse Frequency can be inverted:

Definition 3. *Inverted Reuse Frequency*
Let CS be a set of components. Let DG1,...DGn be all possible resolution graphs of CS. Let INV(DGk) be the inverted graph where all the source and target of

each link is exchanged. Let the inverted component rank ICR(Ci, DGk) be the PR(Ci) in the graph INV(DGk). Let N(C,CS) be the number of DGs for the C in CS. Then the Reuse Frequency of a component C is computed from the ICR of C in all DGi in the following way:

$$IRF(C) = ICR(C,DG1) + ICR(C,DG2) + ... + ICR(C,DGn) / N(C,CR)$$

In other words: the inverted Reuse Frequency of a component C out of a repository R is the average of all component ranks of C in every possible resolving context out of R where for each context the source and target of a dependency is exchanged.

Example 2 from Figure 2 can be used as an example again. INV(DG1) leads to B linking A. INV(DG2) leads to C linking A. It follows that: ICR(A,DG1) = 0.2775, ICR(B,DG1) = 0.15, ICR(B,DG1) = 0.15, ICR(A,DG2) = 0.2775, ICR(B,DG2) = 0.15, ICR(C,DG2) =0.15. Finally: IRF(A) = 0.2775, IRF(B) = 0.15, IRF(C) = 0.15. Component A ends up with a higher inverted Reuse Frequency indicating that it would integrate (i.e., make use of) best with the other components.

3   ComponentGraph

The ComponentGraph is a Java and OSGi [6] based tool for the visualization of component dependencies. Its main purpose is to visualize the component graph of components of a repository.

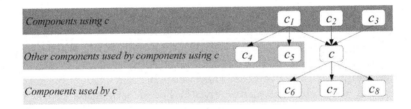

Fig. 3. ComponentGraph showing three possible queries

Like the structure of html documents that are linked to each other, components depending on each other span a directed graph. The component dependencies can be viewed synonymous to the hyper-links in html documents. See Figure 3 for an illustration of an ensemble of components that use each other - the resulting graph looks similar to what we know from linked html documents. The analogy is not complete - it is for example very common to have cycles for the Web Graph while it is seldom for the ComponentGraph. ComponentGraphs are the averaged dependency graphs of entities (See Figure 3 for an illustration of a very small ComponentGraph):

Definition 4. *ComponentGraph*

$$CG = (N,E)$$

where each node $n \in N$ is a component and each edge $e \in E$ is a dependency among two nodes.

After constructing the Graph with components as nodes and component dependencies as edges, the Reuse Frequency of the components is calculated. It is stored along with the Graph nodes. The ComponentGraph is now complete and can be used for assessing components. Figure 4 shows the ComponentGraph tool displaying the averaged dependency graphs of a specific example repository augmented with their popularity and the likelihood of each possible dependency resolver.

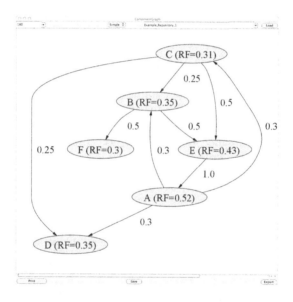

Fig. 4. ComponentGraph Showing an Example Graph

4 Case Study

This section presents the application of our Component Assessment System to a concrete component repository. The next paragraph briefly introduces the three used technologies namely OSGi [6], Eureka [2], and Gravity [7], followed by the case-study.

The Open Services Gateway Initiative (OSGi) framework and service specification, was defined by the OSGi Alliance to deploy, activate, and manage service-oriented applications dynamically. The OSGi framework, that sits on top of a Java virtual machine, is an execution environment for services. It defines a unit of modularization, called a bundle, that is both a deployment and an activation unit. Physically, a bundle is a Java JAR file containing a single component. After installing a bundle, it can be activated if all of its Java package dependencies are satisfied. Package dependency metadata is contained in the manifest of the JAR file. Bundles can export/import Java packages to/from each other - these are deployment-level dependencies. After a bundle is activated it can provide or use service implementations of other bundles within the framework. A service is a Java interface with externally specified semantics. When a bundle uses a service, an instance-level dependency on the provider of that service is created. Technically, the OSGi service framework can be boiled down [8] to a custom and dynamic Java class loader and service registry that is globally accessible within a single Java virtual machine. The custom class loader maintains a set of dynamically changing bundles that share classes and resources among each other and interact via services published in the global service registry.

Eureka is a network-based resource discovery service supporting deployment and run-time integration of components into extensible systems using Rendezvous' DNS-based approach [9]. Publishing and discovery of components can be performed in both wide-area and local-link (i.e., ad-hoc) networks.

Gravity [7] is a research project investigating the dynamic assembly of applications and the impact of building applications from components that exhibit dynamic availability, i.e., they may appear or disappear at anytime. Gravity is built as a standard OSGi bundle and provides a graphical design environment for building application using drag-and-drop techniques. Using Gravity, an application is assembled dynamically and the end user is able to switch at anytime between design and execution mode. Eureka was integrated into the Gravity user interface to enable end user discovery of components for integration into his running application.

4.1   Component Discovery and Deployment Case Study

For this case-study we communicate with an OSGi component repository. The discovered components are then fed back into an Eureka network, annotated with their Reuse Frequency. This allows an ordering of the displayed components in Gravity.

Eureka as a Component Metadata Provider allows extracting dependencies of discovered bundles. Additionally, existing repositories can also be queried using the Eureka API. In the next step, the ComponentGraph is created showing a network of bundles connected by their dependencies. Since our Component Assessment System is component model agnostic deployment and instance level dependencies can be treated equally in the resulting view.

Component Discovery is enabled via a special filter integrated into the Component Assessment System and applied in case a bundle is discovered. Subsequently, the filter uses Eureka to extract the dependencies of the bundle while storing the metadata in an Eureka controlled component repository. The component is now available to clients via Eureka using this repository. Additionally, we write the Reuse Frequency into the component's metadata.

Reuse Frequency used as Order Relation in OSGi based applications has been evaluated using the Eureka enhanced Gravity. As mentioned above, Gravity provides a resource discovery that enables the user to extend an application at runtime. For example, an editor component could be extended by a spell-checker or a buffer switcher. More specifically, the dependencies of the underlying component serve as a means of filtering the suggested components. In a situation where the amount of suggested components is small the order of the suggestions has low importance. If many components are found, that resolve a specific dependency, Reuse Frequency is used to order the displayed suggestions. The order of the suggestion list provides the user with additional information. Firstly, it is likely that by choosing one of the more prominent suggestions (i.e., one with a higher Reuse Frequency) over a less prominent one with a similar or equal functionality (e.g., two different spell-checkers are available) the one with the higher importance is chosen. Secondly, by following the former approach the assembled application will be more extendable since heavily reused components will be added and therefore more suggestions will become available.

4.2   ComponentGraph Case Study

At the moment two free OSGi R3 [10] framework implementations are available. Both projects provide a small component repository. Both contain the implementation of the OSGi R3 service specification. Oscar [11] from Richard S. Hall is part of ObjectWeb [12] and Knopflerfish [13] is based on the Gatespace GDSP OSGi framework. In order to present the ComponentGraph and to intuitively validate the assumption that the visualization of component dependencies combined with the calculation of their Reuse Frequency allows reasoning about the popularity of components both repositories have been inspected. Future work will include empirical analysis of other repositories and focus on conclusions that can be derived directly from the visualizations or the calculated Reuse Frequencies.

Figure 5 shows a subset of the Oscar repository augmented with the Reuse Frequency of the components. Due to the Reuse Frequency of the example one can reason about the importance of the participating components. Furthermore, information about the likeliness that a component may function because all of its dependencies are satisfied is conveyed. The two components with the highest

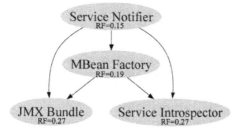

Fig. 5. Partial ComponentGraph of Oscar's Bundle Repository

Reuse Frequency (JMX Bundle and Service Introspector) are self-contained (i.e., deployable without any assumptions about the availability of other components). One step down the hierarchy the MBean Factory can be found - it has dependencies on the two aforementioned bundles. At last the Service Notifier depends on all of the other inspected components and has the lowest rank, because no other components depend on it. This observations empirically support the intuitive assumption that the Reuse Frequency can be used as an order relation as in our Gravity case-study.

Apart from Oscar and Knopflerfish a third free OSGi implementation exists supporting underlying the last release of Eclipse [14]. Eclipse is a kind of universal tool platform. Eclipse uses it's own OSGi framework implementation as a plugin mechanism and provides the possibility to discover, deploy, and dynamically integrate plugins (i.e., bundles) from remote sources. The entry point for the remote repositories is the Eclipse web site. A ComponentGraph using Eclipse plugins promises to be an overwhelming source for empirical validations of our assumptions.

5   Related Work

The problem of selecting the best possible resolver of a dependency applies not only to component or service based systems but to plugin frameworks as well. In plugin based systems the dependencies are not imperative [15] [16].

Automatic component discovery is closely related to other search and matching problems such as: text document matching, web search and web service matching.

Text Document Matching and classification is a well studied problem in information retrieval. Popular solutions to the problem are based on term frequency analysis [17], [18], [19]. In our case term frequency can be used once we extend our infrastructure to also include component documentation into the assessment process. However it will be a supplementary information source to the dependency relations that we are extracting from the source code or the component repositories.

Web Search inspires techniques proposed in this paper. We compare component architectures to the world wide web. We suggest addressing the component searching problem specifically by using component specific information. Web search should nevertheless influence component search since for example component documentation is normally deployed on the web.

Web Service Matching. In Woogle [20] the authors propose unsupervised matching of web services at the operation level. Web services comply to the notion of a software component and the technologies shown for matching on the operation level can contribute to the information stored in the ComponentGraph.

The Oscar Bundle Repository [21] is an incubator and repository for OSGi bundles. It promotes a community effort around bundle creation by increasing the visibility of individual bundles. OBR provides diverse simple access mechanisms for the bundles in the repository.

Knopflerfish's Spin Visualization. Knopflerfish is an open source implementation of the OSGi framework. Apart from other extra functionality it provides a view of installed bundles where the dependencies among bundles are shown. The application used to visualize (Spin) allows selecting an installed bundle and see how its dependencies are resolved.

Gravity's Architecture Viewer allows introspecting the architecture of the running application. In other words, a visualization of the currently installed services together with their dependencies.

6   Conclusion and Future Work

In this paper we defined the Reuse Frequency as a metric for the relative importance of components and presented how Reuse Frequency can be used for component assessment. Together with the Component Assessment System and the ComponentGraph and the Reuse Frequency calculation it contains, our method can be applied to many different component repositories. Using Eureka as a concrete example we demonstrated how Reuse Frequency establishes an order on the components involved and can be used to compare the importance of different components. The possibility to generalize our method to other component technologies or component information of different granularity makes it attractive for general component assessment. Future work includes more assessments on large component repositories like the Eclipse plugins, the Linux RPM archive or the archive of Debian packages. How we will address versioning of components and integrate it with the Reuse Frequency is currently investigated in this context.

Acknowledgments. We would like to thank Max Haustein for his help in the conceptual design of the ComponentGraph and Manuel Oriol for providing us with helpful comments on the draft of this paper. We also thank the anonymous reviewers as well as the reviewers for an earlier version, which appeared as an ETH Zurich technical report [22], for all their valuable comments.

References

1. C. Szyperski: Component Software: Beyond Object-Oriented Programming. ACM Press/Addison-Wesley Publishing Co., New York, NY, USA (1998)
2. Karl Pauls and Richard S. Hall: Eureka - A Resource Discovery Service for Component Deployment. In: Proceedings of the 2nd International Working Conference on Component Deployment (CD 2004). (2004)
3. Sergey Brin and Lawrence Page: The Anatomy of a Large-Scale Hypertextual Web Search Engine (last visit June 2005) www-db.stanford.edu/ backrub/google.html.
4. webrankinfo.com: PageRank   Explained   (last   visit   June   2005) www.webrankinfo.com/english/pagerank/#1.
5. Craven, P.: Google's PageRank Explained and how to make the most of it (last visit June 2005) www.webworkshop.net/pagerank.html.

6. OSGi Alliance: OSGi Alliance. Official Web Site, http://www.osgi.org (2004)
7. Richard S. Hall and H. Cervantes: Gravity: Supporting Dynamically Available Services in Client-Side Applications. In: Poster paper in Proceedings of ESEC/FSE 2003. (2003)
8. Richard S. Hall and H. Cervantes: An OSGi Implementation and Experience Report. In: Proceedings of IEEEConsumer Communications and Networking Conference. (2004)
9. Apple Computer, Inc.: Rendezvous. Official Web Site, http://developer.apple.com/macosx/rendezvous/ (2004)
10. The Open Services Gateway Initiative: OSGi Service Platform. IOS Press, Amsterdam, The Netherlands (2003) Release 3.
11. Oscar Community: Official Web Site (2004) http://oscar.objectweb.org.
12. Object Web: Official Web Site (2004) http://www.objectweb.org/.
13. Knopflerfish OSGi: Official Web Site (2004) http://www.knopflerfish.org/.
14. The Eclipse Foundation: Eclipse Platform - Technical Overview. Technical report, Object Technology International Inc. (2003)
15. Chatley, C.R.: Magicbeans: a platform for deploying plugin (2004)
16. M. Oriol, G.D.M.S.: A disconnected service architecture for unanticipated runtime evolution of code. IEE Proceedings-Software, Special Issue on Unanticipated Software Evolution 151 (2004) 95–107
17. Scott Cost and Steven Salzberg: A Weighted Nearest Neighbor Algorithm for Learning with Symbolic Features. Machine Learning 10 (1993) 57–78 http://citeseer.ist.psu.edu/cost93weighted.html.
18. Larkey, L.S., Croft, W.B.: Combining classifiers in text categorization. In Frei, H.P., Harman, D., Schäuble, P., Wilkinson, R., eds.: Proceedings of SIGIR-96, 19th ACM International Conference on Research and Development in Information Retrieval, Zürich, CH, ACM Press, New York, US (1996) 289–297
19. Yang, Y., Pedersen, J.O.: A comparative study on feature selection in text categorization. In Fisher, D.H., ed.: Proceedings of ICML-97, 14th International Conference on Machine Learning, Nashville, US, Morgan Kaufmann Publishers, San Francisco, US (1997) 412–420
20. Xin Dong et Al.: Simlarity Search for Web Services. In: Very Large Data Bases. (2004) 582–599
21. Richard S. Hall: Oscar Bundle Repository - Official Web Site. http://oscar-osgi.sf.net (2004)
22. Bay, T.G., Pauls, K.: Reuse frequency as metric for component assessment. Technical Report 464, ETH Zürich (2004) www.inf.ethz.ch/research/publications/techreports/show?serial=464&lang=en.

ORYA: A Strategy Oriented Deployment Framework

Pierre-Yves Cunin, Vincent Lestideau, and Noëlle Merle

Adèle team, LSR – IMAG, 220 Rue de la Chimie,
Domaine Universitaire – BP 53, 38041 Grenoble Cedex 9, France
{Pierre-Yves.Cunin, Vincent.Lestideau, Noelle.Merle}@imag.fr
http://www-adele.imag.fr/

Abstract. The current trend consists in deploying, on each machine, a specific version of an application, according to the choices of the enterprise and users, with constraints verified by the target site. To support automated deployment, we propose a model-based deployment framework named ORYA which allows to define and execute deployment strategies. This paper presents and illustrates the concept of deployment strategy supported by the framework.

1 Introduction

Various approaches exist to deploy an application on a set of target machines. One possibility is to create a deployment plan and then to execute it. To produce automatically this plan, we define models which describe *units* to deploy, *target machines* and *enterprise structure* [1]. The *application model* defines the deployment unit (a version of an application) with properties, constraints and dependencies. The *site model* describes the hardware and software configuration of a target machine with properties. The *enterprise model* collects machines into groups and subgroups.

A *property* describes a feature of a unit or a machine. A *constraint*, associated to a deployment unit, expresses a property the target must have. A *strategy*, attached to an enterprise entity (group, machine), expresses a constraint imposed by the enterprise.

Section 2 presents fundamental aspects of our strategy-based approach.Section 3 presents a use case. Section 4 concludes with future works and objectives.

2 Deployment Strategies

Large scale deployment is a complex action that cannot be done by hand. Often the deployers use in-house defined deployment strategies to ensure the right quality level of operation (security, homogeneity, standards, …). In some approaches strategies are included (hard coded) within the deployment tools [2]. Therefore a deployer cannot define new ones, better adapted to his needs. Our objective is to help deployers expressing advanced deployment strategies and to provide a framework for piloting strategy-based deployments. An outcome will be a new version of our deployment environment ORYA [3, 4, 5] based also on the GDF experiment [6].

A. Dearle and S. Eisenbach (Eds.): CD 2005, LNCS 3798, pp. 177–180, 2005.

2.1 Approach and Algorithm Principle

We assume that the strategies are expressed only on sites and groups. Strategies belong to the enterprise and therefore are attached to the entities of the enterprise structure. Each strategy is applied to the current set of deployable units.

A strategy is a 3-uple <LogicalExpression, Activity, Choice> The *Activity* specifies one phase of the deployment. In this paper we consider only the *Initial Deployment* phase. During the *Activity*, the *LogicalExpression* is evaluated for all the current deployable units, i.e. the current *application structure (AS)*. This gives two sub-sets: the "*true* set" and the "*false* set". Then the *Choice*, its associated actions, is applied to these two sets depending on the semantics of the strategy. The result is an *AS* made of the remaining deployable units.

There exist many strategies, for example: enforce the same version on a set of machines, allow replacement of a version by a newer one, favor the deployment of a unit having some characteristic (e.g. choose a unit written in Java instead of the same in C++), deploy the dependencies of a unit before the unit itself, deploy a unit on a group of machines before on another one, roll back during the execution of the plan, due to a change of the environment (e.g. the needed resources are no more available).

The algorithm is a parsing of the *enterprise structure(ES)* with propagation of an *AS* through the whole structure. On each node, strategies are applied in order to prune the *AS*. On a machine node, the constraints of the units are checked.

Strategies can be classified in three main categories: strategies to select units having specific properties, strategies to define the ordering of the plan and strategies used during the execution of the plan (mainly to handle errors).

A strategy is defined by its basic behavior and the following features: 1) the **scope**: a strategy may be attached to a group or a single machine, 2) the **visibility**: a strategy attached to a group may or may not hide - may or may not be overloaded by - any similar strategy expressed on a sub-node, 3) the **propagation**: a strategy attached to a group may impose collecting information about the sub-nodes, 4) the **precedence**: several strategies may have to be applied at the same time on the same node.

2.2 Strategies VERSION-RIGHT and VERSION-SCOPE

To illustrate some characteristics, we focus on two strategies .

1. Strategy VERSION-RIGHT is attached to a group or a single machine and can be applied without additional information (e.g. from sub-nodes, if any). If Choice is NO, units of the "true set" cannot be deployed on the machine(s of the group) and the resulting *AS* is made of the "false set". If Choice is ONLY, only units of the "true set" can be deployed on the machine(s of the group)and the *AS* is made of the "true set".

2. Strategy VERSION-SCOPE. is a complex strategy used to ensure coherence on versions deployed on all the machines of a group. The semantics of the strategy depends on Choice: a) if ANY, each machine may have a different version and the units of the "false set" are discarded. b) if SAME-TRUE, the units of the "false set" are discarded and one same unit, of the "true set", should be deployed on all machines and should be compatible with the configuration of each machine. c) other values are possible, for example *SAME-IF-TRUE* means that each machine may have a unit of the "*false* set" or the same unit of the "*true* set".

The application of the strategy is different for each value of *Choice*: a) if *ANY*, the strategy is immediately applied at the level of the group node and the new *AS* is equal to the "*true* set". b) if *SAME-TRUE*, the "*true* set" is propagated as *AS*, through a recursive parsing of the *ES*, together with a query about what units of this set can be deployed . When this information is made available at the level of the group node, the *AS* is constructed as the set of the units deployable on every machine. During this recursive parsing local strategies *VERSION-SCOPE* or *VERSION-RIGHTS* on sub-nodes have to be applied before treating the "propagated" query and set of units

3   Use Case

The two representations structures are shown in Fig. 1. The *ES* represents the target on which to deploy. The *AS* represents possible units, with their characteristics and dependencies. The deployer wants to deploy the application *U* on the machines of the group *G*. *G* is composed of two groups *G1*, composed of machines *M1* and *M2*, and *G2*. *G2* contains the machine *M3* and the group *G3*, itself composed of machines *M4* and *M5*. The machines have properties specifying operating system (*OS*), memory capacity (*Mem*) and available disk space (*Disk*). Strategies *VS* (*VERSION-SCOPE* strategy) and *VR* (*VERSION-RIGHTS* strategy) are defined, on nodes *G* and *G1*.

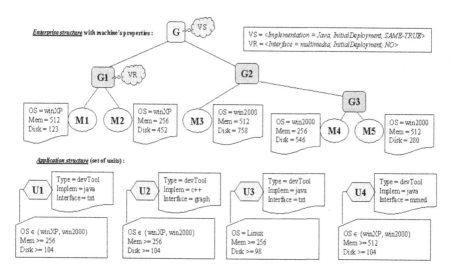

Fig. 1. *Enterprise structure (ES) and Application structure (AS)*

The application *U* is available in four versions, described by properties: type, programming language, interface type. Each unit forces constraints : a set of possible operating system, a minimal memory capacity, a minimal available disk space.

On G, the application of the strategy *VS* requires information from the sub-nodes. The "*true* set" of units *{U1, U3, U4}* is propagated to *G1* and *G2*. **On G1**, the strategy VR is applied and the set *{U1, U3}* is propagated to *M1* and *M2*. Then the constraints are checked and *U3* is discarded because it imposes *Linux* as OS. So the set *{U1}* for

M1 and *M2* is sent back to *G* through *G1*. **On *G2***, the set *{U1, U3, U4}* is propagated to *M3* and *G3*. The set *{U1, U4}* for *M3* is sent back to *G* through *G2*. **On *G3***, the set *{U1, U3, U4}* is propagated to *M4* and *M5*. The sets *{U1}* for *M4* (*U4* is discarded due to the memory capacity) and *{U1, U4}* for *M5* are sent back to *G* through *G3* and *G2*. **Back to *G***: the strategy VS is finally applied and the $\underline{AS}$ is build as the intersection of the sets of all the machines: *{U1}*. Therefore, in that example, only this unit could be installed on all the machines.

4 Future Work and Objectives

We have defined and prototyped a design and execution framework. A set of basic strategies has been defined The approach has been validated through real size experiments [7] with simple strategies.

In the example we have not taken into account the dependencies that may exist for each unit. Dependency units are units themselves. Trying to apply strategies to dependencies introduces "meta" strategies, e.g.: should a strategy, applied to a unit, be also applied to its dependencies ? Should we evaluate the *LogicalExpression* of a strategy on (all) the dependencies of a unit ? Should we consider dependencies as being standard units on which apply the strategy algorithm ? The approach we use is an MDE (Model Driven Engineering) compatible one based on three interacting levels: strategy instances, strategy model and strategy metamodel (meta-strategies).

References

1. Merle N., Un méta-modèle pour l'automatisation du déploiement d'applications logicielles. DECOR'04. Grenoble, France. Octobre 2004.
2. Ayed D., Taconet C., Sabri N., Bernard G.: CADeComp : plate-forme de déploiement sensible au contexte des applications à base de composants. 4ème Conférence Française sur les Systèmes d'Exploitation (CFSE'05). Le Croisic, France. 5-8 avril 2005
3. Lestideau V., Belkhatir N., Cunin P.-Y.: Towards automated software component configuration and deployment. PDTSD'02. Orlando, Florida, USA. July 2002.
4. Lestideau V.: Modèles et environnement pour configurer et déployer des systèmes logiciels. PHD Thesis, Université deSavoie, December 2003, http://www-adele.imag.fr/Les.Publications/BD/PHD2003Les.html
5. Merle N., Belkhatir N., Open Architecture for Building Large Scale Deployment Systems The 2004 International Conference on Software Engineering Research and Practice (SERP'04), Las Vegas, Nevada, USA, June 2004
6. On-demand Service Installation and Activation with OSGi. ObjectWebCon05 : Fourth Annual ObjectWeb Conference. January 2005,Lyon, France.
7. Centr'Actoll web site : http://www-adele.imag.fr/Les.Groupes/centractoll/index.html

Deployment of Infrastructure and Services in the Open Grid Services Architecture (OGSA)*

Paul Brebner[1] and Wolfgang Emmerich[2]

[1] CSIRO ICT Centre, PO Box 664, Canberra, ACT 2601, Australia
Paul.Brebner@csiro.au
http://www.ict.csiro.au/staff/paul.brebner
[2] Department of Computer Science, University College London,
London WC1E 6BT, United Kingdom
W.Emmerich@cs.ucl.ac.uk
http://www.cs.ucl.ac.uk/staff/W.Emmerich

Abstract. The ability to deploy Grid infrastructure and services across organizational boundaries (rapidly, reliably, and scalably) is critical for the success of large-scale service based grids such as OGSA. We report the results of the UK-OGSA Evaluation Project infrastructure and services deployment experiments, and analytically compare application versus service deployment. The use of a 3rd party component deployment technology to remotely automate installation and service deployment is discussed, and outstanding problems and potential solutions and benefits are presented. We conclude that grid deployment must be treated as a first-order activity by integrating secure deployment capabilities into the middleware, to enable deployment of secured infrastructure and services across organizations.

1 Grid Deployment Introduction

The UK Open Grid Services Architecture (OGSA) Evaluation [1] was a one year project to establish an experimental OGSA-based [2] grid for the UK E-Science community. The novel focus of the project was to gain insight into issues related to deploying OGSA across organizational boundaries from software engineering and architectural perspectives. Globus Toolkit 3.2 (GT3.2 [3]) was chosen as the exemplar OGSA technology, but the evaluation was designed for the conclusions to be valid for other Service Oriented Architecture (SOA) infrastructures, including GT4. This paper is based on reports and presentations documenting the experimental outcomes of the project [4, 5] and an analytical evaluation of Globus mechanisms [6].

A SOA supports distinct lifecycle steps, namely service development, service deployment, service registration, service discovery and service consumption. In an intra-organizational enterprise context, there are two distinct roles associated with these steps: Provider and Consumer. The provider is responsible for development, deployment and registration of services behind a firewall. The consumer is typically

---

* This research was funded under EPSRC grant GR/S78346/01.

A. Dearle and S. Eisenbach (Eds.): CD 2005, LNCS 3798, pp. 181–195, 2005.
© Springer-Verlag Berlin Heidelberg 2005

external to the organization, outside the firewall, and discovers and consumes services. The provider role is therefore intra-organizational, while the consumer role is inter-organizational. However, in the Grid community the role division is different. End-user scientists typically develop their own applications, locate resources to run them on, deploy and execute them on these resources, and manage them. The focus is on end-user development, deployment and use, resulting in an overlap of provider and consumer roles, crossing organizational boundaries and firewalls.

GT3 supports end-user deployment of *applications* using mechanisms including: Grid Services, Grid Security Infrastructure (GSI), Master Managed Job Factory Service (MMJFS), Resource Specification Language (RSL-2), data transfer services (Grid File Transfer Protocol - GridFTP, Global Access to Secondary Storage – GASS) and index services (Globus Monitoring and Discovery System - MDS3). For authorized users these allow: job submission services (MMJFS) to be discovered; applications and data to be transferred onto the target machine; resources requested, scheduled and allocated; jobs submitted, run and monitored; and end-users notified upon completion - across organizational boundaries and firewalls.

However, GT3 does not support cross-organizational end-user deployment of grid *services*. This means that an end-user can not easily deploy their science code to resources behind firewalls as a "1st order" grid service. A grid service is an implementation of a Grid Service port type, described (with GWSDL a grid extension of WSDL 1.1), packaged (in a Grid Archive "GAR" file), deployed across organizations to all the containers available to a Virtual Organization (VO), registered in a VO index service, and is discoverable and callable by all the users in the VO who are authorized to use it.

Support for end-user deployment of applications, but not services, reflects two different ways of using a SOA for Grid computing: resource-centric versus service-centric. Scientific applications have typically been large monolithic applications written in legacy languages (e.g. Fortran), for proprietary high performance computing (HPC) architectures. GT3 is designed as a resource-centric infrastructure to allow legacy applications to portably utilize heterogeneous Grid resources. GT3 uses services as *infrastructure* services, to resource science as *applications*. End-users are not expected to deploy new services, but to use pre-existing services to deploy and run their applications. This approach is resource-centric, resourcing *by* services, Web Services enabling of Grids. We define this as a "2nd order" approach, since science is not exposed directly as grid services, only indirectly via infrastructure services. The other approach is service-centric, resourcing *of* services, Grid enabling of Web Services. We define this as a "1st order" approach, since it enables science to be deployed, resourced, and used directly as distinguished grid services.

SOAs exhibit a number of desirable features that are lost if direct execution of science as 1st order services is not supported, including: rich SOA patterns (e.g. proxies for monitoring service use); work-flows for the design and execution of flexible and portable applications and services (through recursive composition); loose coupling of client and service by registration/discovery of services and service descriptions and dynamic binding; and interoperability by conformance to Web Standards.

The original intention of GT3 was also to enhance the *implementation* of Grid services by extending Web Services with a rich component model. In fact, OGSI [7] was explicitly based on J2EE [8]. The OGSI component model includes a set of conventions for service naming and reference, common and extended interfaces and behaviour support for dynamic instance-specific meta-data, and run-time support to manage service lifecycles. Service level security provides a fine-grained security model allowing different levels of access to services, instances and methods. The component model can be used for the development of 1st order science services as well as infrastructure services.

A non-trivial aspect of deployment is Grid infrastructure installation. We consider this to be in the scope of deployment requirements since correct installation and configuration of infrastructure is a precondition for service deployment.

This paper focuses on GT3 infrastructure, application, and service deployment by end-users across organizational boundaries. Sections 2 and 3 compare GT3 installation and deployment for 1st and 2nd order approaches. Scenarios for installation and deployment for each approach are described and an analysis is performed based on the impact of GT3 components and mechanisms on quality attributes. Section 4 details the results of experiments to automate remote installation and deployment, and section 5 reviews related work. Finally, in section 6 we conclude with outstanding problems, potential solutions and benefits of supporting deployment as a 1st order activity in OGSA.

2   Installation of Grid Infrastructure

The grid infrastructure installation scenario steps are as follows: obtain infrastructure components (Globus, and supporting software); discover and select hosts to install to; determine host specific configuration information; install on selected hosts; configure installation on each host; secure installation on each host; start/stop container and services. Related tasks include: Validate installation; discover installation state (what is installed, versions, and configurations); trace installation progress; detect and debug installation failures; reinstall selected components; un-install selected components; install client-side infrastructure and security.

Several months were spent installing GT3 infrastructure across the project's four test-bed sites [4]. The installation experiences varied because of a combination of factors including: platform heterogeneity; site-specific security, and access policies; degree of familiarity with Globus technology; and GT3's fragile build process and complex package structure. Consequently, substantial effort was expended diagnosing and rectifying installation, configuration and access problems, resulting in the following insights.

2.1   Common Infrastructure for 1st and 2nd Order Approaches: Core Package, Tomcat Container, Security, Globus Monitoring and Discovery System (MDS3).

Core Package. Installation of the Core package (pure java container related services) and container (e.g. Tomcat) is relatively straightforward, but requires understanding and configuration of Globus and site-specific requirements and policies for installation, access, accounts, and security. On some sites Globus was treated as production software and installed by systems administrators, entailing extra effort to separate and support roles (for installation, configuration, container management, and deployment). Testing the core installation without security is feasible and is an important step, since it is critical to ensure basic access and functionality before enabling security, as security interferes with remote testing.

Security. Security infrastructure is required for the 2nd order approach, but only for a secured production version of the 1st order approach. In theory the 1st order approach does not require the complete "All Services" package to be installed (the complete middleware stack, which is not pure Java), but some sites installed it for a variety of reasons making security more difficult to install, configure and use than expected [4].

In order to emulate a realistic production grid environment we requested and obtained host and client certificates from the UK e-Science Certification Authority [9]. Accounts were requested and created for users on each site, and client certificate subjects and account mappings configured in "grid-map" files on all nodes. Hosts were configured to use host certificates, client-side security infrastructure was installed and configured, and client-side code was modified to call services with the required security protocol. Unfortunately there is no portable client-side package including security and we were unable to get secured client-side code working under Windows. There are significant problems with certificate management, including the application, acquisition, storing, use, renewing, and revocation processes. A major problem is the lack of scalability of installation and management of security, particularly due to the necessity to provide a unique local account per user, and to map user certificates to local accounts in grid-map files.

It may be possible to run services securely without having individual client accounts on the host machines, making the security process more scalable. It is also not obvious that the GSI approach to security is either sufficient or necessary for a 1st order approach, since GSI was designed for the 2nd order approach and supports proxy certificates, single sign-on, and delegation of credentials. A different security infrastructure may be more appropriate for a 1st order approach, for example, one supporting role based authorization.

Testing and debugging the installation with security enabled is difficult. It is impossible to determine the security configuration of containers and services remotely and to debug calls to secure stateful service instances, since these preclude the use of non-invasive tracing techniques such as proxy interception of calls. It is essential to install infrastructure with tracing and debugging components enabled (E.g. the Axis SOAP handler, SOAPMonitor, and remote Tomcat management; although these have their own security requirements).

MDS3. MDS3 supports a rich index service model, allowing Service Data Elements (SDEs) to be collected, updated, aggregated, cached, persisted and queried for service instances in a variety of configurations. MDS3 was relatively easy to install, configure and test across sites, although it is not part of the core package, many manual configuration and testing steps were required, and configuration errors were not discovered until run-time.

Data Transfer. For 1st order services we assume that SOAP attachments are sufficient for data transfer. In practice they are unlikely to be adequate due to bugs in SOAP attachments in Axis/Globus, a practical upper limit to attachment sizes of 1GB, limited scalability, and incompatibility with security. Otherwise the OGSA data transfer services must also be installed (but are problematic to use with services, see [5]).

2.2   Extra 2nd Order Infrastructure: "All Services", and Data Transfer

The 2nd order approach needs the "All Services" package to be installed and configured, including MMJFS (the Job Manager, part of the Web Service Globus Resource Allocation Manager, or GRAM, component), a resource scheduler, and data transfer services. We did not attempt to use a real resource/batch scheduler as Globus does not come with one by default, but used the simpler MMJFS fork instead.

The non-Java packages, and even some of the Java packages, require compilation as part of the installation process. Correct versions and in some cases "brands" of supporting software must be used to guarantee a successful build. Globus is primarily targeted at Linux and support for other flavours of UNIX and other platforms is limited. We experience compilation issues on both Linux and Solaris and the build process was fragile and error prone. Due to version churn and build problems this process had to be repeated frequently, starting from a clean slate each time to eliminate dependencies on previous attempts. Some sites reported issues installing different versions of "All Services" on the same machine.

GridFTP is a legacy Globus component and not well integrated with GT3 services and the container. To support file staging with MMJFS, GridFTP, or a GASS server (for smaller files) must be installed on both server and client machines [10]. Due to problems originating from poor documentation, lack of example code, bugs in the GridFTP server, and certificate issues, we were unable to get data transfer working correctly across sites [5].

2.3   Analysis

Infrastructure weaknesses include portability, build-ability, and packaging. There is a need for well-supported binaries or portable code (i.e. pure Java), better integration and packaging of components, support for adding (or removing) selected components from a working installation, and a portable client-side package (including security). Portability contributes directly to the ability to automate the installation process remotely and therefore scalability of installation. The 1st order approach is intrinsically more portable, since only a container and security are essential, whereas the 2nd order approach relies on legacy non-Java components which are less portable and require more effort to build, install, configure and test before use.

Support for remote viewing of installation state is minimal, with no way to determine what packages and versions have been installed, or how far the installation has proceeded. One obvious problem for security scalability is creating and mapping user certificates to local accounts. Security infrastructure processes and management, including certificates and accounts, need improvement in order to be more useable, scalable and easier to automation. Apart from security, any organization, machine or site-specific configuration makes it more difficult to automate a scalable installation process. For example, installation location, port number, user access, and site-specific security policies must be successfully negotiated and configured.

We conclude that the infrastructure for 1st order services is amenable to automatic remote installation since it can be better packaged, requires less building, is more portable, requires less configuration, is easier to test incrementally (without security, and then with security), and in theory can utilise a simpler security model. However, improvements in processes, tools and technologies are also required to support: remote automatic installation and configuration; separation of installation roles; monitoring of installation progress and state; visibility of components installed and versions, and security infrastructure; and debugging of installations.

3   Deployment of Services and Applications

In the standard 1st order SOA world, services are deployed within an enterprise, behind firewalls, by enterprise developers and deployers. End-users typically do not (and can not) deploy services. However, in the grid community deployment needs to be supported across firewalls and enterprise/organizational boundaries (i.e. inter-enterprise), for different types of deployers, some of whom are essentially end-users. For the deployment scenario, we assume: a set of Grid resources (possibly heterogeneous); shared by a number of VOs, but with at least one centralised index service for each VO listing the resources available to the users of that VO; end-user deployment; portable service/application code; and, manual deployment of 1st order services by Systems or Grid Administrators on each site.

3.1   Grid Service Deployment (1st order)

The scenario for grid service deployment is as follows: Configure service specific security; validate deployment; discover hosts available; select hosts to deploy to; deploy service to selected hosts; register the services in an index service; enable or disable the services. Related tasks include: Test to ensure that services are registered, discoverable and callable by specified users; un-deploy service; redeploy service; trace progress of deployment; debug deployment failure.

Security Configuration. Given a GAR file, the deployer unpacks it, configures security for the target host, and then repacks ready to deploy. We assume that authentication is specified at development time in a custom service security configuration file. This allows the developer to specify the minimum level (and other permissible levels) of security for each service and method, but not *who* is authorized to use them. Authorization is specified in service specific gridmap files. A gridmap is an Access Control List that specifies which users have access to a service. It has a list of distinguished names and maps each name to a user account. The requirement to map user certificates to unique local accounts in gridmap files reduces the scalability of the deployment process. This is the default approach, but a number of alternatives are possible. Using role based security would reduce the complexity of managing gridmap files, but authentication is still a problem, requiring user certificates, proxy certificates, and certificate subjects. One simplification is to allow anonymous users (users who share the same credentials) so that nodes only need to know about the mapping between classes of anonymous users and roles. However, this allows the possibility for rogue users to misuse their roles without being able to be traced as individuals. It is possible that a common account could be used in gridmap files (every user would still have a unique certificate). Even though there would then be no privacy or isolation between users mapped to the same account (the common account functioning more as a "role") this may be a reasonable compromise.

Validation and Testing. Ideally the GAR file, deployment descriptors, and security configuration, could be validated before deployment, but this is not supported. Errors may be discovered during deployment, or worse, at run-time, which impinges on scalability, availability and reliability of deployment and use.

Host Discovery and Selection. We assume that services are portable, and that they will be deployed to all resources in a VO without reference to the base capacity, current resources, or load on each machine. This is a reasonable assumption since newly developed Grid Services are more likely to be portable compared with legacy applications deployed using MMJFS.

Deployment. For the experiment deployment was initially performed locally on each machine with the GT3 deployment scripts. The mechanism for manual deployment is to make the GAR file available to the deployer on each site and then wait for them to deploy it, restart the container, and register the service in the central VO index service. Restarting the container is problematic if services are in use unless they support persistence across container restarts. So-called "hot" deployment would be an advantage; otherwise a workaround is to have separate containers (or multiple Web Application Contexts using Tomcat) for each service, user, or VO. To un-deploy/redeploy a service, the container is stopped, the service un-deployed, a new version of the service deployed if required, and then the container is started again. The MDS3 entry for the service must be updated or removed.

Service Registration. MDS3 is designed to support a meta-data oriented registry service, various topologies (e.g. hierarchical aggregation), and soft-lifecycle management/update of service instance state changes. This makes it more than a simple UDDI registry service. It takes multiple steps to register a service in one container into a remote index service. This requires manual local server-side editing of configuration files, and information entered during configuration is not checked until execution time. In a typical SOA the directory service contains information about the service location, along with service description (WSDL). Our experiments did not require dynamic discovery of service descriptions since client-side code (including stubs) was developed at the same time as services. However, this capability is critical for scalable, flexible and robust SOAs, and we are obliged to assume that MDS3 supports registration and discovery of GWSDL service descriptions.

Non-functional Deployment Attributes. Using a manual deployment process the performance (time to deploy to a node), scalability (how many nodes can be deployed to with increasing nodes, services, and users), reliability, repeatability, traceability, and debuggability are all extremely poor. The security of deployment is only moderate since the process is manual and error-prone. It assumes secure transfer of GAR files to the deployers, that they are not tampered with by the deployers, and that only services from permitted developers are deployed. Validating the security configuration of deployed services remotely is non-trivial. Scalability of security configuration maintenance is an issue, requiring authorized users to be added/removed from service specific security configuration files. This currently entails editing of grid-map files and then redeployment and restarting of the container. More seriously, in the absence of automated/remote deployment there is no formal security model for inter-organizational/VO deployment.

In the absence of any other resource management mechanism, deploying a service on a machine and giving users permission to use it gives them the "right" to consume resources on that machine simply by invoking it. The default service resourcing model is shared, not exclusive, but with no guaranteed QoS unless the hosting environment can provide it at the time of use taking into account both base-level capability and actual load. Extra resource scheduling or load-balancing mechanisms are required to ensure QoS, fair sharing of resources, and to prevent resource saturation.

3.2 2nd Order Application Deployment

The 2nd order application scenario is different, as using MMJFS an executable is deployed (or "staged") immediately prior to use as part of the same invocation of MMJFS by the same user. The steps are as follows: Prepare RLS-2 file based on application requirements; discover and select MMJFS services; call selected MMJFS with RSL-2 file; wait for success of staging, notification of job submission, and eventual termination.

MMJFS. MMJFS/GRAM is a basic job submission service (without scheduling) that takes an RSL-2 XML file and a user certificate as input, and submits the job to the underlying queue with the proper invocation syntax, running as the user account mapped to the certificate. MMJFS supports staging of executables using a GASS server which runs on the GRAM client and negotiates data transfers with the remote MJS service [12]. MMJFS services are assumed to be registered in a VO index service to be discovered at deployment time. We assume that deployment occurs to all of the resources available to a VO simplifying the problem of matching application requirements to resources (for example, platform and concurrency). Otherwise, the resource management system in each organization is responsible for discovering and allocating appropriate resources, although how this is coordinated globally across organizations is unclear. The distinction between Deployment and Use phases is somewhat artificial as file staging (i.e. deployment) is just one of the operations performed by MMJFS once invoked. The MMJFS Start Operation steps are as follows: client credential delegated to MJS instance, file staging performed, submit job to scheduler. There is a strong assumption that an application is deployed and then used immediately by the same user, although there may be a substantial delay before the job is executed if using a job scheduler. This limits the options for deploying/staging an executable in advance, splitting deployer and user roles, and may impact scalability, performance and flexibility [11].

Security. One distinction between the 1st and 2nd order approaches is security related to deployment – both configuration of security during deployment for subsequent use and security of deployment. The 1st order approach enables services and methods deployed in a container to have different security settings. Due to the lack of an automated/remote deployment mechanism there is no explicit security model for deployment. The 2nd order approach imposes one security model on deployment and execution, due to the use of one mechanism for both tasks – i.e. the security configuration of MMJFS. Therefore only one set of security policies can be applied, to both the deployment and execution, of all jobs in a container. If a user has permission to use MMJFS in a given container, then they can deploy and use any application in that container. However, finer grained security may be provided by a resource manager and the use of virtual containers as sand-boxes would reduce security problems.

Data Transfer, Index Services, and Tracing. GridFTP and a GASS server must be installed and working on servers and client machines. It is unclear if there is any explicit un-deployment capability and if/when or how files are cleaned up/deleted. MMJFS is already registered in the index service, but MJS instances (returned from the MMJFS Create Service operation) can also be registered to enable management of individual jobs (allowing for long-running batch jobs). There is some support for tracing the progress of MMJFS events and exceptions since MMJFS was designed to manage job execution. However, only minimal information is available remotely.

3.3 Analysis

Remote deployment of "applications" is straightforward with the 2nd order approach, although more infrastructure must be installed (MMJFS, security, resource manager, data transfer services). There is support for resource matching and some support for deployment tracing/debugging. There is no capability for "application" registration, explicit deployment packaging, or validation of the deployment prior to use. There is an explicit security model for deployment, which is just the MMJFS security settings, and therefore identical for deployment and job submission for the whole container. Deployment and Use are therefore indivisible, both temporally, for identity/authentication, and for authorization. There is some support for tracing/debugging, but it is impossible to test MMJFS deployment without security being enabled. Deployment at least guarantees job submission and therefore (eventually) resourcing.

There is no in-built support for remote deployment of Grid Services and therefore no formal model of deployment security, no support for resource matching (although portability of services can reasonably be assumed), and very poor non-functional deployment characteristics. There is explicit Grid Service deployment packaging (GAR file) and it would be possible in principle to validate at least parts of the deployment prior to, or during, deployment. Service registration is well supported and we assume that it is possible to register GWDSL service descriptions. The scalability of the default 1st order service security model is poor, requiring configuration for each site to map local accounts to user certificates. However, testing service deployment is feasible prior to security being enabled and a simpler more scalable security model may be possible. Deployment allows for immediate invocation but does not guarantee QoS.

4 Remote Deployment with SmartFrog

Due to the lack of support for automated remote deployment of Grid infrastructure and services across organizations in the Globus middleware stack we trialled Smart-Frog (a 3rd party component deployment technology [14]) for Grid deployment and conducted five experiments as follows: intranet deployment; internet deployment; secure deployment; deployment of secured infrastructure; and deployment of services.

Deployment on an Intranet: Within the Laboratory. A project at UCL [15] investigated the use of SmartFrog to deploy GT3.2 on an intranet in a laboratory setting. This involved: configuring SmartFrog to remotely install and start the core GT3 package and Tomcat container; deploy sample grid services across multiple machines in the laboratory; and the development of a management console to control the process. The solution worked well in the laboratory but relied on the freedom to install and run a new installation of GT3 and supporting software as an unprivileged user on a public file system. It was also constrained to the deployment of core/container infrastructure only, over a LAN, with no security (either for deployment, or for the GT3 infrastructure), with an identical configuration for each installation. A GUI management console was provided for selecting target machines (based on available resources) and installing, configuring, starting and stopping the infrastructure or services. The progress of the installation along with any exceptions could be monitored and a partial (services) or complete (infrastructure) uninstall performed. The deployment process was scalable for increasing numbers of machines and was portable across different versions of Linux/UNIX.

Deployment on the Internet: Across Sites and Firewalls. Given the success of the intranet experiment we moved out of the laboratory setting and applied the experimental SmartFrog infrastructure across the internet to the OGSA test-bed sites. However, the new environment introduced a number of difficulties. We were unable to get the collection of components developed in the laboratory (a version of Smart-Frog, Grid specific deployment files, and GUI management console) working together correctly across sites, although deployment was demonstrated across an unsecured port in a limited test situation using the default unmodified SmartFrog package and examples. Because of differences in site security policies and the perception that SmartFrog is a perfect virus propagation mechanism it was impossible to open a new SmartFrog daemon listener port across all the test-bed sites. In theory RMI over HTTP (tunnelling [16]) could be used over the already open grid container port, but secure deployment was still a precondition.

Secure Deployment. SmartFrog and Globus use different security models and certificates. In order to deploy infrastructure securely with SmartFrog an independent (and therefore redundant) security infrastructure, process, and certificates is required, which introduces yet another layer of complexity into already complex infrastructure and security environments. Nevertheless, the SmartFrog security architecture is relatively sophisticated and includes code signing and multiple trust domains, and is well designed for the deployment domain. Issues related to SmartFrog security configuration, use, and debugging prevented us from getting it working correctly across sites, illustrating the difficulties of debugging security infrastructure, and secured infrastructure. Security and debugging are mutually exclusive.

Deployment of Secured Infrastructure. The next challenge was to use SmartFrog to install, configure and run a *secure* GT3 installation and container. The first problem is the requirement for the deployment infrastructure to have access to host certificates, user certificates, and local accounts, and to prepare customised deployment configurations (e.g. the gridmap files) for each site. It is possible in theory to use a generic single user to run all the jobs for a node and it may even be the case that for non-mmjfs services a real user account is not needed at all [17]. However, there are significant issues to do with trust, security and auditing if the binding between users and accounts is weakened. A role-based security mechanism is an alternative [18]. A fundamental obstacle is if the SmartFrog daemon needs to run as a privileged user such as "root", as is the case for configuration of the standard GT3 production security environment. The "–noroot" option is an alternative for configuring GT3 security without root permission, but it is unlikely to be appropriate for production environments [19]. One workaround for the security installation problem is for the first installation and security configuration to be done locally and manually, enabling subsequent updates or (re-)installations for different user communities to proceed automatically/remotely by reusing the first security configuration. As long as there is one correctly installed and secured version, other versions (of at least the GT3 core package) can be installed by non-root users.

Deploying Services. The final goal was deploying *services* to an already deployed infrastructure. In the laboratory SmartFrog demonstrated the ability to deploy services to a container and then start the container. However, because of the lack of "hot" deployment in GT3 stopping and restarting a container that is in use is unlikely to be acceptable. "Hot" deployment and/or running multiple real (or virtual) containers (one per user or VO) are possible tactics. However, another problem is deploying *secured* services since these may require both service and site specific configuration.

5 Related Work

This section reviews related work in deployment and security. Because of the functionality available at deployment time and the complexity of deployment, deployment is an explicit role in the EJB/J2EE specification [20] and is supported in J2EE products. Some products go further than the specification and provide remote deployment, automatic updating of client-side code from a server, and one-step deployment of components to a cluster. Java Web Start and the underlying Java Network Launch Protocol (JNLP) provide a simple way of end-users installing and running new (client-side) Java programs over the Web [21]. Operating System patch management systems such as Microsoft's Windows Update could be applied to middleware [22].

In the Java community there is a view that J2EE is too heavy-weight and POJOs (Plain Old Java Objects) are enough. With the support of light-weight containers such as Spring/Hibernate POJOs can be deployed with close to zero effort, as deployment dependencies are resolved by containers using reflection [23]. Inversion of Control (IoC) and Aspect Oriented Programming (AOP) approaches to component portability could be applied to Grid deployment [24, 25].

Problems with deployment in Globus have been documented [26], as have Grid deployment Use Cases which complement our deployment scenarios [27, 28]. Other approaches and tools for Grid deployment include GITS [29], distributed Ant [30], the IBM autonomic deployment framework [31], deployment planning [32], PACMAN [33], GPT [34], and Virtual Machines [35]. None of these deal adequately with the deployment of services.

Work that specifically targets Grid service deployment includes model based deployment [35], dynamic deployment [37], QoS-aware deployment [38], dynamic service architecture [39], hot service deployment [39], grid service GUI [41], remote deployment interface [42], and two projects using SmartFrog [43, 44]. Related work on web services deployment includes remote deployment in Tomcat [44], Axis [46], and P2P web services deployment [47]. However, despite acknowledging the importance of the problem and providing a variety of solutions, we do not believe that any single existing approach adequately deals with all aspects of secure deployment of secured Grid infrastructure and services across firewalls.

An increasing number of projects are working on solutions to security issues and better tools and procedures are likely [11, 18, 47-50]. However, it is critical to ensure that these work seamlessly with services. CAS [50] does not work with grid services.

6 Conclusions

Remote grid deployment infrastructure needs to: support deployment of infrastructure and services across organizational boundaries and firewalls; be secure; be able to deploy secure infrastructure; be manageable (deployment state, progress and errors monitored, and debugged and fixed); support configuration and version management, recovery and audit trails; be reliable and repeatable; maintain consistent versions and sets of components and services for a VO across heterogeneous resources; support multiple scenarios (e.g. un-deployment), roles, and role/trust delegation; be scalable (with increasing users, nodes, and services); be usable (easy to install, use and administer, portable, GUI tool support).

A fundamental problem is how to bootstrap the installation process. Which comes first: The deployment infrastructure or the grid infrastructure, the deployment security or the infrastructure security? On the face of it, the easiest solution is to start with a light-weight, portable, easy to install and secure, deployment infrastructure which is then used to bootstrap the installation of the Grid infrastructure, security and services. This is the approach we took with SmartFrog and which was demonstrated to work in the laboratory albeit with a number of simplifying assumptions. However, out of the laboratory, installing, configuring, securing, and debugging extra and redundant infrastructure for deployment presents the same types of problems as does the installation of grid middleware itself. The duplication of the security infrastructure and extra issues of trust by Systems Administrators, and use of the deployment infrastructure to secure grid infrastructure are significant barriers to this approach.

An alternative approach is to first remove the requirement for a redundant deployment-specific security infrastructure by using a lightweight security mechanism as the core of both the deployment and grid infrastructure. This allows the security mechanism to be set up once correctly and then used as the basis of deployment and infrastructure security. We believe this is feasible as the security requirements for 1st order service security and deployment are simpler, or at least different, to what the GSI model is designed for. Ideally the security model would be composable (or extensible) so that its capabilities could evolve [53]. We have observed that the core GT3 package is relatively lightweight and portable compared with the other packages. It is therefore possible to remove the requirement for a redundant deployment infrastructure by including basic remote deployment capabilities in the core GT3 package. Assuming initial manual deployment of the core grid infrastructure, including basic deployment and security, the grid infrastructure itself can then be relied upon to support subsequent remote automated infrastructure re-installation/updates and service deployment. That is, deployment is a first-class citizen and adding it as an after-thought, or as an extra redundant infrastructure is best avoided. It needs to be built into the middleware stack. It would also be feasible to expose the middleware's remote deployment capability as a "service deployment service" in the container (using SOAP attachments to transfer GAR files). Finally, we suggest that the problem of debugging and rectifying run-time failures can be (partially) solved by making critical deployment context information available at run-time, along with the ability to redo some of the deployment steps. We call this approach "Deployment-aware debugging" which will be addressed in another paper.

Building a loosely coupled distributed grid system across organizational boundaries using OGSA is non-trivial and different from building a system over a LAN. This paper demonstrates that there is a need for better understanding of, and support for, cross-cutting non-functional inter-organizational roles such as deployment. There is a lot more work to do before we realize the vision of the Grid.

References

1. The UK-OGSA Evaluation Project. http://sse.cs.ucl.ac.uk/UK-OGSA/
2. Foster, I., Kishimoto, H., Savva, A. (eds.): The Open Grid Services Architecture, Version 1.0 (2005). http://www.gridforum.org/documents/GFD.30.pdf
3. Globus Toolkit 3.0. http://www-unix.globus.org/toolkit/3.0/ogsa/docs/
4. Brebner, P. (ed.): UK-OGSA Evaluation Project Report 1.0: Evaluation of Globus Toolkit 3.2 (GT3.2) Installation (2004). http://sse.cs.ucl.ac.uk/UK-OGSA/Report1.pdf
5. Brebner, P. (ed.): UK-OGSA Evaluation Project Report 2.0: Evaluating OGSA Across Organizational Boundaries (2005). http://sse.cs.ucl.ac.uk/UK-OGSA/Report2.pdf
6. Brebner, P., Two Ways to Grid: A Service-centric vs. Resource-centric evaluation of the Open Grid Services Architecture (OGSA), CSIRO Technical Report (2005).http://www.ict.csiro.au/staff/Paul.Brebner/TwoWaysToGrid.htm
7. S. Tuecke, et. al.: Open Grid Services Infrastructure (OGSI) Version 1.0. Global Grid Forum Draft Recommendation (2003)
8. An Interview with Argonne's Steve Tuecke. IBM developerWorks (2003). http://www-106.ibm.com/developerworks/java/library/j-tuecke.html?dwzone=java
9. UK e-Science Certification Authority. http://www.grid-support.ac.uk/ca/
10. Girard, J.: Staging Files for Grid Jobs using Globus GASS Server. IBM developerWorks (2003). http://www-106.ibm.com/developerworks/grid/library/gr-cglobus3/
11. Workspace Management Service. http://www-unix.mcs.anl.gov/workspace/tech_preview_2/docs/index.html
12. Elwasif., W., Plank, J., Wolski, R.: Data Staging Effects in Wide Area Task Farming Applications. IEEE International Symposium on Cluster Computing and the Grid. Brisbane, Australia (2001)

13. Yahyapour, R.: Grid Resource Management and Scheduling. Europar 2004 Tutorial. http://www.di.unipi.it/europar04/Tutorial3/Europar_Tutorial_GRMS_Yahyapour.ppt
14. Goldsack, P., Guijarro, J., Lain, A., Mecheneau, G., Murray, P., Toft, P.: SmartFrog: Configuration and Automatic Ignition of Distributed Applications. HP (2003). http://www.hpl.hp.com/research/smartfrog/papers/SmartFrog_Overview_HPOVA03.May. pdf
15. Kong, D., Novov, V., Tsalikis, D., Koukoulas, S., Karampaxoglou, T.: Deployment in Computational Distributed Grids. Main Report. UCL MSc Data Communications, Networks and Distributed Systems Project (2004).
16. jGuru: Remote Method Invocation. Sun Developer Network. (2000). http://java.sun.com/developer/onlineTraining/rmi/RMI.html
17. Globus 3.2.1. Job Submission Errors. Globus-discuss (2004). http://www-unix.globus.org/mail_archive/discuss/2004/10/msg00276.html
18. The PERMIS project. http://www.permis.org/en/index.html
19. GT3.2 Installation Guide. http://www-unix.globus.org/toolkit/docs/3.2/installation/install_installing.html#rootNonroot
20. Enterprise JavaBeans Specification, Version 2.1. Sun Microsystems, http://java.sun.com/products/ejb/docs.html
21. JNLP. http://java.sun.com/products/javawebstart/faq.html, http://java.sun.com/developer/technicalArticles/Programming/jnlp/
22. Dadzie, J.: Understanding Software Patching. ACM QUEUE. March (2005)
23. Matthew, S.: Examining the Validity of Inversion of Control. The Server Side. (2005). http://stage.theserverside.com/articles/article.tss?l=IOCandEJB
24. Fowler, M.: Inversion of Control Containers and the Dependency Injection Pattern. (2004). http://www.martinfowler.com/articles/injection.html
25. Spille, M.: Inversion of Control Containers. (2004). http://www.pyrasun.com/mike/mt/archives/2004/11/06/15.46.14/index.html
26. C. Mattmann, S. Malek, N. Beckman, M. Mikic-Rakic, N. Medvidovic and D. Crichton. GLIDE: A *G*rid-based, *L*ightweight, *I*nfrastructure for *D*ata-intensive *E*nvironments. European Grid Conference (EGC2005), pp. 68-77. Amsterdam, February (2005)
27. Lamanna, M., Rocha, R.: Grid Deployment Use Cases. LHC CERN (2004). http://lcg.web.cern.ch/LCG/peb/GTA/GTA-ES/es-008.doc
28. Foster, I., Gannon, D., Kishimoto, H., Von Reich, J. (eds.): OGSA Deployment Use Cases. Global Grid Forum (2004). http://www.ggf.org/documents/GWD-I-E/GFD-I.029v2.pdf
29. Fenglian X., Eres, M., Baker, D., Cox, S.: GITS, Grid Integration Test Script. IEEE International Conference on Services Computing (2004) 281 - 287
30. Goscinski, W., Abramson, D.: Distributed Ant: A System to Support Application Deployment in the Grid. IEEE/ACM International Workshop on Grid Computing (2004) 436-443.
31. Small, L.: The IBM autonomic deployment framework. http://www-128.ibm.com/developerworks/autonomic/library/ac-abc2/
32. Lacour, S., Perez, C., Priol, T.: Deploying CORBA Components on a Computational Grid: General Principles and Early Experiments Using the Globus Toolkit. In: Emmerich, W. Wolf, L. (eds.): Proceedings of the 2nd International Working Conference on Component Deployment (CD 2004). Number 3083 LNCS. Edinburgh, Scotland, UK. Springer-Verlag (2004) 35-49
33. PACMAN: http://physics.bu.edu/~youssef/pacman/
34. Grid Packaging Tools (GPT): http://www.ncsa.uiuc.edu/Divisions/ACES/GPT/

35. Childs, S., Coghlan, B., O'Callaghan, D., Quigley, G., Walsh, J.: Deployment of Grid Gateways using Virtual Machines. Proceedings EGC'05. Amsterdam (2005). https://www.cs.tcd.ie/coghlan/pubs/egc-vm-deployment.pdf

36. Huang, G., Wang, M., Ma, L., Lan L., Liu, T.: Towards architecture model based deployment for dynamic grid services. IEEE International Conference on E-Commerce Technology for Dynamic E-Business (2004) 14 – 21

37. Ting, A., Caixia, W., Yong, X.: Dynamic Grid Service Deployment (2004). http://www.comp.nus.edu.sg/~wangxb/SMA5505-2004/xieyong-report1.pdf

38. Musunoori, S., Eliassen, F., Staehli, R.: QoS-aware component architecture support for grid. WET ICE 2004. 13th IEEE International Workshop on Enabling Technologies: Infrastructure for Collaborative Enterprises (2004) 277 - 282

39. Weissman, J.: Enabling communities of collaborating users and services on the Grid. http://www.dtc.umn.edu/resources/weiss.ppt#1

40. Friese, T., Smith, M., Freisleben, B.: Hot service deployment in an ad hoc grid environment. ICSOC (2004) 75-83

41. Wood, M., Ferner, C., Brown, J.: Towards a GUI for Grid Services. Proceedings of the IEEE Southeastern Conference. Greensboro NC (2004) 316-324 http://people.uncw.edu/cferner/papers/IEEESECON2004_047.pdf

42. Wu, Y.: CGSP 1.0 (China Grid Support Platform). Asia Summit Grid (2005). http://www.gridforumkorea.org/asiagridsummit2005/data/WuYongWei.pdf

43. Talwar, V., Milojicic, D., Wu, O., Pu, C., Yan, W., Jung, G.: Approaches for Service Deployment. IEEE Internet Computing Vol. 9 No. 2 March/April (2005).

44. Anderson, P., Smith., E.: OGSAConfig. http://groups.inf.ed.ac.uk/ogsaconfig/

45. Tomcat Manager. http://jakarta.apache.org/tomcat/tomcat-4.0-doc/manager-howto.html

46. CypressLogic ObjectView Axis Deployment Product. http://www.cypresslogic.com/home.html

47. Harrison, A., Taylor, I.: WSPeer - An Interface to Web Service Hosting and Invocation. 19th IEEE International Parallel and Distributed Processing Symposium (IPDPS 2005)

48. Beckles, B.: Removing digital certificates from the end-user's experience of grid environments. UK eScience All Hands Meeting (2004)

49. Virtual Organizations Membership Service (VOMS). http://edg-wp2.web.cern.ch/edg-wp2/security/voms/

50. Pearlman, L., Welch, V., Foster, I., Kesselman, C., Tuecke, S.: A Community Authorization Service for Group Collaboration. 3rd International Workshop on Policies for Distributed Systems and Networks. Monterey, California. IEEE (2002).

51. Emmerich, W., Butchart, B., Chen, L., Wasserman, B., Price, S.: Grid Service Orchestration using the Business Process Execution Language (BPEL). Submitted to Journal of Grid Computing. (2005)

52. Lamport, L.: http://research.microsoft.com/users/lamport/pubs/distributed-system.txt

53. Llewellyn-Jones, D., Merabti, M., Shi, Q., Askwith, B.: Secure Component Composition for Personal Ubiquitous Computing. ProgNet Workshop (2003). http://www.cms.livjm.ac.uk/pucsec/dnload/pucsec02.pdf

54. Brebner, P.: Grid Middleware: Principles, Practice and Potential. UCL Computer Science Department Seminar (2004). http://sse.cs.ucl.ac.uk/UK-OGSA/GridMiddlwarePPP.ppt

Author Index

Lecture Notes in Computer Science

For information about Vols. 1–3702

please contact your bookseller or Springer

Vol. 3754: J. Dalmau Royo, G. Hasegawa (Eds.), Management of Multimedia Networks and Services. XII, 384 pages. 2005.

Vol. 3753: O.F. Olsen, L.M.J. Florack, A. Kuijper (Eds.), Deep Structure, Singularities, and Computer Vision. X, 259 pages. 2005.

Vol. 3752: N. Paragios, O. Faugeras, T. Chan, C. Schnörr (Eds.), Variational, Geometric, and Level Set Methods in Computer Vision. XI, 369 pages. 2005.

Vol. 3751: T. Magedanz, E.R. M. Madeira, P. Dini (Eds.), Operations and Management in IP-Based Networks. X, 213 pages. 2005.

Vol. 3750: J.S. Duncan, G. Gerig (Eds.), Medical Image Computing and Computer-Assisted Intervention – MICCAI 2005, Part II. XL, 1018 pages. 2005.

Vol. 3749: J.S. Duncan, G. Gerig (Eds.), Medical Image Computing and Computer-Assisted Intervention – MICCAI 2005, Part I. XXXIX, 942 pages. 2005.

Vol. 3748: A. Hartman, D. Kreische (Eds.), Model Driven Architecture – Foundations and Applications. IX, 349 pages. 2005.

Vol. 3747: C.A. Maziero, J.G. Silva, A.M.S. Andrade, F.M.d. Assis Silva (Eds.), Dependable Computing. XV, 267 pages. 2005.

Vol. 3746: P. Bozanis, E.N. Houstis (Eds.), Advances in Informatics. XIX, 879 pages. 2005.

Vol. 3745: J.L. Oliveira, V. Maojo, F. Martín-Sánchez, A.S. Pereira (Eds.), Biological and Medical Data Analysis. XII, 422 pages. 2005. (Subseries LNBI).

Vol. 3744: T. Magedanz, A. Karmouch, S. Pierre, I. Venieris (Eds.), Mobility Aware Technologies and Applications. XIV, 418 pages. 2005.

Vol. 3740: T. Srikanthan, J. Xue, C.-H. Chang (Eds.), Advances in Computer Systems Architecture. XVII, 833 pages. 2005.

Vol. 3739: W. Fan, Z.-h. Wu, J. Yang (Eds.), Advances in Web-Age Information Management. XXIV, 930 pages. 2005.

Vol. 3738: V.R. Syrotiuk, E. Chávez (Eds.), Ad-Hoc, Mobile, and Wireless Networks. XI, 360 pages. 2005.

Vol. 3735: A. Hoffmann, H. Motoda, T. Scheffer (Eds.), Discovery Science. XVI, 400 pages. 2005. (Subseries LNAI).

Vol. 3734: S. Jain, H.U. Simon, E. Tomita (Eds.), Algorithmic Learning Theory. XII, 490 pages. 2005. (Subseries LNAI).

Vol. 3733: P. Yolum, T. Güngör, F. Gürgen, C. Özturan (Eds.), Computer and Information Sciences - ISCIS 2005. XXI, 973 pages. 2005.

Vol. 3731: F. Wang (Ed.), Formal Techniques for Networked and Distributed Systems - FORTE 2005. XII, 558 pages. 2005.

Vol. 3729: Y. Gil, E. Motta, V. R. Benjamins, M.A. Musen (Eds.), The Semantic Web – ISWC 2005. XXIII, 1073 pages. 2005.

Vol. 3728: V. Paliouras, J. Vounckx, D. Verkest (Eds.), Integrated Circuit and System Design. XV, 753 pages. 2005.

Vol. 3726: L.T. Yang, O.F. Rana, B. Di Martino, J.J. Dongarra (Eds.), High Performance Computing and Communications. XXVI, 1116 pages. 2005.

Vol. 3725: D. Borrione, W. Paul (Eds.), Correct Hardware Design and Verification Methods. XII, 412 pages. 2005.

Vol. 3724: P. Fraigniaud (Ed.), Distributed Computing. XIV, 520 pages. 2005.

Vol. 3723: W. Zhao, S. Gong, X. Tang (Eds.), Analysis and Modelling of Faces and Gestures. XI, 4234 pages. 2005.

Vol. 3722: D. Van Hung, M. Wirsing (Eds.), Theoretical Aspects of Computing – ICTAC 2005. XIV, 614 pages. 2005.

Vol. 3721: A. Jorge, L. Torgo, P.B. Brazdil, R. Camacho, J. Gama (Eds.), Knowledge Discovery in Databases: PKDD 2005. XXIII, 719 pages. 2005. (Subseries LNAI).

Vol. 3720: J. Gama, R. Camacho, P.B. Brazdil, A. Jorge, L. Torgo (Eds.), Machine Learning: ECML 2005. XXIII, 769 pages. 2005. (Subseries LNAI).

Vol. 3719: M. Hobbs, A.M. Goscinski, W. Zhou (Eds.), Distributed and Parallel Computing. XI, 448 pages. 2005.

Vol. 3718: V.G. Ganzha, E.W. Mayr, E.V. Vorozhtsov (Eds.), Computer Algebra in Scientific Computing. XII, 502 pages. 2005.

Vol. 3717: B. Gramlich (Ed.), Frontiers of Combining Systems. X, 321 pages. 2005. (Subseries LNAI).

Vol. 3716: L. Delcambre, C. Kop, H.C. Mayr, J. Mylopoulos, Ó. Pastor (Eds.), Conceptual Modeling – ER 2005. XVI, 498 pages. 2005.

Vol. 3715: E. Dawson, S. Vaudenay (Eds.), Progress in Cryptology – Mycrypt 2005. XI, 329 pages. 2005.

Vol. 3714: H. Obbink, K. Pohl (Eds.), Software Product Lines. XIII, 235 pages. 2005.

Vol. 3713: L.C. Briand, C. Williams (Eds.), Model Driven Engineering Languages and Systems. XV, 722 pages. 2005.

Vol. 3712: R. Reussner, J. Mayer, J.A. Stafford, S. Overhage, S. Becker, P.J. Schroeder (Eds.), Quality of Software Architectures and Software Quality. XIII, 289 pages. 2005.

Vol. 3711: F. Kishino, Y. Kitamura, H. Kato, N. Nagata (Eds.), Entertainment Computing - ICEC 2005. XXIV, 540 pages. 2005.

Vol. 3710: M. Barni, I. Cox, T. Kalker, H.J. Kim (Eds.), Digital Watermarking. XII, 485 pages. 2005.

Vol. 3709: P. van Beek (Ed.), Principles and Practice of Constraint Programming - CP 2005. XX, 887 pages. 2005.

Vol. 3708: J. Blanc-Talon, W. Philips, D.C. Popescu, P. Scheunders (Eds.), Advanced Concepts for Intelligent Vision Systems. XXII, 725 pages. 2005.

Vol. 3707: D.A. Peled, Y.-K. Tsay (Eds.), Automated Technology for Verification and Analysis. XII, 506 pages. 2005.

Vol. 3706: H. Fukś, S. Lukosch, A.C. Salgado (Eds.), Groupware: Design, Implementation, and Use. XII, 378 pages. 2005.

Vol. 3705: R. De Nicola, D. Sangiorgi (Eds.), Trustworthy Global Computing. VIII, 371 pages. 2005.

Vol. 3704: M. De Gregorio, V. Di Maio, M. Frucci, C. Musio (Eds.), Brain, Vision, and Artificial Intelligence. XV, 556 pages. 2005.

Vol. 3703: F. Fages, S. Soliman (Eds.), Principles and Practice of Semantic Web Reasoning. VIII, 163 pages. 2005.